# THE INTELLIGENT GUIDE TO TEXAS HOLD'EM POKER

*2nd Edition*

# THE INTELLIGENT GUIDE TO TEXAS HOLD'EM POKER

## 2nd Edition

### Sam Braids

**Intelligent Games Publishing**

Baltimore

The Intelligent Guide to Texas Hold'em Poker, 2nd Edition

ISBN-10   0-9677551-4-X
ISBN-13   978-0-9677551-4-4
Library of Congress Control Number: 2009943249

Book Cover Writing:  Graham Van Dixhorn, Write to Your Market, Inc.

Publisher's Cataloging-In-Publication Data
(Prepared by The Donohue Group, Inc.)

Braids, Sam.
  The intelligent guide to Texas hold'em poker / Sam Braids. -- 2nd ed.

    p. : ill., charts ; cm.

  Includes bibliographical references and index.
  ISBN-13: 978-0-9677551-4-4
  ISBN-10: 0-9677551-4-X

1. Poker.  2. Poker--Rules.  3. Game theory.  4. Gambling systems.  I. Title.

GV1251 .B73 2010
795.412/01                              2009943249

**PLEASE NOTE:** The material contained in this book is for informational
purposes only. In no manner should this book be construed to offer legal advice
on the issue of online gambling. It is the reader's responsibility to know and
follow the laws that apply in his or her state and jurisdiction. Seek appropriate
legal advice from a qualified attorney if unsure. The publisher does not endorse
or guarantee any of the services described in this book. The reader assumes
all risks and responsibility for his or her actions.

# Contents

## List of Figures and Tables

# Preface

It has been six years since the publication of the first edition of this book. At that time, I was absolutely amazed by the demand for the book and the enthusiastic and positive letters I received from readers. When I first conceived of the book in the year 2000, Texas Hold'em was actually an obscure game. Relatively few books on poker, let alone Texas Hold'em, were available. I saw the need for a concise guide that would explain the rules, vocabulary, concepts, and tactics that are essential to the play of Texas Hold'em. I wanted to provide a guide that would inform readers without overwhelming them and bring them quickly up to speed so that they could compete in the popular low-limit games found online and in public cardrooms.

Much has happened in the poker world over the past six years. The game of poker has experienced an unprecedented boom followed by a predictable contraction. However, the contracted poker economy is still huge compared to pre-2000 levels. An American game is now played in countries all over the world and in all the inhabited continents. The first edition of this book has even appeared in translation, and I understand that the Norwegian-language edition sells well in Norway. Even though poker growth has leveled off somewhat in the United States, the game's worldwide spread insures steady growth and interest in poker for years to come.

Texas Hold'em is now the most popular variation of poker in the world. The game has become a part of popular culture. Poker-themed merchandise and tournament sets are displayed in department stores. Expressions such as "all-in" are now part of ordinary language. A tournament Hold'em competition even made for a memorable scene in the 2006 James Bond film, *Casino Royale*.

A confluence of factors resulted in the poker boom. Television producers found that tournament poker could be presented as entertainment. Televised World Series of Poker events and shows such as *Celebrity Poker Showdown* earned high ratings. This is actually a counterintuitive discovery. Successful poker requires extreme patience and careful observation. Experienced poker players would not ordinarily think of the game as made for TV entertainment. Poker works on TV because of the use of hole-card cameras and heavy editing. Making all the hole cards known to the audience gives them an omniscience not shared by any of the players. The audience can follow along in the decision-making, understand the strategies and tactics, and know immediately which decisions will work.

Even with hole-card cameras, heavy editing is necessary because most hands dealt are unremarkable and have little drama. The editing makes for better entertainment, but presents a distorted view of the game. The hours of folding hands before making the big move are lost and with it, much of the context players use when faced with a big decision. Viewers see the tactics, but do not get a sense of the hours of patient study and maneuvering that are necessary for success. There is also confusion about the difference between tournament and cash-games.

The other factor driving the poker boom was the Internet. Widespread access to the Internet did not exist prior to the 1990s. Online poker came about with the growth of the World Wide Web in the late 1990s and it has proven to be an incredibly popular activity. The Internet allows access to poker for millions of people all over the world from the privacy of their homes any time of day or night. It allows people to participate in poker without the need for travel or to round up a group of friends. While online poker is a different experience than poker played in-person—in ways that this book will discuss—the online game still has the same rules, strategies, and tactics.

Online poker sites also promote what is now termed "brick-and-mortar poker," which means poker played in-person at a physical place. Many sites have promotions that allow online players to win entry into events such as the annual World Series of Poker held in Las Vegas. Because of extensive television coverage of brick-and-mortar events, such as the World Series of Poker, the cross-marketing has been extremely effective. Players can watch poker on television and go immediately to their computers to play.

A result of all the media, cultural, and online focus on poker is an explosion of books offering information and advice. When I wrote the first edition of this book, I read just about every book in print on Texas Hold'em. It was easy to do because there were not that many books on the subject. I can no longer do that because today hundreds of books are available, with many additional ones published each year. In terms of shelf space at a bookstore, poker books now occupy as much space as books on the ancient game of chess. Each year, dozens of books on chess are published because millions of people worldwide have a fascination with the game. With its simple rules, yet subtle and complex strategies, poker, like chess, is becoming a permanent part of the world's shared cultural experience.

Why update this book, given all the literature now available? I believe my original intent—a concise summary and guide to the game—is needed now more than ever. While the book is expanded from its original edition, it retains the original focus on the essential facts, tactics, strategies, and psychology needed to play Texas Hold'em successfully. The intended readers are the recreational players who comprise the vast majority of poker players. However, professional and semi-professional players will find the information and resources in this book valuable as well.

As an expert on correspondence chess, I also offer a unique perspective on poker. I see parallels between the games, and differences. As I write, I find that chess makes a good framework for understanding many poker topics—tournament structures, online play, the role of luck, and the psychological attributes needed for success. How the games of chess and poker differ is also instructive. Why has it taken researchers on artificial intelligence until 2007 to build a computer that can compete with world-class poker players, when a computer in 1997 beat the World Chess Champion? The reasons for this decade of additional effort—discussed in Chapter 10—provide instruction on the requirements for success in poker.

Features unique to this book are the following:

• **Useful tables and charts that render an easy-to-comprehend visual representation of the essential mathematical facts for Texas Hold'em.** This information, found in Chapter 5, is expanded from the earlier edition and includes:

— A listing of the expected value of all 169 starting hands determined from analysis of tens of millions of actual hands played online.

— Three-dimensional charts showing the combined effects of card rank and player position on the expected values of starting hands.

— Charts showing the minimum pot size for the correct pot odds, given the number of outs available and the number of cards to come.

• **A strategy section that explains how to adjust your play to different game conditions.** Successful poker players use a dynamic approach, constantly fine-tuning their play to prevailing game conditions. An additional chapter has been added on how strategies and tactics differ online. It is essential reading for anyone making a switch from in-person to online poker.

• **A section with essays on the mathematical and psychological considerations necessary for success.** A series of stories are told that illustrate key concepts in action. These vignettes, mostly real-life examples, should aid the reader in putting into practice all the principles and information contained in this book. This section has been revised and expanded with additional essays on the role of luck and how knowledge of behavioral finance applies to poker.

• **A guide on how to choose an online poker room.** There are many online venues that offer poker. This guide will lead you through the considerations necessary to choose one that is right for your circumstances.

• **Locations and contact information for places to play poker throughout the United States and Canada.** Legal poker games exist in about half the states and most of the Canadian provinces. Included are names, addresses, phone numbers and Websites of over 200 brick-and-mortar cardrooms. If you travel, this book is a resource to help you find the nearest cardroom.

Players at all levels will find this book valuable:

**For the beginner:** This book will teach the rules of Hold'em poker, conduct in both public cardrooms and online poker games, the fundamental tactics and strategies for play, and will point you towards further resources, both in print and online.

**For the experienced player:** The book is meant to provide a framework for thinking about Hold'em poker and serve as a reference. The carefully-planned tables, charts, graphs, illustrations, and strategic summaries are provided to efficiently assist players in their real-time poker decisions. With the growth of online poker in recent years, it is possible for players to have charts and tables in front of them while they play. Some of these charts were designed with that use in mind.

Texas Hold'em poker is a complex and subtle game. Simply following a set of instructions will not make you a successful player. Mastering the game requires hours of both study and practice, and a commitment to a long-term, disciplined approach to play. This book is a road map to use on your journey.

Sam Braids
January 2010

# Introduction

This book provides a concise summary of Texas Hold'em poker, including rules, conduct, tactics, and strategies. Read this book to:

- Learn the rules of Texas Hold'em.
- Learn poker terminology.
- Learn to play Texas Hold'em in a public cardroom.
- Learn to play Texas Hold'em online.
- Learn the fundamental tactics and strategies.
- Learn to become a winning poker player.

*The goal of this book is to provide the tools you need to play an intelligent game of Texas Hold'em in any venue, and to give you a greater understanding of poker, in general.*

Texas Hold'em is one of the many variations of poker. In all poker games, money is wagered on the outcome of each hand, but each variation of poker has its own structure for dealing cards, betting, and awarding the money wagered. *Winning money is the object of all poker games*. Without monetary stakes, poker is a meaningless game. Poker combines elements of both skill and luck. The structure of the game determines the extent to which skill is more of a factor than luck.

The variations of poker that have become standards in cardrooms online and throughout the United States fall into two broad categories: flop games (Texas Hold'em, Omaha, and Omaha High-Low Eight-or-Better) and board games (Seven-

Card Stud, Razz, and Seven-Card Stud High-Low Eight-or-Better). Of these variations, Texas Hold'em is the most popular. All these poker variations require a high degree of skill to be successful. Only players with the knowledge, discipline, and patience to execute correct strategies will win over the long-run.

Compared to the board games, flop games, such as Hold'em, are characterized by:

- More players: Unlike Seven-Card Stud, in which a deck supports only seven players, in Texas Hold'em, the deck can support 23 players. In practice, cardrooms seat up to 10 players at a Hold'em table.

- Faster play: More hands per hour are played in Hold'em because fewer cards are dealt from the deck. No more than 25 cards are dealt in a 10-player game. With a fast dealer, it is possible to play as many as 40 hands per hour.

- Less memorization: All exposed cards in Hold'em remain on the table. There is no need to remember the contents of previously folded hands.

- More competitive hands: The characteristic feature of Hold'em is the use of shared cards to make up a hand. Since most of your cards are also everybody else's, there will not be a great disparity between the strengths of the winning and losing hands.

Hold'em is a complex, exciting, and aggressive game. For both the recreational and serious gambler, mastering Hold'em is a source of much enjoyment and many rewards.

# Part I

# The Game of Texas Hold'em

This book begins with a discussion of how to play Texas Hold'em, covering the rules of the game (Chapter 1), the actual conduct of games in: public cardrooms (Chapter 2), online poker rooms (Chapter 3) and tournament play (Chapter 4).

If you are completely new to Texas Hold'em, it is a poker variation that will seem strange at first. People with little knowledge of poker usually have a familiarity with *board* and *draw* variations of the game because of their portrayal in popular culture. Board games—Seven-Card Stud is the most popular version—deal hands that are a mix of cards known only to the holder and cards seen by everyone. As cards are dealt and bets placed, only the player has complete knowledge of his or her hand, but others make guesses based on partial knowledge from the exposed cards. For draw games—Five-Card Draw is the most popular—there are no exposed cards. Only betting patterns and the number of cards drawn for improvement provide information to the other players.

Texas Hold'em is in a completely different class of poker variants known as *flop* games. Flop games have elements of both board and draw games. Also like draw games, the cards dealt to the players are not exposed and are known only to them. Like board games, hands are improved through exposed cards. The twist is that *the exposed cards belong to everyone*. The use of shared (or community) cards to complete a poker hand is the defining characteristic of flop games. Some of the other flop variants (Omaha and Omaha High-Low Eight-or-Better) are described in the Appendix. Of the flop games, Texas Hold'em is the most intricate and challenging to play. The annual *World Series of Poker* uses Texas Hold'em to determine the champion. My book specifically addresses Texas Hold'em. While some of the information presented is relevant to the other flop games (and poker, in general), the correct strategy and tactics for a game

3

such as Omaha are different from Texas Hold'em, even though on the surface, the games look remarkably similar.

Opportunities to play Texas Hold'em are more widespread than most people realize. Aside from the obvious locations (Atlantic City and Las Vegas), there are public cardrooms throughout California and the Northwest, on Native American reservations throughout the United States, and on riverboats up and down the Mississippi River system in the country's heartland. Chapter 2 describes what to expect in a public cardroom and how to conduct yourself. To locate a public cardroom near you, or near a place you plan to visit, check the listings in Chapter 12 for public cardrooms in the United States and Canada. The listings are sorted geographically and include locations and contact information for more than 200 cardrooms.

The Internet has provided unlimited opportunity to play Texas Hold'em because of the growth of online poker games in which you can compete for real-money. Chapter 3 explains the nuts and bolts of playing online, and Chapter 11 provides advice on how to choose an online poker site. Be aware that the legal issues surrounding online gambling are murky. **Discussion of online poker is for informational purposes only. In no way should anything in this book be construed as legal advice or an endorsement or guarantee of any online services.** It is the reader's responsibility to know the appropriate laws governing any activity undertaken and to consult with a lawyer when unsure. Online poker play is covered in this book because the Internet — and the opportunities and risks brought by the Internet — are here to stay. It will become increasingly difficult for the government to regulate online activities. Therefore, it is more important than ever to be informed and responsible when online.

# 1. Rules

The object of Hold'em is to accumulate money. As in any variation of poker, money is obtained by winning the *pot*—all the bets made during the course of a hand. There are two ways to win the pot:

• *Be the last remaining player.* During the play of a hand, players will fold and forfeit their interest in the pot. You win if you are the last remaining player.

• *Have the highest ranking hand.* If more than one player remains after the last round of betting, there is a *showdown*. All remaining players show the contents of their hands. If you have the highest-ranking hand, you win the pot.

## A Hand in Hold'em

At the beginning of a hand, each player is dealt two cards face down—their *pocket cards*. During play of the hand, a total of five additional cards are exposed in the center of the table in three stages, creating the *board*. Each stage of dealing has a different name, and before each stage is a round of betting. There is a fourth and final round of betting after the last card.

The *flop*—the first three exposed cards.
The *turn*—the fourth card.
The *river*—the fifth and last card.

In Hold'em, cards on the board are *community cards*—they are used by all the players in forming their hands. Your hand is the best five-card combination possible, using your two pocket cards and any of the five community cards. If the best five-card hand consists of the five cards on the board, that is your hand. Your pocket cards only matter if one or both of them improve what is on the board.

## Hand Rankings

The recognized five-card combinations are summarized next in order of rank (the highest-ranked hand, which is the least likely to occur, is listed first). To reinforce the concept of pocket cards and community cards, a sample hand is shown for each hand ranking. Pocket cards are on the left, and the complementing community cards follow each description. Learn to spot patterns in the formation of hands. The use of community cards creates possibilities for hands in Hold'em that players of Seven-Card Stud don't think about. For example, in contrast to Stud, it is possible for two Hold'em players each to have three cards of the same rank. However, it is impossible for two Hold'em players to have flushes in different suits. These new possibilities and new limitations are discussed.

  STRAIGHT FLUSH—five sequentially ordered cards of the same suit. The value of the highest card determines the value of the straight flush. Therefore, the highest-ranked hand possible is a *royal flush*: – A, K, Q, J, 10 (all of the same suit).

FOUR OF A KIND—four cards of the same rank, such as four 9s or four Aces. In Hold'em, at least one pair must appear on the board for someone to have four of a kind.

For example: if you are dealt two 9s, the other two 9s must appear on the board for you to have four 9s. You can also have four 9s if three 9s appear on the board and you hold the remaining 9. If two pairs are on the board, it is possible for two players to have four of a kind. In this case, the rank of the cards forming the hand determines the rank of the hand (four 9s beat four 8s). If all four 9s appear on the board, then all players have four 9s as their hand. To win the hand in this circumstance, one of your pocket cards must be higher than anyone else's pocket card and higher than the fifth card on the board. This illustrates an important concept in Hold'em—the *kicker*. A kicker is a pocket card that is not part of the combination, but decides ties. If the fifth card on the board is higher than anyone's kicker, all players have the exactly the same hand and the pot is split.

FULL HOUSE—A full house (also referred to as a *boat*) is three of one kind and two of another. For someone to have a full house, at least a pair must appear on the board. There are several card combinations that allow you to have a full house. One is to have a pair of pocket cards that match one card on the board, and an unrelated pair also appears. A full house also occurs with two unmatched pocket cards when one matches a pair on the board and the other matches one of the other board cards. For example, you have two 4s as pocket cards and the board has 10, 10, 4, J, A (you have 4s full with 10s). Notice that in this case, you could lose to someone holding 10, A. They would have 10s full with Aces. That person could lose to someone with a pair of Jacks who would have Jacks full with 10s. When multiple players have full houses, the person with the highest three of a kind wins. The pair only comes into play when players have the same three of a kind. Given this board, a person holding A, 10 beats a player hold 10, J. Each player has 10s full, so the pairs play and the Aces beat the Jacks. A less common way to have a full house is when three of kind appears on the board and you hold a pair in the pocket. Again, if two or more people hold a pair in the pocket, the highest pair wins.

  FLUSH—five cards of the same suit. In Hold'em, at least three suited cards must appear on the board for someone to have a flush. Note that since only five cards appear on the board, it is not possible for two players in the same hand to have flushes in different suits. All flushes will be of the same suit and the highest card wins. For example: If three Hearts appear on the board, a person holding A, 2 of Hearts beats someone holding K, Q of Hearts. If four Hearts appear on the board, a person holding an Ace of Hearts, and a 2 of a different suit beats someone holding any other pair of Hearts, because only one card is needed to complete the flush. Having an Ace-high flush is referred to as having the *nut-flush*. Of course, if the board showed 3, 4, 5, 6 of Hearts, someone holding a 2 of Hearts beats someone holding an Ace, since the 2 completes a straight flush.

STRAIGHT—five cards of differing suits in sequential order. The higher the rank of the top card, the higher the straight. The highest possible straight is an Ace-high straight (A, K, Q, J, 10) . The lowest possible straight is A, 2, 3, 4, 5, and is often referred to as a *bicycle* or *wheel*. At least three of the cards in the straight must come from the board.

THREE OF A KIND—three cards of the same rank, also referred to as *trips* or a *set*. You have trips if a pocket pair matches one of the cards on the board, or if one of your pocket cards matches a pair on the board, or if three of a kind appears on the board. Note that more than one player can hold three of the same kind. If a pair of Aces is on the board, and you hold one Ace and an opponent holds the other Ace, you both have three Aces. If three of a kind appears on the board, all players have at least three of a kind.

TWO PAIR—two cards of one rank in combination with two cards of a different rank. This is a very common hand in Hold'em and illustrates a concept discussed earlier—

the kicker. Suppose the board shows K, K, 3, 7, 5. You hold J, 3 and another player holds a 10, 3. Both of you have two pair, Ks and 3s, but you win, since your J-kicker beats the 10-kicker. As mentioned before, it is possible for the top kicker to appear on the board, in which case, the pot is split. Suppose for the same pocket cards, the board showed, K, K, 3, 7, A. Both of you have Ks and 3s with an Ace kicker. Your Jack does not get to play and the pot is split. When comparing hands with two pair, the top pair determines who wins. Which brings us to another important concept in Hold'em—the *overcard*. Suppose you have K,Q in the pocket and the board comes up K, 3, 3, Q, A. The Ace on the board is an overcard to your King. Your hand is two pair, Kings and Queens, but you lose to anyone holding a single Ace in the pocket, since they also have two pair (Aces and threes).

  ONE PAIR—two cards of the same rank. If you have two pocket cards of the same rank, you have one pair. If two cards of the same rank appear on the board, everyone has at least one pair. Any card you hold that matches at least one card on the board gives you one pair.

HIGH CARD—If none of the combinations described can be formed, the high card wins at showdown. If players share the same high card, the second highest card plays, and so on.

*Reading the Board*

Determining the rank of a hand is called "reading the board." Here are some useful facts to remember.

- Unless the board has a pair, it is impossible for any player to hold a full house or four of a kind.
- Unless the board has at least three cards of the same suit, it is impossible for any player to hold any kind of flush.
- It is impossible for two or more players to hold flushes in different suits.
- Pairs on the board can "counterfeit" pocket pairs. Suppose you hold pockets 8's and the board has J,J, 9, 9, 3. Your hand is two pair—Jacks and 9s, with an 8 kicker. Your pair of 8s do not play. You lose to any player with a single pocket card higher than an 8.

## Betting in Limit-Hold'em

A hand of Texas Hold'em has four rounds of betting. In a *limit* game, the first two betting rounds are set at a limit (such as $2), and the last two betting rounds are at twice the limit of the early rounds. All bets and raises must be in increments of the limit. Hold'em games are referred to by their limits. In a $2–4 limit game, the betting increments in the first two rounds are $2, and in the last two rounds, $4. The flowchart on page 13 shows the four betting rounds and the possible decisions in each round.

*Seeding the Pot:* Before any cards are dealt, two designated players must place *blind bets* to seed the pot. The player selected as the *small blind* must bet half the smaller limit. Then the player to the immediate left of the small blind, designated as the *big blind*, must bet the full amount of the smaller limit. In a typical $2–4 game, the small blind bet is $1 and the big blind bet is $2. After each hand, the blind positions shift to the left by one seat.

*Round 1—After the Deal:* The first round of betting occurs after all players are dealt their pocket cards. Betting begins with the player to the immediate left of the big blind, who must *call*, meaning match the big blind bet in order to stay in the game. Betting proceeds to the left. To stay in the game, each player must call the current bet. All players, including the blinds, have the option of raising when it is their turn. *Raises*, which are a match and increase of the previous bet, are in increments of the big blind bet (if $2 is the blind bet, then all raises are in increments of $2). Usually, raises are capped at three: if three raises have been made, no further raising is allowed. When play reaches the small blind, that player must make up the difference between the small and big blind bets, plus any raises, to stay in the game. The big blind player has the option to raise (if the cap has not been reached) after all the other players have acted.

*Round 2—After the Flop:* After betting on the pocket cards is complete, the dealer exposes the first three community cards (the flop) on the table. In a $2–4 game, bets and raises after the flop are again in $2 increments. Betting starts with the small blind and continues to the left. The small blind may either bet or *check* (pass on making a bet). Because each player has the option of checking, it is possible for everyone to check after the flop, which will result in no additional money going into the pot. If a player checks and someone bets later on, the player who checked gets a turn to call the bet or even raise. Raising after checking is a play referred to as a *check-raise*. Once a bet is made, all players must at least call the bet to stay in the game, and raising is an option. To stay in the game, a player must call all bets and raises, which results in all remaining players contributing equally to the pot.

*Round 3—After the Turn:* After betting on the flop, a fourth card (the turn) is exposed on the board. Play again starts with the small blind, who either checks or bets. As play proceeds to the left, the increments for bets and raises are doubled. In a $2–4 game, bets are $4 after the turn card and raises are in increments of $4.

# Betting Structure of $2– 4 Texas Hold'em

**Blinds**: small – $1, big – $2.

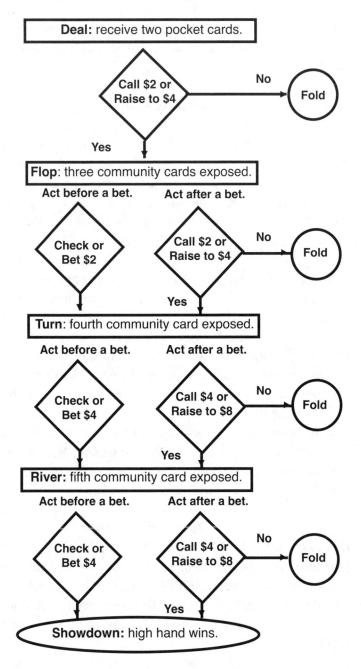

*Round 4—At the River:* After the third round of betting, the fifth card (the river card) is exposed. There is a final round of betting at the same level as the turn card.

If more than one player remains after the fourth round of betting, there is a showdown. The player with the highest-ranked hand wins the pot.

## Table Stakes

In public cardrooms, both brick-and-mortar and online, poker is always played for table stakes, meaning that you cannot put additional money in play, or take money out of play during a hand. All your playing money must be on the table at the start of the hand. If you run out of money during the course of a hand, you are tapped out, and are allowed to go all-in. When you go all-in, you do not have to call any more bets to stay in the hand. If only one opponent remains, he or she cannot bet more money. The remaining cards are dealt and the person with the highest hand wins the pot. If you go all-in against two or more opponents, they may continue betting. The money they bet goes into a separate pot, the side pot, for which you cannot compete. If one of your opponents has the highest-ranked hand at showdown, that person wins both pots. If you have the highest hand, you win only the main pot. The side pot goes to the person with the second highest hand. You may purchase chips after going all-in, but it must be for at least the table minimum. You are allowed to buy-in (put more cash on the table or purchase more chips) any time between hands, but not during a hand.

## Rule Variations

*Spread-limit games:* Some cardrooms offer limit games in which the betting is not in fixed increments. In a $5–10 spread-limit game, the allowed bets and raises are any amount up to $5 in the first two rounds, followed by any amount up to $10 in the second two.

**No raising caps when head-to-head:** Some cardrooms cap raises at three until there are two remaining players. Two players going head-to-head are allowed to have a raising war and raise as many times as they like.

**Structure variations:** Different cardrooms can have variations on the traditional blind and betting-round structure. Some variations I have experienced include $2–$5–$5–$10, which means that if there are no pre-flop raises, everyone pays $2 to see the flop, but must bet $5 to see the turn card. Bets then double again after the river card. I also played in a game that did not have a rake; instead, the player on the button (the last player to bet in each round) paid the house an amount equal to one big blind. In exchange, that person was included in the hand, and unless there was a pre-flop raise, saw the flop without betting additional money. The first time you play in a cardroom, ask the poker manager to explain all the house rules, and take notice of unfamiliar variations.

*Jackpot games:* Some cardrooms set aside a portion of the rake to form a jackpot that is awarded to players under special circumstances. The most common kind is the "bad-beat" jackpot. In order to win, a player must have a losing hand. The catch is that the losing hand must be ranked Aces-full or better. Since bad-beats of this nature are rare, jackpots can become enormous before someone wins and the jackpot rebuilds. I once witnessed a $4–8 Hold'em table on a Missouri riverboat hit a $20,000 jackpot. In that instance, the casino awarded the losing hand 50% ($10,000), the winning hand 25% ($5,000), and the remaining six players split the remaining 25%. Again, ask for the details before you play. If a casino has a jackpot, there will be house rules regarding which events hit the jackpot and how the pot is awarded.

## Pot-limit and No-limit Hold'em

Television coverage of poker tournaments has popularized the no-limit and pot-limit forms of Hold'em, which in the past were played primarily by professionals for high stakes. Today, many cardrooms, both brick-and-mortar and online, offer no-limit Hold'em for small buy-ins that recreational players can afford.

No-limit Hold'em is played the same way as limit, with a small and big blind and the same four rounds of betting. The difference is that in any betting round, a player may bet any amount of money up to the total he or she has on the table. Raises can also be in any amount. No-limit Hold'em is much more complex than limit because players must decide both whether to bet or raise, and how much to bet or raise. It also means that a player can lose all the money he or she has on the table, no matter how much, on any hand. The total amount a player has on the table at a given time is referred to as his or her "stack." Usually, cardrooms that offer no-limit Hold'em specify minimum and maximum allowed buy-ins when joining a table so that initial stack sizes are roughly equal. For example, a table with a $1 small blind and $2 big blind might require a player to buy at least $50 of chips to join, but no more than $200. By capping the buy-ins, players who compete for modest stakes can afford to play in no-limit games.

A close relative of no-limit Hold'em is pot-limit in which bets and raises are limited by the size of the pot. For example, if the pot holds $10, a player may bet any amount up to $10. Suppose $10 is bet into a $10-size pot, bringing the total pot to $20. The next player to act has the option of calling the $10 to make the pot $30 or placing a bet up to $40—the $10 to call, plus a raise up to the new pot size of $30. A player who responds with the maximum bet of $40 would increase the pot size to $60 and expose him or her to a potential $140 response—the $40 to call making the pot $100, plus a possible $100 pot-size raise. In relation to the size of the player's stacks, bets in pot-limit might be small at the beginning of a hand, but the potential growth of the pot in the later betting rounds can easily allow players to go all-in.

> ### *The difference between pot-limit and no-limit Hold'em*
>
> Pot-limit and no-limit Hold'em differ the most in pre-flop play. In no-limit Hold'em, the all-in move can be used at any time in the play of a hand. That means a no-limit player with a large stack can raise all-in prior to the flop. In pot-limit Hold'em, initial pre-flop raises are limited by the blind structure, not a player's stack size. Initial post-flop bets are limited by the size of the pot prior to the flop. That means there are more flops in pot-limit games and more post-flop play. But once a post-flop bet has been placed, the pot-size can grow drastically and pot-size raises can allow any player to go all-in. Like no-limit Hold'em, a player who continues after the flop in pot-limit Hold'em often has the option of putting his or her entire stack in play at any time.

## Unique Features of Texas Hold'em

**Hold'em has a small number of starting hands.** Only 169 unique starting hands exist, since many of the initial two-card combinations are equivalent. All suits are considered equal, so hands such as A♣ J♠ and A♥ J♦ are the same, and likewise, suited combinations such as A♦ J♦, and A♠ J♠ are also equivalent hands.

**Hold'em is a fixed position game.** Position refers to the order in which players act in a round of betting. During a Hold'em hand, your position does not change. The small blind always acts first, the big blind second, the player to the left of the big blind next, and so on. In stud games, position changes as the cards are dealt since the player with the highest exposed cards acts first. Position is important because in all forms of poker, it is advantageous to act last in a round of betting. Your position at the start of a hand of Hold'em stays the same for all four rounds of betting, conferring either a permanent advantage or disadvantage.

**In Hold'em, it is possible to have the nuts.** The nuts is the highest possible hand that can be formed with a given set of community cards. For example, if you hold K♠ K♣, and the board has K♥ 10♦ 7♠ 5♣ 2♥, you can bet and raise to the maximum, knowing that you cannot lose. No straights or flushes can be formed from this board, and, without a pair, neither can a full house or four of a kind. Your three Kings are the nuts. Suppose instead, with the same hand, K♠ K♣, the board has A♣ A♠ K♥ 7♥ 3♣. Even though you have a much higher hand than in the previous situation (Kings-full with Aces), you can lose. Someone holding A♥ K♦ wins with Aces-full, but that is not the nuts. In this case, the nuts is A♦ A♥.

**The winner takes all.** In Hold'em, the highest ranking hand wins the pot. It is not a split-pot game like some variations of poker. Split pots in Hold'em occur only if two or more players have identical high hands at the showdown.

---

### *Spotting the Nuts*

Critical to success at Hold'em is knowing when you have the "nuts" and cannot lose. Sometimes, it is obvious that you have the nuts, but other times subtle changes in the board can drastically change the kinds of hands possible. Consider the following cases.

1. You hold...

The board is...

You have the nuts because Aces full with Kings is the highest hand that can be formed. No one can have four Aces if you hold the A♥.

Now consider holding...

The board is...

You hold the exact same hand as above—Aces full with Kings, but it is now possible for someone to have the other two Kings and make four-of-a-kind. Even that would not be the nuts, because for this board, someone with a Q♦ J♦ would complete a royal.

2. You hold...

The board is...

You hold the nuts because no hand higher than trips can be completed with this board and you have the top set of trips.

Now consider holding the same...

The board is...

A similar looking board, but the change of a 6♦ to a 5♦ means that anyone with 2 and 3 completes a five-high straight. Your three Aces are no longer the nuts.

# 2. Texas Hold'em in a Cardroom

In a casino or public cardroom, poker games are dealt on a large, oval, felt-covered table. The table, shown in the figure below, seats the dealer and up to 10 players. There usually are no markings on the table.

The dealer sits in front of a tray of *chips*. A plastic circle, imbedded in the table to the right of the dealer, provides a spot for separating the cardroom's percentage of the pot, called the *rake*. There is a slot in the table where the dealer deposits cash from players who are buying in, and a box to the dealer's left where tips are placed.

## Table Layout

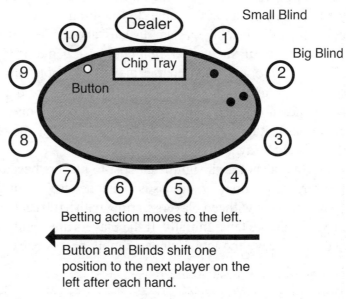

Betting action moves to the left.

Button and Blinds shift one position to the next player on the left after each hand.

A small plastic button is used to indicate which person acts last in the hand. The person to the left of the button is the *small blind*, and the next person to the left is the *big blind*. Play proceeds from right to left: You act after the person on your right and before the person on your left. At the end of each hand, the button is passed to the next player on the left and the blind positions are shifted accordingly.

The dealer conducts the game. All players receive their cards from the dealer, and the dealer exposes the community cards. The dealer collects the bets from each player and, if necessary, makes change. Players never reach into the pot or handle any chips but their own. They never handle any cards other than the two that are dealt to them. If there is a showdown at the end of the hand, the dealer inspects the hands and awards the pot to the player with the highest hand. In cardroom poker, *cards speak,* meaning that you do not have to state the contents of your hand. If you mistakenly state your hand, you still get the pot if your hand is the best. Always show your cards at the showdown and let the dealer inspect them. Pay attention in case the dealer makes a mistake.

Cardrooms make money from poker, either by taking a percentage from every pot (the rake) or by charging players for the time they spend at the table. In low-limit games ($5–10 and below), cardrooms take a rake, usually about 5% of the pot, up to a certain limit, such as $5. In higher limit games ($10–20 and above), cardrooms often charge players for table time instead of taking a rake. In a game paid for by a rake, the dealer takes the money after each round of betting and puts it on the plastic circle on the table. After each hand, the money is moved to the dealer's chip tray.

The rake is not an insignificant cost to players because poker is a zero-sum game—your loss is someone else's gain. Suppose there is a game with ten players starting with $100 each, resulting in $1000 on the table initially. If the players are evenly matched and never leave the table, money simply passes back and forth between them, with the cardroom taking a little each time. It's easy to see that if this game goes on indefinitely, the cardroom will end up with all the money. To make money at poker, not only do you have to be better than the other players, but you have to beat the rake. You must win enough money to afford to give about 5% to the cardroom and play in games with new money entering.

In addition to the cost of the rake, it is customary to tip the dealer. Tips are usually given by a player after winning a pot. Usually, players give the dealer a $1 chip after a win. Tipping is not obligatory and for small pots, $1 is a large cut and not always given. It is polite to tip dealers, but tips are another poker expense that need to be controlled for profit to be realized.

## Joining a Game

Not all casinos have poker rooms, and not all casinos offering poker have Texas Hold'em. Call ahead to find out what games and betting limits are offered at the casinos that you plan to visit.

**Betting Limits:** Once you decide where to play, select a game with affordable limits. For a $3–6 game, you should have at least $100 in front of you. In a $5–10 game, you need at least $200. For higher-limit games, you need proportionally more money. It must be money you can afford to lose. Not even the best poker players make a profit every time they play. You cannot fear losing money or you won't be able to play correctly. Placing bets that lose is an integral part of the game. You cannot win in the long-run without the ability to absorb losses along the way. If you are new to Hold'em, start with lower-limit games, even if you can afford higher ones. Players in higher-limit games are better. To make money at poker, you must not only have a sufficient bankroll to stay in the game; you must be better than your opponents. Learning poker by playing in high-limit games against expert players is a sure way to lose a lot of money fast.

**Signing up to play:** When you arrive at the cardroom, tell the manager what games you are interested in playing. They will put you on lists for those games. You can sign up for more than one game and play in the first one. You can also switch games later on. If you want to play $5–10 Hold'em, but that game has a waiting list, you can take an available seat in a $3–6 game. Ask the manager to notify you when a space in the $5–10 game becomes available.

**Buying in:** Most tables have a minimum buy-in. Before you begin to play, you must buy a minimum amount of chips, usually $50 in a low-limit game ($5–10 or less). Chips come in standard denominations that are color coded: $1 (white), $5 (red), $25 (green) and $100 (black). Occasionally, players will purchase chips from each other, but some cardrooms have rules against this. If there is a question, ask the dealer.

**Games in progress:** When you join a game in progress, you will be required to *post* if you take a seat that the blind position has just passed. To post, you must place a bet equal to the big and small blinds combined in order to receive cards. This money goes into the pot, in addition to the money from the current blinds. Like the big blind, you automatically get to see the flop, unless there are raises that you decide not to call. When joining a game in progress, you also have the option to wait until the blind position gets to you, and then enter the game as a normal blind. Many people do this because it is cheaper in the long-run and lets them observe the game before they play. The blind bets are your cost for receiving those initial pocket cards during the times you are not in the blind position.

**Leaving the table during play:** You are allowed to temporarily leave your seat. Either leave your chips on the table, or tell the dealer you are taking a break, and the dealer will hold your seat for a specified interval of time, usually a half-hour. No cards will be dealt to your spot unless you are seated at the table. If you miss your turn as a blind, the dealer marks your spot with a button that says "missed blind." When you return, you will be required to pay the missed blind to get back into the game, or you can wait for the blind position to rotate back to you.

**Leaving the game:** You can leave a poker game at any time. Tell the dealer your seat is open, pick up your chips and take them to the cashier's window to exchange them. Dealers do not buy chips back from you.

## General Conduct

Poker is a fast-moving game, and for beginners, it is intimidating to play. Poker has many unspoken norms for behavior, and you risk quick ostracism if you violate them carelessly. If you are new, don't hesitate to ask questions of the dealer. Also, most poker players are friendly and will assist newcomers with proper conduct.

**Don't pick up your cards:** Leave your cards face-down on the table. Look at them by cupping your hands over them and turning up the corners. Get in the habit of looking at your cards once and leaving them face-down. There are many other things to observe at the table, so avoid looking at your cards repeatedly. In addition, many cardrooms have rules against taking your cards off the table. Even when it is permissible, picking up and holding cards is still a bad habit to acquire. It is easy for the players next to you to see your cards if you are holding them in front of you.

**Protect your cards:** If you win a pot, return the cards to the dealer after the money is pushed to you. If you sit next to the dealer, leave a chip on top of your cards to prevent the cards from being accidentally scooped up. Once your cards are gone, you do not get them back.

**Act in turn:** Don't broadcast actions before it is your turn—such as reaching for chips or giving cards back to the dealer. If you fold before someone has a chance to bet, they don't have to worry about a raise from you. If you bet a good hand before people ahead of you have acted, they may fold, which will cost you money. Acting out of turn gives information to opponents that they should not have.

**Actions are to fold, check, bet, call, and raise:** While most communication is non-verbal, all communication of your intended action, including verbal statements, is binding.

- To fold—Return your cards to the dealer. Do not expose them to anyone.
- To check—Tap the table with your hand.
- To bet or call—Place the money in front of you. State the amount if ambiguous.
- To raise—Place the money in front of you. State the amount if ambiguous, or if the dealer needs to make change from the pot.

**Don't *splash the pot*:** Always put bets in front of you where the dealer can clearly see the amount. Let the dealer handle the money and make change if necessary. If you throw your money directly into the pot, no one is absolutely sure if you bet the correct amount. The game will be interrupted while the dealer counts all the money in the pot, and the other players will be upset with you for causing the break in the action.

**Don't make *string bets*:** A string bet is when you call a bet and then reach back to your pile of chips to raise. You must place all the chips for a raise at once, or state your intention to raise out loud.

**Don't give information (especially after you've folded):** This especially angers other players because it can have a big effect on a hand. If you threw away the A♦ and now there is a Diamond flush possible on the board, a person holding a King-high flush has the highest possible hand. If you comment out loud about throwing away the Ace, the person with the King can raise to the maximum, now knowing they can't lose. If cards are exposed in any way (which happens occasionally by accident), everyone at the table must be shown the card. If you expose your cards to another player, all players at the table can demand to see your cards.

**Don't delay the game:** Pay attention! Act in a timely fashion when it is your turn.

**Respect the dealer:** If the dealer makes a mistake, be polite. If you have just received pocket Aces for example, and there is a misdeal before you have a chance to play them, do not give the dealer a hard time. The cards are not yours until everyone has been properly dealt. If the dealer makes a mistake that negates the deal, that is part of the game.

**Respect the other players:** Some players become angry when an opponent who makes a bad play happens to win. Berating another player for his or her play of hand is inexcusable. There is no reason to ever get angry with opponents even if they make playing decisions that are poor or illogical. You should either be happy that your opponents play poorly or respect them for playing well.

# 3. Texas Hold'em Online

Any game that does not require physical contact can be played over the Internet. Board games such as chess and popular card games, including many poker variations, now have online playing venues and informational Websites. This chapter describes how to get started playing poker online and discusses how the online experience differs from a brick-and-mortar cardroom.

Online games have grown in popularity because the Internet has made it possible for real-time interactions to occur between groups of people scattered all over the world. The term "real-time" means that no significant delay occurs in the transmission of information to any location in the world. To understand the impact of the Internet on competitive activities, consider the example of chess players, who have for centuries recognized two distinct forms of competition. Players who meet in-person, sit at the same table, and take turns moving one set of chess pieces on one board are said to engage in "over-the-board" competition. This is the most familiar version of chess, with the two players totally immersed until the game ends, usually in one sitting.

A less familiar form of competitive chess, although it appears to have existed throughout the history of chess, is "correspondence" chess. Two players compete without ever meeting in person or entering the same room. Each player uses his or her own chess set. Moves are communicated via the mail with long transmission delays. Because each player must act in turn, a single game usually takes one year or longer to complete. Obviously, the players are not totally immersed in the game during the year and many activities that are forbidden in over-the-board competition such as studying chess books or analyzing by actually moving the pieces about, are a normal part of correspondence play.

The real-time transmission of information on the Internet has blurred the distinction between correspondence chess and over-the-board chess. Two players in two widely-separated locations can meet online at a "virtual" chess club and conduct a game in one sitting, at the same pace as a normal over-the-board game. However, it is important to note *that an online chess game is still a correspondence game.* The two players do not meet in person, they do not share the same chess set, and most importantly, they can talk to other people and refer to chess books. While this distinction between correspondence chess and over-the-board chess may appear off subject in a poker book, these models for chess are relevant to Internet poker. If you are considering online poker, remember that poker games played over the Internet are correspondence games. You will compete against unseen people in remote locations, who are able to engage in unseen activities (talk to others, refer to books, etc.).

## A Brief History of Online Poker

As of this writing, online poker rooms operate from locations outside the United States. It is illegal to operate an online poker room from within the United States, although the law on this is vague, and is changing. Federal law on playing online poker for real-money is unclear and state laws vary. **In no manner should this book be construed to offer legal advice on the issue of online gambling.** It is your responsibility to know and follow the laws that apply in your state and jurisdiction. Seek appropriate legal advice from a qualified attorney if unsure.

The first online poker rooms that allowed players to compete for real-money opened in 1998. The activity proved incredibly popular, and within a few years, dozens of online cardrooms opened on the Internet. A convergence of two trends—televised poker tournaments and the explosive growth of the Internet— made poker a pop-culture phenomenon. Because of extensive television coverage and the popularity of TV shows like *Celebrity*

*Poker Showdown,* many professional poker players became household names. Millions of poker fans flocked to online sites and by 2006, the average number of real-money players online at any given time was approximately 100,000. The average total value of the pots each day was estimated at $250,000,000.

The Internet turned a classic American game into a worldwide pastime. It became common for a single online table to have players from multiple countries and continents competing. Some companies that got in early on the Internet poker boom, such as Party Poker, went public with billion dollar stock offerings. Inevitably, consolidation within the industry occurred with larger companies buying up smaller ones.

In October 2006, the United States government tried to stop the flow of money from U. S. residents to online gaming sites, poker included. Congress passed and President Bush signed into law The Unlawful Internet Gambling Enforcement Act (UIGEA) that directed U. S. banks to block all transactions with offshore gaming sites. The act did not change the legal status of online poker, or for that matter, any kind of online gaming. The law forbids banks from processing any transactions involving U. S. residents and offshore gaming companies. The law resulted in a bizarre schism within the online poker industry. Many major companies, such as Party Gaming (operator of Party Poker) and Bwin (operator of Pokerroom.com), immediately pulled out of the U. S. market. They refused to accept deposits from U. S. players and blocked U. S. players from competing in real-money games. But many large online poker rooms noted that the legal status of online poker had not been changed by the law and continued to serve the U. S. market. As will be explained in this chapter, U. S. banks did not process most online gaming transactions before the law took effect, so the industry was already positioned to operate without them.

I call this schism in the poker industry "bizarre" because most of the revenue in the online poker industry comes from U. S. players. While poker is becoming a worldwide phenomenon, and people outside the United States are potentially a huge untapped market, U. S. residents as a group control a large amount of wealth relative to other populations. When Party Poker quit the U. S. market, they jettisoned close to 90% of their revenue stream. Party Poker and many other companies believe that they can survive without U. S. customers. But, as long as companies operate that do serve the U. S. market, I am skeptical about the long-term viability of companies that do not. For example, European customers can choose between cardrooms that serve everyone, including U. S. players or cardrooms that serve only people outside the U. S. For a game like poker, in which the object is to win money from the other players, it makes more sense to go to poker rooms where the other players have the most money.

Of course, it is particularly true for poker that the money must come from other players. For casino style gaming, in which players compete against the house, it matters less. As long as the house pays off its bets, a slot, blackjack, bingo, or any other player in a betting game does not care about the other players present and whether those players win or lose. *Poker is unique because the players compete against each other, not the house.* How many players compete in a cardroom and how much money each brings to the game does matter to a poker player, because it is not possible to win more in a poker game than is brought to the table. Because highly-skilled poker players can win consistently, the poker industry argues that poker should not be classified with casino games. Skilled poker players are not "gambling" in the traditional sense; rather they are taking calculated risks that will pay off over the long-run. And from the point of view of the poker room operator, a legal case could be made that the companies that offer online poker are not engaged in gambling because these companies never wager on the game. The profits from online poker come by collecting a rake, just like in a brick-and-mortar cardroom. A poker room operates much like a brokerage house. It facilitates transactions between other people and takes a percentage off the top in exchange for its services. It has no direct stake in which party profits from the transaction. This argument has never been tested in court.

The U. S. government, at the time of this writing, is committed to the prohibition of offshore online gaming, poker included. However, the international legal battle over online poker is far from over. The United States has lost two rulings before the World Trade Organization (WTO) in a legal case brought by the tiny Caribbean nation of Antigua—a host country for many online gaming companies. Antigua charged, and the WTO agreed, that U. S. laws prohibiting U. S. residents from participating in online gaming offered by foreign sites constitute an unfair trade practice. The reason the U. S. lost is because of the blatant hypocrisy in U. S. law, particularly the UIGEA act. That law carved out exceptions for favored domestic gaming industries, such as horse racing and state lotteries. The WTO position is that unless *all* online gaming is banned within the United States, laws that block foreign competitors constitute an unfair trade practice. Antigua is seeking trade sanctions against the United States.

The U. S. government's response to losing the WTO ruling was to announce that the U. S. would not abide by the ruling. Instead the U. S. will unilaterally rewrite the trade rules it agreed to in the 1995 GATS (General Agreement on Trade in Services) treaty. Such a position makes it legal for Antigua to place retaliatory trade sanctions—such as withdrawing copyright protection on U. S. intellectual property—against the United States. However, Antigua has too small an economy for any trade sanctions it imposes to significantly damage the U. S. economy.

What the history of online poker shows is that the transnational nature of the Internet presents a unique set of problems to authorities that seek to proscribe certain kinds of private behavior. Traditionally, gaming is an activity that the states have regulated, not the federal government. But only a few jurisdictions have laws that forbid people from playing online poker. (In June 2006, the state of Washington criminalized the act of playing poker online.) Most U. S. residents can play online poker without fear of prosecution. But, online poker sites still must operate outside the United States—out of reach of both U. S. gaming and U. S. banking laws. However, an Internet site outside of the United States is still accessible to anyone in the world.

It is unlikely that online poker will go away. The demand is too great and the amount of money involved too large for all the participants and operators to simply quit. Unfortunately, the U. S. government's position is making it difficult for meaningful regulation and taxation of online poker to take place. The situation has some similarity to the recording industry's failure to recognize that the Internet had destroyed their traditional business model. Rather than invent a new business model that would meet the new demand for downloadable music, the industry took the bizarre action of suing its customers. Because the industry was so late in providing legitimate sources of downloadable music, online piracy mushroomed. Music piracy would certainly exist in some form either way, but record companies made matters far worse by failing to meet the demand for online music and angering their customers with lawsuits.

As of this writing, most U. S. residents can still play online poker for real-money. As will be explained, it is possible to legally work around the UIGEA law. That law limits what U. S. banks are allowed to do, not the actions of online poker players. It is possible to move money to an online poker site without the direct involvement of a U. S. bank. Of course, anyone can play on any poker site for play-money. U. S. residents should learn about their local and state laws, which in some places do forbid participation in real-money online poker. Poker players in the U. S. should also join the Poker Player's Alliance (PPA), a grassroots organization that lobbies for the legal right of all Americans to play the game. The PPA Website is *http://www. pokerplayersalliance.org*.

*Government and Corporate Collusion*

Americans should be alarmed by the extent to which their rights are being eroded by bullying tactics of the U. S. government in collusion with major corporations. I discovered this firsthand when I logged into my PayPal account one day to find that all my funds had been frozen for violating their "acceptable use" policy. My infraction had been the sale of the first edition of this book through my Website and accepting payment for it via PayPal. I did not know at the time that PayPal forbids using their services to sell advice on how to play poker. Unfreezing my account required that I explicitly agree to their acceptable use statement that prohibited the sale of gambling related services "such as providing gambling tips or instructions," and listed poker as gambling activity "whether or not it is considered a game of skill in the gambler's jurisdiction." Now, I have spent many years in the writing business and in order to be paid, I've had to negotiate agreements on content with publishers, editors, producers, designers, and advertisers. But this is the first time a financial institution inserted itself into the process as a condition for handling the monetary transaction.

## Setting Up To Play Online

To play poker online, you will need:

- A computer.
- A software package called a *Web browser.*
- A connection to the Internet.

I will make some general comments on all of the above; in

particular, how your choices relate to online poker games. It is not my intent to review specific computers or make recommendations. Consumer choice changes weekly and there are thousands of publications on computers, software, and accessories for those who need guidance.

**Computers:** Personal computers come in two basic types that are defined by their operating system. The operating system is the program that appears when you first turn on the computer and allows the user to perform all the basic tasks—launch application programs, manage files, connect to peripherals. The Microsoft Windows operating system runs on more than 90% of the personal computers manufactured. The Macintosh operating system runs only on computers manufactured by Apple Computer and accounts for less than 10% of the market. There are other operating systems (for example, Unix and its variants such as Linux), but most people rarely encounter them. Windows dominates the market so most online poker rooms require the use of a Windows-based computer. If your primary purpose for owning a computer is for online activity, poker or otherwise, a Windows-based computer will give you more online options.

The Macintosh operating system is used heavily for education, graphics design, and desktop publishing (this book was produced on a Macintosh). If you have a Macintosh computer, you can still play online poker, but your choices will be limited. While all online poker rooms work on Windows machines, not all work on a Macintosh. You can check the list of recommended cardrooms at *http://www.IntelligentPoker.com* to find online poker rooms that are Macintosh compatible.

Owners of Macintosh computers manufactured starting in 2006 have an additional option available to them. Beginning that year, Apple switched to using Intel processors—the same processors that power Windows-based computers—inside all Macintoshes. That allows owners of Intel-based Macs to purchase and run full versions of the Windows operating system. The computer can be started up in either the Windows or Macintosh operating system. With the purchase of an additional software package called Parallels (*http://www.parallels.com*), an Intel-based Macintosh can run both operating systems simultaneously. The user can then seamlessly switch between different programs that run under the Macintosh or Windows operating systems just by activating different desktop windows. Obviously, this is a more expensive configuration than a machine that uses only one operating system, but it allows the user many more choices.

**Web browser:** The software that allows you to download and view Web pages is called a *Web browser.* The most popular browsers are Firefox and Microsoft's Internet Explorer. Apple has a browser called Safari that runs on Macintoshes. While browsers are slightly different in appearance, they are similar in function. Use of one over another is a matter of personal preference. Most computers come with at least one browser preloaded. Once you are using a browser to surf the Web, the difference between the Windows and Macintosh operating systems is not readily apparent. From the user's point of view, Firefox works close to the same way in either operating system. Once your Web browser is launched, you go to specific Web sites by typing the Uniform Resource Locator (URL) into the window at the top of the screen. The URL is the Web address that usually begins with http://www. For example *http://www. IntelligentPoker.com* will take you to the Website for this book assuming you have established an Internet connection.

**Internet connection:** By itself, your computer will not connect to the Internet. You must subscribe to an Internet Service Provider (ISP) to have access to the Web and other Internet features, such as e-mail. There are two basic kinds of Internet service: dial-up and broadband. Dial-up subscriptions range from between $15 to $25 per month and work over your existing phone line. You connect the cable that goes into your phone, into your computer instead and program the computer to dial the phone number provided by your ISP. Dial-up connections are inexpensive and easy to set up. The disadvantages are that they tie up your existing phone line and are slow, unstable, and unreliable. For real-time poker, the transmission delays and sudden disconnects in the middle of hands are a nuisance. Online poker games are programmed as a courtesy to automatically put players "all-in" if, when it is their turn, they don't respond within 30 seconds. What going "all-in" means is that a player does not have to match further bets to contest the pot. If the disconnected player's hand is the winning hand, his or her account is awarded the fraction of the pot present at the time of the disconnection. Bets placed after the disconnection go into a side-pot and are awarded to the second-best hand. However, the "all-in" courtesy is usually extended only once per day to avoid intentional disconnects motivated by players who want to finish the hand without paying. Also, players in pot-limit and no-limit games are not given "all-in" protection in the event of a disconnection.

Broadband connections are faster and more stable. However, they are more expensive ($40 to $60 per month), more difficult to set up, not available in all areas of the country, and not completely free of glitches. Your broadband connection will also experience sudden disconnects, though not as often as a dial-up. Broadband ISP's include providers that connect through the cable TV lines with use of a cable modem, and providers that work through the local phone company by using ISDN (Integrated Services Digital Network) or DSL (Digital Subscriber Line) services. Find out what services are available in your area and their set-up costs and procedures. Set-up of a broadband connection is more complicated than plugging the phone line into your computer and entering a number. Often, the set-up takes several weeks and requires an on-site visit from a technician. Unless you live in a densely populated area, dial-up may be your only choice. If broadband is available and you try it, you will quickly become addicted to the increased download speeds. Also, you will not tie-up your phone line. If you are a serious Internet user, consider getting broadband. The extra cost (compared to dial-up) is about the cost of the extra phone line that you might want if you spend hours online using a dial-up connection. If you are just getting started, try dial-up first and find out what the Internet is about.

In recent years, wireless Internet service (know as "Wi-Fi") has become more available and most laptop computers sold are equipped to receive wireless Internet. It is very common for hotels, airports, and coffee shops to have a wireless signal available on the premises. In some locations, wireless Internet is provided complementary as a customer service. In many locations, the user must pay an access fee for the time spent online. If your computer has the special card needed for wireless reception, launching your Web browser will bring up a window with instructions on how to use and possibly pay for Internet access in that location. Wireless service is always broadband and is usually fast and reliable. It is also possible to set up a wireless network in your home by feeding a broadband signal to a piece of a equipment called a "wireless router" that broadcasts the signal throughout the house. This allows multiple wireless equipped computers to be online at the same time.

One final note on Internet service for users of WebTV deserves mention. Televisions do not have computer processors and hard drives and, therefore, cannot download and run poker-playing software. WebTV users are only able to view (browse) sites. You cannot play in any online poker room that requires a software download unless you have a computer.

## Conduct of Online Games

Once you are connected to the Internet, use your Web browser to visit the Website of the online poker room of your choice or visit *http://www.IntelligentPoker.com* for recommendations of places to play. The poker room's Website will have instructions on how to participate in the games offered. The usual method in which online games operate is for the participant to download software from the poker room's Website, that runs locally on the user's computer. Each online poker room has its own proprietary software. Most poker rooms require the user to download software that runs in a Windows environment, meaning that the choices of online poker rooms for the Macintosh user are limited.

Once you register and download the required software, you usually can observe games in progress and participate in play-money games against other online players. When the software is in operation, it provides you with a real-time view of the games in progress through animations, complete with sound effects. First, you are presented with a window known as the "lobby" that lists all active games, betting limits, number of active players, available seats, and play or real-money status.

The figure shows the lobby from the Full Tilt Poker cardroom. Like most online cardrooms, Full Tilt offers a choice of popular flop games—Hold'em, Omaha, and Omaha High-Low Eight-or-Better—and popular board games—Seven-Card Stud, Seven-Card Stud High-Low Eight-or-Better, and Razz—for real and play-money. To see the available games, a player selects the real or play-money button and then clicks on the tab below the button to select the game of interest.

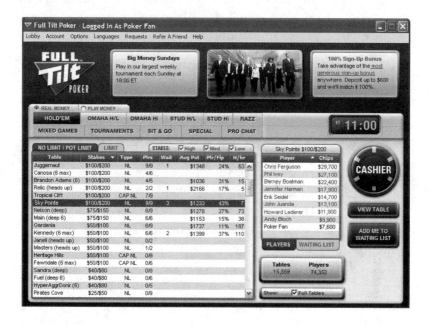

A second row of tabs includes additional playing options. "Mixed Games" refers to a recent trend of rotating poker variations at a single table. The most popular mixed game format is HORSE, which at Full Tilt consists of 10 hands each of limit **H**old'em, **O**maha High-Low Eight-or-Better, **R**azz, Seven-Card **S**tud, and Seven-Card Stud High-Low **E**ight-or-Better. The rotation continues in that order. Clicking on other tabs in the second row will show available tournaments. "Sit and Go" is a popular tournament format that consists of a single-table that runs as soon as it fills up and has no additional advancement beyond the one table. Clicking on the poker chip icon labeled "cashier" will cause the pop-up window shown in the next figure. It provides information on current funds in your account with buttons to click to deposit and withdraw money.

After selecting a tab for the kind of game and format of interest, you will see a list of available tables and statistics on the active games. A single click to highlight a table will show the current players seated and their chip counts. You choose a game by double-clicking on a selected table. A graphic of a poker table will pop up with the button, cards, chips, and players. A Full Tilt table is shown in the next figure. You take a seat at the table by clicking on an empty seat graphic. A dialog box will appear showing the amount of your current bankroll, along with a prompt to enter the amount for your table buy-in. Most tables have a minimum buy-in and pot-limit, and no-limit tables will have a maximum buy-in. Once you buy in, an avatar will appear in your seat and you have the choice of playing immediately, by posting a blind bet, or waiting until the blind position rotates to your seat.

After the deal, your cards and the community cards are displayed face-up to you; the other players' cards are face-down. A row of buttons corresponding to available actions appears on your screen. When it is your turn, you point and click with your mouse to one of the actions— *Check, Fold, Call, Bet, Raise.* In the situation shown in the figure, the actions of check and bet are not allowed, so those buttons do not appear. The software will never offer forbidden actions.

The rules are the same as in a brick-and-mortar cardroom and the software rigorously enforces them. It is not possible to make the kind of etiquette violations—fold out of turn, string bet, splash the pot, etc.—because the software does not allow those actions. You can still annoy people by delaying the game, but even that is limited by a 30-second timer placed on each player's action. If you don't act within the 30 seconds, your hand is either checked or folded for you, depending on the circumstance.

Each online poker room has its own software with its own look and feel. You can try out several poker rooms to see which interface is more comfortable. I recommend a lot of practice in play-money games before opening a real-money account. Online poker has a different "feel" to it than in-person poker. For example, it is not possible to verbally state your intentions online. If you accidentally move the mouse-pointer a little too far over and click the fold button, when you meant to hit raise, your hand is gone.

Surprisingly, online poker games often move faster than in a cardroom: 60–70 hands per hour are not uncommon. While slow, unstable Internet connections can sometimes put a drag on the game, there are many time-saving features of online games that make up for the delays. The software instantly handles routine tasks. It will shuffle cards, issue chips, give change, award pots, and determine the winning hand. All these actions take time for a real dealer to perform. As a result, online play requires greater attention on your part, since most of your waiting is for other players to act, which means you must be ready when they are. In a real cardroom, most of the downtime is waiting for the dealer, whose actions do not require your careful attention.

## Funding Your Online Poker Account

After you have set up an account with an online cardroom and downloaded the software, you can participate in play-money games. However, to play for real-money, it is necessary to transfer funds to your online account. It is this step that has become the most difficult and complicated. Unlike most online purchases, credit cards are often not an option for funding an online poker account. Even before the UIGEA law, most U. S. banks that issue credit cards would not accept charges for any online gaming site, poker included. As mentioned previously, PayPal, a popular service for conducting credit card transactions online, will also not allow money to be transferred to or from online poker rooms. Most online cardrooms will accept checks for deposit and issue checks for withdrawal. Because checks must travel via regular mail out of the country and be cleared with your bank, the process can take one to two weeks.

To avoid the hassles of checks and restrictions on credit cards, a variety of online services appeared that provided secure, electronic methods to transfer funds. Prior to October 2006, online poker players could set up accounts with services such as Neteller, Firepay, PrepaidATM, or Moneybookers. These services acted as intermediaries, not just for poker, but also for many other Internet transactions. For example, an account with Neteller could be funded with a credit card and then the owner would have an electronic wallet to go shopping online without ever having to use the credit card again.

But after the UIGEA law passed, many of the intermediaries, even though most were non-U. S. companies, (Firepay, Moneybookers, PrepaidATM, Neteller) announced that they would comply with the new U. S. banking law and not allow their U.S. customers to conduct transactions with online cardrooms. Neteller was forced by the U. S. government to abandon the U. S. market completely. Even if the online cardroom still served U. S. players, those players could no longer use their existing Neteller, Firepay Moneybookers, or PrepaidATM account to transfer money. Obviously, cardrooms that remain in the U. S.

market are still accepting deposits and issuing withdrawals to U. S. players. What happened is that new methods for payment processing evolved.

As of this writing, the available methods to fund an online poker account continue to change. I cannot predict the best funding method(s) in the future once this book goes to press. The methods used to fund online poker accounts have evolved and will continue to evolve in response to actions by the U. S. government to limit the ability of its residents to play poker online. But, I think it is safe to say the following about the future:

- It is not, nor will it be, illegal for U. S. citizens to transfer money out of the United States. There are no laws against U. S. citizens having bank accounts in other countries.
- Funds sent out of the United States and legally deposited in foreign banks are no longer subject to monitoring and reporting by U. S. banks.
- U. S. citizens with money deposited in foreign banks must abide by the banking laws of the host country.
- Online poker is legal in many countries throughout the world.
- Online cardrooms operate legally in the countries in which they are based.
- Online poker is not going to go away. Millions of people wager billions of dollars each year.

Therefore, I believe that market forces will continue to operate and produce solutions for people who want to play real-money online poker.

In regard to real-money, I do recommend that your poker bankroll be kept in a separate bank account and a budget for withdrawing and depositing money established. Mingling wins and losses from poker play with personal expenses makes budgeting difficult. Play should always be conducted with cash that you have set aside for poker and never on credit. If you are a U. S. player, serious about online poker, and plan to play with substantial sums of money, I recommend that your separate bank account be kept outside the United States. Most online poker sites will issue withdrawals through wire transfer to non-U.S. banks.

Tempting as it might be, I would not treat the online cardrooms as banks. Do not keep on deposit any more than you need to play with comfortably at your usual limit. When you deposit money with an online cardroom, you are essentially making a purchase. Like any purchase, if the company you paid goes out of business or does not deliver as promised, it is difficult to recover your funds. This is especially true for online poker where the funds are in another country and you have limited legal recourse.

---

### The greatest risk is not with the poker rooms

Players are rightly concerned about the safety of the funds deposited with online poker rooms. But the past has shown that U. S. residents have more to fear from the "protective" actions of their government than the poker rooms or payment processors. The government's moral justification for prohibiting the transfer of money to online poker rooms is to prevent people from wagering more than they can afford to lose. But, consider the case of Neteller, a company that until 2007 provided the most popular service for moving money in and out of online poker accounts. After the UIGEA law passed, the U. S. government seized the Neteller funds that belonged to U. S. customers. Owners in the U. S. of funds that totaled about $55 million in Neteller accounts could not withdraw their money. A spokesman for Neteller stated that in regard to the money: "There is a difference between being *able* to cover it and being *allowed* to cover it." Neteller eventually negotiated a settlement with the U. S. government that allowed it to return the money to its customers, but it took many months.

---

## Risks Unique to Online Poker

There are two major problems unique to online real-money play necessitating that each online poker room establish and enforce a policy. One is the unreliability of Internet connections. If you play online, the possibility exists of losing a large pot with a monster hand because of a sudden disconnect. To protect players against such an occurrence, online poker rooms typically have a rule that automatically places players all-in should their connection to the game suddenly vanish. If you are suddenly locked out of a game because of a faulty Internet connection and have what turns out to be the winning hand, you still win all the money wagered up to the point you left. Of course, such a rule can also be abused. You could disconnect yourself whenever you wanted to try to draw someone out without having to call bets. To avoid abuse of all-in rules, the poker rooms usually limit their application to an individual to no more than once per day. If you are forced to go all-in because of an interruption, you lose the protection of the rule if you immediately resume play.

But, the "all-in" protection provided to online players usually applies to limit forms of poker only. For pot-limit and no-limit games, all-in protection is usually not given. It would be too easy for a player facing a tough decision on whether or not to call a large bet to simply unplug the computer. If you play no-limit or pot-limit poker online, be aware that there is a risk that a sudden disconnect could cost you a large pot. Always read the all-in policy carefully before you play in an online poker room, and know the rules.

The second major problem is the possibility of collusion between players. Because of the remote and anonymous nature of the Internet, it is possible for participants in a game to all be together in the same room, or in communication via telephone, so that they can share information and defraud the honest players in the game. Online poker rooms use software that records the events of every hand and searches for suspicious betting patterns. The software flags players who appear to be in collusion. Warnings are posted threatening to permanently ban players caught colluding, and all online rooms post vigorous assurances of the integrity of their games. It is not possible to know how much of a problem online collusion is or the effectiveness of the detection methods that are employed. Be wary of the game circumstances as you play. If something feels wrong, even if you cannot articulate what is wrong, get out and find another game.

## Differences Between Online and In-person Poker

With the growth of online poker, much can be written comparing the experience of online poker to that of what is now called a "brick-and-mortar" cardroom. If you have tried one venue and not the other, or must decide in which venue to begin, here are some general considerations.

Games with much lower limits exist online than are found in brick-and-mortar cardrooms. You can start your real-money poker career online much cheaper than in a brick-and-mortar cardroom. It is possible to find $0.05–0.10 Hold'em games online, whereas stakes that low would never produce enough profit for the house in a brick-and-mortar cardroom, where an actual person has to deal the cards. The lowest limit games found in brick-and-mortar cardrooms are usually $2–4.

Online play has much less overhead than a brick-and-mortar cardroom. As a result, it is easier to be more selective about the games you choose to join. If you go to a brick-and-mortar cardroom, you must incur the travel expenses. For many people, the travel is out-of-town with expenditures required for airline, taxis, dining, and overnight stay. Even if you live close to a brick-and-mortar cardroom, it costs money to drive your car and park. At the tables, waitresses will provide drinks and snacks, for which they expect a tip. Dealers also expect a tip from each pot that you win. All these expenses are in addition to the rake the house takes for conducting the game. In a brick-and-mortar cardroom, all expenditures constitute overhead that must be paid from your winnings before a profit is realized.

Psychologically, overhead makes it difficult to be selective with the games in which you choose to compete. All poker books stress the need for choosing the right game: one that is within your betting limits and populated with enough poor players to be profitable. Much has been written on choosing the right seat at the right game. But suppose after spending substantial time and money getting to a cardroom, you can't find an ideal seat at a good game. Naturally, you will play in the available seat in whatever game is underway.

Another feature of online play is the impossibility of violating conduct rules during play. You cannot act out of turn, place string bets, see other player's cards, show your cards to others, or squirrel money away unseen in a table-stakes game. The software rigidly enforces the rules of the game and precisely displays all the game parameters. At all times, you know precisely the number of active players, how much money each has, and how much money is in the pot.

In the privacy of your home, you can have poker charts and tables open to aid in your decision-making, and make notes as you play. It is easy to know the exact pot odds (a concept that will be discussed in the next chapter) when you bet, because the exact amount in the pot is displayed and you can tape a chart on odds from this book above your computer screen. The chart in Chapter 5—*Minimum Pot Size for Correct Pot Odds*—is especially useful for online play. When online, there is no one blowing smoke in your face, an uncomfortable distraction to many. If you do smoke, no one will complain.

In contrast, poker in a brick-and-mortar cardroom is a social event. Players talk, joke, and get angry with one another. If you get confused, people help you out. The waitress brings drinks and snacks. The dealers switch tables frequently and banter with the players. There is sensuality in a cardroom that fancy graphics and sound effects cannot create on a computer screen: the feel of the weight of real chips when you bet, the stiff shiny cards that you lift slightly off the table to view, the many kinds of people who play poker—all races, ages, professions, and economic backgrounds.

The social environment of a brick-and-mortar cardroom also means you can observe mannerisms and gestures that are clues to your opponents' thoughts, which are called "*tells*." Is someone who was staring off into space now paying close attention? Is someone so anxious to bet that their chips are in hand well before it is their turn? Is someone visibly disgusted with the river card? Obviously, none of this is observable online. However, that does not mean online play is completely free of "tells." Online players have their own response rhythms that will vary with the decisions they make. Most poker room software allows players to click an action button at any time before their turn, even though the action will not be executed until it is their turn. Pre-planned actions show up as instant responses, a possible "tell" that the player had an easy decision to make. Players may also use the instant response buttons as a bluff. Player personalities, as manifested by their betting patterns, are discernable in any environment. A player who bets aggressively is obvious both online and in-person.

However, you will never be able to get as good a psychological read on your opponent online as when playing in-person. You also never have as much information about the way your opponent plays online as you get in-person. In online play, the software automatically mucks losing uncalled hands at showdown. Success at online play requires a more mathematical approach to the game.

My recommendation is that if you are learning poker, go online and check out the resources. Participate in play-money games as a way of learning the mechanics and structure of the game. However, the first time you play for real-money, do so in-person, in a cardroom surrounded by people you can observe and talk to. Do not play online until you have developed a good poker sense and can know immediately if the game situation is not working for you. However, once you are comfortable with poker and know yourself and your limits, online poker allows you to play anytime from anywhere.

# 4. Texas Hold'em Tournaments

As a result of widespread television coverage, poker tournaments have grown tremendously in popularity. Hold'em, because it is a fast-paced game, is a favorite for tournament play, although tournaments for all popular poker variations are held. Many cardrooms offer tournaments as well as "cash" or "ring" games. A "cash" or "ring" game refers to the kind of games in which all the chips used have a cash value. In a tournament, the chips issued have no cash value, but there are cash prizes at the end for the winners. If you contact a cardroom, inquire about the tournament structures and schedules. Online poker rooms also offer tournaments.

For poker players, tournaments offer high entertainment value for a fixed dollar amount that is paid up-front. Many tournaments have modest buy-ins (less than $100), which means that for beginners, they offer a low-risk venue for learning the game. The object of a tournament is to determine a winner who will be awarded a cash prize from a prize pool formed from the entry fees. Rarely does one person take all the cash. Usually, there are prizes for the various runner-ups (2nd, 3rd, and so on).

Poker tournaments are analogous in many ways to chess tournaments, which for decades, have used cash prizes to attract chess players. A chess tournament is easier to understand, so I will first explain the concept of tournament chess. Each entrant in a chess tournament pays an "entry fee." From the pool of money created by the entry fees, a cut goes to the organizers for running the event, but the bulk of the money becomes a prize fund that is awarded to the winners. The entrants play a series of scheduled and timed chess games. Players who exceed their allotted time to make their moves automatically forfeit their games. After each round of games, the winners are paired against winners so that the number of players with perfect scores reduces by half each time. Usually, the pairing process results in a single perfect score or a small group of people tied with nearly perfect scores who share the prize money.

Poker tournaments are financed in the same way as chess tournaments. The entrants pay a fee up-front that forms the prize fund and pays the organizers. Each entrant is issued a fixed amount of chips to play with that have no cash value. All entrants start play together with the same number of chips. The winner is the person who at the end has accumulated all the chips. The problem becomes how to structure a poker game so that, like a chess tournament, on a timed and scheduled basis, winners are forced to play winners and losers are forced out.

To force losing players out, the betting stakes are continually increased, either at regularly scheduled time intervals or after a specified number of hands. If you don't win chips, the escalating stakes make it more difficult to stay in the game. For example, suppose at the start, you are issued $500 worth of chips and play starts at $5–10. With $500 to start and only $5 blinds to pay, you could sit at the table for many hours without playing a hand. However, in a tournament, stakes rise as time passes. Each tournament will have its own schedule for upping the stakes. For example: stakes could start at $5–10, then a half-hour later, the stakes could become $10–20, then in another half-hour, $20–40, followed by $40–80, and so on. With this kind of doubling, players who sit tight with their chips, or lose them, will eventually be forced all-in just to cover their blinds. As time goes on, only the winners will have enough chips to keep playing. Those forced to go all-in and lose are eliminated from play. Some tournaments do allow "re-buys" in the early stages of play; others do not. If you choose to re-buy, you pay additional money for a second set of chips to continue play.

Obviously, luck has more to do with tournament outcomes than it does the results of cash-games. The degree to which luck is a factor depends on how fast the stakes escalate. Imagine an extremely fast schedule in which the stakes increase every 10 minutes. Those lucky enough to be dealt winning hands in the first few minutes will have an advantage. But, if the scheduled escalation is over a period of hours, the tournament becomes more like cash poker, with the better players accumulating more chips over the long-run.

The most famous poker tournament is the annual World Series of Poker, in which anyone willing to pay the $10,000 buy-in can play for the World Championship. Success at qualifying tournaments is not a requirement, which it usually is for championship tournaments in most other games. The poker variant used to determine the World Champion of Poker is No-Limit Texas Hold'em.

## Tournament Formats

There are many formats for poker tournaments, and each format has its own unique strategic considerations. Many regular tournament players become specialists in particular formats. The World Series of Poker, held each summer in Las Vegas, is actually a series of over 50 different events, each with its own format. While the $10,000 buy-in, No-Limit Texas Hold'em tournament is the headline event, there are thousands of players competing in the dozens of events held throughout the summer. The elements that define a tournament are the game(s) played, the buy-in, the number of players and tables, the betting structure, and the payout structure.

**The Game:** All forms of poker can be played in a tournament format. The games of Hold'em, Omaha, Omaha High-Low Eight-or-Better, Seven-Card Stud, Seven-Card Stud High-Low Eight-or-Better, and Razz are all played in tournament formats online and in brick-and-mortar cardrooms. The World Series of Poker includes championship events for all these games. Recent years have seen a rise in popularity of mixed-game tournament formats such as HORSE. The acronym stands for a mix of five games—Hold'em, Omaha High-Low Eight-or-Better, Razz, Seven-Card Stud, Seven-Card Stud High-Low Eight-or-Better— that are played in that order.

**The Buy-in:** The prize pool for a tournament is formed from the buy-ins that each player pays at registration. Buy-ins vary considerably from as low as $1 for some online events up to $50,000 for the championship HORSE event held as part of the World Series of Poker.

There are some tournaments called "freerolls" that have no entry fee, but players can enter to compete for cash or non-cash prizes. Freerolls are popular promotional events. Many online cardrooms have regularly scheduled freerolls to allow new players to add real-money to their accounts without risk.

Entrants also pay an additional 5 to 10% to pay the organizers. An online tournament with a buy-in listed as $30 + $3 means that it costs $33 to enter, with $30 allocated to the prize pool and $3 to pay the organizers. Another option, common for the World Series of Poker events, is to list a single number for the buy-in, such as $10,000, and the tournament organizers take a fixed percentage of the total money collected to pay for expenses and staffing.

A variation on buy-in formats is the "re-buy" tournament in which players may purchase additional chips for a specified period of time after play begins. Players who go broke before the re-buy period ends have the option of paying an additional fee for more tournament chips and continuing play. Only after the re-buy period ends, are players who go broke eliminated. Some re-buy tournaments also allow add-ons during the re-buy period, when players who are not broke have the option of purchasing more tournament chips.

The tournament chips issued on registration or after a re-buy have no cash value and their denominations have nothing to do with the prize structure. An event with a $2 buy-in might issue $20,000 in tournament chips to each player. The chips are only used for keeping score and determining the order of finish.

**Number of Players and Tables:** The simplest table structure is a single-table tournament with a fixed number of players. A Hold'em table usually seats 10 players at the most. Play can begin with up to 10 players at the start and continue until one player remains with all the chips. For tournaments to include more than 10 registrants, multiple tables must be used. As players thin out and tables become short-handed, the organizers break-up the games and move the players along with their chips to other tables. Eventually, one table remains—the "final table"—and it essentially becomes a single-table event. Play continues until one player remains.

Another format is the "satellite" event when the winner of a smaller tournament gains entry into a larger tournament that has higher stakes. For example, many players in the World Series of Poker No-Limit Hold'em event gain entry by winning satellite tournaments held either in brick-and-mortar cardrooms or online. This allows players to compete in the main event without putting up the entire $10,000 entry fee.

There is also nothing magic about seating 10 players at a Hold'em table. Any number between 2 and 10 will work. Tournaments for shorthanded poker are held that restrict the number of players seated at a table to six or less. There are even heads-up tournaments in which players compete one-on-one to knock each other out. Shorthanded poker requires a different skill set and strategy than poker played at full tables. Again, there are players who specialize in shorthanded events.

The number of players competing in a tournament depends on the format and scheduling. Tournament organizers may schedule an event for a particular time, or begin as soon as enough players have arrived to fill the table(s). For example, World Series of Poker events do not limit the number of registrants. The 2008 World Championship No-Limit Hold'em event had 6844 entrants and a prize pool of $64,333,200. It had a strict schedule over a 12-day time period—July 3 – July 14, 2008—that determined 9 players for the final table. In order to give organizers more time to promote the event in the media, the final table did not play until November 2008, a break of four months.

# World Championship Limit Hold'em Structure Table

*$10,000 Buy-in 3-day event*
*Rio Hotel & Casino*
*Sunday, June 15, 2008 to Tuesday, June 17, 2008*

| Level | Blinds | Limits |
|---|---|---|
| 1 | $100-$200 | $200-$400 |
| 2 | $200-$300 | $300-$600 |
| 3 | $200-$400 | $400-$800 |
| 4 | $300-$500 | $500-$1,000 |
| 5 | $300-$600 | $600-$1,200 |
| 6 | $400-$800 | $800-$1,600 |
| 7 | $500-$1,000 | $1,000-$2,000 |
| 8 | $600-$1,200 | $1,200-$2,400 |
| 9 | $800-$1,600 | $1,600-$3,200 |
| 10 | $1,000-$2,000 | $2,000-$4,000 |
| 11 | $1,300-$2,500 | $2,500-$5,000 |
| 12 | $1,500-$3,000 | $3,000-$6,000 |
| 13 | $2,000-$4,000 | $4,000-$8,000 |
| 14 | $2,500-$5,000 | $5,000-$10,000 |
| 15 | $3,000-$6,000 | $6,000-$12,000 |
| 16 | $4,000-$8,000 | $8,000-$16,000 |
| 17 | $5,000-$10,000 | $10,000-$20,000 |
| 18 | $6,000-$12,000 | $12,000-$24,000 |
| 19 | $8,000-$15,000 | $15,000-$30,000 |
| 20 | $10,000-$20,000 | $20,000-$40,000 |
| 21 | $13,000-$25,000 | $25,000-$50,000 |
| 22 | $15,000-$30,000 | $30,000-$60,000 |
| 23 | $20,000-$40,000 | $40,000-$80,000 |
| 24 | $25,000-$50,000 | $50,000-$100,000 |
| 25 | $30,000-$60,000 | $60,000-$120,000 |
| 26 | $40,000-$80,000 | $80,000-$160,000 |
| 27 | $50,000-$100,000 | $100,000-$200,000 |
| 28 | $60,000-$120,000 | $120,000-$240,000 |

Players begin with $20,000 in Tournament Chips. All levels will last 60 minutes. Breaks will be every two levels and last 20 minutes. There will be a 30-minute break after level 4. Play will continue on Day 1 until the completion of level 8. Play will resume at 3 PM on June 16, 2008, and play down to the final table. Day 3-Final Table at 3 PM.

**Prize Pool: $2,049,200**
**Entrants: 218**
**Places paid: 27**

| | | | | | | | |
|---|---|---|---|---|---|---|---|
| 1 | $496,931 | 10 | $35,861 | 19 | $20,492 | | |
| 2 | $307,380 | 11 | $35,861 | 20 | $20,492 | | |
| 3 | $194,674 | 12 | $35,861 | 21 | $20,492 | | |
| 4 | $158,813 | 13 | $30,738 | 22 | $20,492 | | |
| 5 | $128,075 | 14 | $30,738 | 23 | $20,492 | | |
| 6 | $102,460 | 15 | $30,738 | 24 | $20,492 | | |
| 7 | $81,968 | 16 | $25,615 | 25 | $20,492 | | |
| 8 | $66,599 | 17 | $25,615 | 26 | $20,492 | | |
| 9 | $51,230 | 18 | $25,615 | 27 | $20,492 | | |

But, another approach is to first decide on the initial number of tables and players. The tournament begins as soon as all the seats are filled. This is known as a "sit & go" tournament and is used for many online events.

**Betting Structure:** The seven-card board games—Razz, Stud, Stud High-Low Eight-or-Better—are always played in limit form. But tournaments based on flop games—Hold'em, Omaha, Omaha High-Low Eight-or-Better—can have limit, pot-limit, or no-limit betting structures. Each tournament will post a "structure table." Shown on the these pages are some examples of structure tables—one for the $10,000 buy-in limit Hold'em event at the World Series of Poker; the other, for a $2 + $0.25 online "sit & go" tournament hosted by Full Tilt Poker.

The limit Hold'em event has 28 betting levels that each last 60 minutes. The structure table for a limit event lists both the blinds and limits for each level. The amounts are in tournament chips, not the cash equivalent. Notice that the $10,000 buy-in purchases $20,000 in tournament chips.

The structure table for the online no-Limit Hold'em event has 32 levels. Because there are no limits, the table only lists the blinds for each level. Online play is much faster, and each level will last only 3 minutes. Again, the amounts listed are in tournament chips. Each player in this $2.25 buy-in event starts with $1500 in chips.

# Full Tilt Poker Sit & Go No-limit Hold'em Structure Table

*$2 + $0.25 Buy-in single-table event*
*www.fulltiltpoker.com*
*Play begins as soon as 9 players are seated*

| Level | Small Blind | Big Blind |
|---|---|---|
| 1 | $15 | $30 |
| 2 | $20 | $40 |
| 3 | $25 | $50 |
| 4 | $30 | $60 |
| 5 | $40 | $80 |
| 6 | $50 | $100 |
| 7 | $60 | $120 |
| 8 | $80 | $160 |
| 9 | $100 | $200 |
| 10 | $120 | $240 |
| 11 | $150 | $300 |
| 12 | $200 | $400 |
| 13 | $250 | $500 |
| 14 | $300 | $600 |
| 15 | $400 | $800 |
| 16 | $500 | $1,000 |
| 17 | $600 | $1,200 |
| 18 | $800 | $1,600 |
| 19 | $1,000 | $2,000 |
| 20 | $1,200 | $2,400 |
| 21 | $1,500 | $3,000 |
| 22 | $2,000 | $4,000 |
| 23 | $2,500 | $5,000 |
| 24 | $3,000 | $6,000 |
| 25 | $4,000 | $8,000 |
| 26 | $5,000 | $10,000 |
| 27 | $6,000 | $12,000 |
| 28 | $8,000 | $16,000 |
| 29 | $10,000 | $20,000 |
| 30 | $12,000 | $24,000 |
| 31 | $15,000 | $30,000 |
| 32 | $20,000 | $40,000 |

Players begin with $1,500 in Tournament Chips with blinds initially $15-30. Each level lasts 3 minutes.

**Prize Pool: $18**
**Entrants: 9**
**Places paid: 3**

**1st $9**
**2nd $5.40**
**3rd $3.60**

**Payout Structure:** Tournaments are rarely winner-take-all events. Usually, prizes are awarded to the top finishers with the exact number of paid players dependent on the number of entrants. For example, a 20-player event could pay the top four finishers according to the following allocation: $1^{st}$ —50%; $2^{nd}$ —25%; $3^{rd}$ —15%; $4^{th}$ —10%. Payout structures can vary greatly between tournaments, with some "top-heavy," which favor the winner, and others "flatter" that pay more money to players further down. It's important to know the payout structure before you begin and the number of players who will be paid.

Along with the example structure tables shown are the payouts for those events. Notice that the World Championship event had a top-heavy payout. Only those who finished in the top 12% of the field were paid. The winner received about a half-million dollars, or about 50 times the buy-in. In contrast, the top third of the field (3 out of 9 players) for the online sit & go finish in the money. But, the winner only receives 4 times the buy-in.

Of course, a player who finishes one place away from the money receives nothing, the same as a player who finishes last. The player who is knocked out one place away from being paid is said to finish "on the bubble." As the field narrows to close to the number of paid places, it is said that "the bubble is approaching," and this obviously has an effect on strategy and the kinds of chances players are willing to take.

It is not uncommon for the top-finishing players to negotiate private deals before the tournament is over and agree to split prize money in alternative ways. Such deals do not involve the tournament organizers and are usually frowned upon. But, top-heavy payout structures provide a great incentive for private deals because as the betting levels increase, luck can become a big factor. For example, the three remaining players in a tournament might agree to split the prize money equally for the top three places, rather than risk coming in second or third place.

## Tournament Conduct

The rules and conduct of tournament poker follow those of cash poker, but there are some additional requirements.

**Seating:** A random draw determines the initial seating and location of the button. Players are only allowed to change seats when the director assigns them a new seat. Tables are broken up in a preset order, with a reasonable effort made to balance the number of players per table. There is a redraw for seating at the final table. In large events, there are redraws for seating at the final two or three tables.

**Absent players:** Blinds, antes, and forced bets are collected from all remaining players, even if they are not present at the table. Hands are dealt to absent players, but the hand is dead if the player is absent when it is his or her turn to act. This includes live blinds who are not present to exercise the option to check or raise. An automatic check is not assumed; instead, the hand is declared dead.

**All-in:** If a player is all-in and the betting action complete (no side-pot action possible), all remaining hands are turned face-up.

**Multiple players knocked out:** If two or more players are eliminated in the same hand, the order of finish is determined by the chip count at the beginning of the hand. For example, if there are three remaining players with $350, $250 and $150 in chips at the beginning of the hand and the leader wins all the chips, the player with $250 before the hand began finishes second, and the player who had $150 finishes third.

## Tournament Considerations

If you have experience in cash-games and decide to play in tournaments, here are some differences to consider.

• You need to have the time available to play the entire event. The only way to cash out of a tournament is to play it through and finish in the money. This is the most important difference for tournament play. In cash-games, you can pick up your chips and leave at any time. You don't have to play a single hand. But you should not enter a tournament unless you have the ability to play serious poker until the end. Behavior such as "chip dumping" or "soft playing," when a player intentionally gives away chips to another player by calling large bets and then folding, is unethical. Penalties and disqualifications can result. If for some reason, it becomes impossible to continue play, your chips should be left on the table and the forced blinds will eventually shrink your stack to zero. In an online tournament, that is how the software handles the stacks of players who become permanently disconnected during a tournament. The blinds will eventually remove their stacks.

• An hourly win-rate has no meaning for tournament play. Instead of expectation per hand, you need to think in terms of expectation per tournament. Top tournament players enter hundreds of tournaments each year. Professional golf is a good model for regular poker tournament players. A golf-pro does not expect to finish in the money or even make the cut in every tournament entered. The expectation is that he or she will finish in the money enough times to pay the expenses for all the tournaments entered and turn a profit.

• The skill versus luck factor is a much longer-term consideration for tournament players. Winning a tournament requires both skill and luck. If you don't know how to play well, you won't win a tournament. But a series of bad beats can still knock you out even if your play is perfect. It is also hard to win without hitting one or more miracle draws along the way. Again, golf is good model. It requires a great deal of skill to play professional golf, but random wind gusts and bad bounces can alter the distribution of thousands of dollars in prize money at the end.

• Tournament play requires a more aggressive approach than cash-game play. The escalating blinds make it impossible to wait out long periods of bad cards. Tournament players are often forced to take chances that cash-game players would have no reason to take. A tight-passive player might make a small steady income in cash-game play, but not be able to win tournaments. Conversely, a loose-aggressive player might do well in tournament play, but go broke facing careful patient players in a cash-game.

• Poker is still poker and the differences between cash and tournament play, while real, are not as great as many people think. Many tournament novices make the mistake of over-aggression, especially at the beginning, thinking that they need to come out swinging and accumulate chips as soon as possible. Patience is still important in tournament poker, especially in the beginning. At the start, the blinds are small compared to the average stack size and that means play should be close to that of a cash-game. Also, remember that in tournament play, the goal is not to win pots; it is to eliminate opponents by taking their stacks. That means patiently waiting for the right moment when you can set a trap or induce a major mistake.

The poker skill that tournament play will test to the utmost is your ability to adjust to changing circumstances. Sit in a cash-game and you might play for several hours in the same seat with the same relative position to the same opponents. The stakes will not increase and you can be as patient as necessary during the long periods of bad cards. But a tournament is by definition a constantly changing situation. Opponents are eliminated, players are moved, stack sizes grow and shrink, short-handed play is common, and winning often requires prevailing in a heads-up format. Success requires understanding each new situation as it develops and making the appropriate changes to your play.

---

*Tournament Format Lingo*

**Shootout:** Players have to win their table before advancing. There is no movement to keep tables balanced while the tournament is in progress.

**Knockout Bounty:** The buy-ins are split between creating a prize pool and funding bounties on each player. Knocking out a player will win an immediate cash bounty.

**Freeroll:** An event with no buy-in, but cash and/or prizes awarded to the winners.

**Satellite:** A tournament in which the winners are awarded entry into another tournament.

# Part II

# Winning Poker

Mastering Texas Hold'em, like mastering any competitive activity, requires three kinds of knowledge: factual (Chapter 5), tactical (Chapter 6), and strategic (Chapters 7, and 8).

Factual knowledge includes the vocabulary, basic concepts, and sought-after goals that define the activity. Without the facts, you cannot make sense of the game. A golfer must know the difference between an iron, a wood, and a putter, and why all three are in a golf bag. Facts are learned by committing them to memory.

Tactics are the various actions taken to achieve the goals. Tactical knowledge is acquired through practice. You play the game and, through experience, gradually obtain the skills necessary for success. Golfers learn to swing their clubs and read the greens by repetitive practice.

Strategic knowledge is obtained after the facts are memorized and the tactical skills are acquired. Strategy is learning to see the game in a broad context. Once you possess strategic knowledge, your actions are no longer a direct response to individual events, but are considered in the context of a broad purposeful plan. Only after you reach the level of strategic thinking can you truly master a game. Great golfers don't play individual holes. They think about the course as a whole.

While I have used golf as an example, any activity that involves performance requires these three kinds of knowledge. Musicians have the factual knowledge of how to read music, the tactical knowledge of how to play their instrument, and the strategic knowledge of how to interpret the music. The facts, tactics, and strategies must be learned in order. It is not possible to shortcut the learning process by skipping ahead to strategy without learning facts and tactics, nor is it possible to learn music, golf, or poker from reading alone. You must play.

This section of the book presents the facts, tactics, and strategies of Texas Hold'em. The underlying theme is that you win at poker by making better decisions than your opponents make because over time, cards (and hence situations) are equally distributed. Poker decisions are based on five factors: your cards, your position, the number of opponents, the cost, and how your opponents play. The factual basis for each decision factor is presented first. How these facts enter into tactical play will then be discussed. Strategy is learning to give some factors more weight than others, depending on the game conditions. To plan strategy, you must learn to analyze the reasons and motivations for a poker game. In essence, poker is a social game. The competition for money takes place within a social context that must be understood before a correct strategy can be formulated.

# 5. Facts

The key to making intelligent poker decisions is to understand that successful poker is not about winning hands; it is about winning money. Since everyone has the same chance of being dealt a winning hand, winning hands are, in the long-run, equally distributed among the players. Over time, money is accumulated by the players who make the best decisions.

Poker decisions require knowledge of mathematical probabilities, but the game is far more complex and cannot be completely described mathematically. In blackjack, in which the dealer always plays the same way, it is possible to calculate the best decision for each hand. No such calculation is possible in poker, because you are competing against different players, all of whom play in their own ways. Not only do individual players differ, but each poker table develops its own group dynamics that changes as players enter and leave the game. The replacement of a single passive player with an aggressive one can instantly alter the mood of a poker table and necessitate changes in decision making.

The combination of mathematics, psychology, and social dynamics makes poker a rich and fascinating game. Mastering poker requires hours and hours of playing in different settings with different people. However, many people place too much emphasis on the psychological aspects of the game. They think poker is all about bluffing and reading body language. The fact is, poker has an underlying strategy that must be followed for there to be any chance of survival, let alone winning.

Correct strategy bases decisions on the knowledge available to you of the cards and your opponents. You never have perfect knowledge of your opponents, their cards, and the cards to come. Given imperfect information, you must assess what is most likely to happen. Decisions must be based on the most probable outcome of a hand, not on what you hope will happen.

Before discussing the actual play of hands, it is necessary to have the facts that intelligent decisions are based on. This section, which is meant to be used as a reference, contains tables, graphs, and summaries of important information and concepts. There are five factors to consider in every poker decision. After summarizing the five decision factors, each one is discussed in detail. How knowledge of these factors translates into actual play is the subject of the next chapter.

## The Five Decision Factors

The decisions you make during the course of a hand should always take the following five factors into consideration:

**Your cards:** Betting in poker means you wager that, at showdown, your hand will be ranked the highest. Unless you believe that to be a likely possibility, you should not bet. Statistically, in a ten-handed game, you will only have the highest hand 10% of the time. Knowing when it is your time to have the best hand is, of course, the difficulty. When you have a strong hand, bet aggressively and force the other players to chase you. It is rarely correct to slow-play; that is, not bet a strong hand. If you don't have a strong hand, fold. In poker, money saved is the same as money won, and staying out of the 90% of the hands you are destined to lose is as important as being in the hands you win.

**Your position** is an important factor in Hold'em because it is a fixed-position game. When you are in an early position (close to the blind), you have no way of knowing how large the pot will be at the end of a betting round, and how many players will be contesting it. To compensate for this disadvantage, you need to play stronger cards than you would from later positions.

**The number of players** contesting a pot determines the kinds of hands that are playable. The irony is that you can play weaker starting cards when many players contest the pot, but you must have a stronger final hand at showdown. A high pair is a strong favorite to win against one or two opponents, but if ten players enter the hand, someone is likely to beat a high pair with a flush or a straight. Conversely, drawing hands (weak initial cards that may give you a flush or straight) are playable against a large field since the final pot will be large, but drawing hands are seldom worth playing for small pots against one or two players.

**Pot odds** are the costs of staying in the hand compared to the pot size. In each betting round, you decide if the amount of money it will cost you to finish the round is worth the size of the pot being contested. The cost to play can range from nothing (if everyone checks) to four large bets (if raising is capped late in the hand). Like any sound investment decision, riskier plays must have greater rewards for success.

**Opponents' playing styles:** During the hands that you don't enter, observe the playing style of each player and of the group as a whole. Does a certain player only bet when he has good cards or does he bet with anything? Does a player buy-in for a small amount of money and carefully guard it, or does she buy new chips from the dealer frequently? For the table as a whole, are showdowns frequent or rare? How do your opponents react to your play? A big mistake beginning poker players make is playing only their cards and not considering how other people are playing theirs. Your opponents' actions are a source of information that must be used.

Over the course of a hand, some of these factors become more important than others. Early in the hand, your position, the initial strength of your cards, and the potential number of opposing players are the most important factors. Later in the hand, pot odds and the playing styles of the remaining players become more important. Before presenting a detailed discussion of these five factors, I need to clarify some mathematical language.

## Math Concepts for Poker

Poker is inherently a game of incomplete information and uncertainty. Correct decisions do not always lead to desired outcomes. Even with the best possible play, the outcome of any single hand is unpredictable. To profit over the long-run, it is necessary to make decisions that are correct in a probabilistic sense, because events at the table are not determined. To understand the decision-making process, it helps to have some ideas and language from the mathematics of probabilities.

*Probabilities and Odds*

Throughout the discussion that follows and in the mathematical charts and tables, references will be made to the *probabilities* of events occurring and the *odds* against events occurring. Judging by the mail I received following the first edition of this book, the two terms—*probabilities* and *odds*—are frequently confused. Probabilities are related to odds, but these quantities are defined differently.

*Probabilities* are expressed either with a number between zero and one, or as a percentage. A probability of zero means the event will never happen, while a probability of one means that the event is a certainty. When the probability is between zero and one, that means the outcome is uncertain. Consider the common occurrence of having four cards of the same suit (a four-flush) with one card to come. There are nine remaining cards that complete the flush out of 46 that have not been seen (you see the two cards in your hand and four on the board). You will make a flush 9 out of every 46 times this situation happens, or about one-fifth of the time, and not make the flush four-fifths of the time. The probability for a flush can be expressed as one-fifth, as its decimal equivalent 0.2, or as 20%. The probability for not making a flush is four-fifths, or 0.8, or 80%. Note that these combined probabilities add to one, or 100%, because it is certain that you will either make the flush or not.

*Odds* are expressed ratios. The odds are the average number of failures for each success. For the example of the flush, in which success occurs 20% of the time, there will be four failures on average for each success. That means the odds against making the flush are 4 to 1. If the probability of an event is 50%, then there is one success on average for every failure. In this case, the odds against success are 1 to 1.

### Converting from probabilities to odds

If you know the probability of an event (p), the odds against the event occurring are $[(1/p) - 1]$. For the example of the flush, 1 divided by 0.2 equals 5, subtract 1 to get 4, and the odds are 4 to 1. For unlikely events, the probabilities are small, which means $1/p$ is a large number and is very close to the odds against the event happening. For example, the probability of receiving two Aces for pocket cards is 0.004525 or 0.4525%. That means $1/p$ is 221, so the odds against receiving two Aces are 220 to 1. On average, for every hand with two Aces, there are 220 without. For events that are much more likely, $1/p$ is not very close to the odds. The probability of completing a flush with two cards to come, when you have a four-flush, is 0.35 or 35%. In this case, $1/p$ is 2.86, so the odds are 1.86 to 1 (almost 2 to 1). You will have about 2 failures for each success when drawing to flush if you already have four of the cards.

In the charts that follow, the frequencies of events are expressed as probabilities in some cases and odds against in other cases. The probabilities are expressed in percentages. For example, if you start with a pocket pair, 71.84% of the time your five-card hand after the flop will be one-pair. The remaining 38.16% of flops will improve your hand to better than one pair (two pair, trips, full house or quads). For frequent events, percentages are a useful way of thinking. But for remote events, it is often easier to remember the odds. The odds against being dealt pocket Aces are 220-1, while for Ace-King, the odds against are 82-1.

*Expected Values*

When betting on an uncertain outcome, it helps to think in terms of the average profit that results if the same bet in the same situation is made repeatedly. It is useful to define the *expected value* of a bet as the average profit that results after many repetitions. Expected values can be positive, negative or zero, depending on whether the bet wins money over the long-run, loses money, or breaks even. The expected value of a bet depends on the odds against success and the payoff if the bet succeeds.

For example, consider having four cards to a flush, with one card to come, and it costs $1 to contest a $5 pot. The odds against success are 4 to 1, which means on average, four out every five times, this bet will lose. It costs $5 to make this bet five times and its one success will return $6—the $5 already in the pot, plus the $1 put in to contest it. The ratio of 6 to 5 is 1.2. That means the expected value of the bet is $1.2 -$1 or $0.20. The bet expects to return a profit $0.20 per dollar on average every time it is placed.

Consider the same situation with the cards, but with a $3 pot. It now costs $1 to contest a $3 pot. Again, it will cost $5 to make this bet 5 times, but the one success will return $4. The ratio of 4 to 5 is 0.8, so the expected value is $0.8 - $1 or –$0.20. On average, this bet will lose $0.20 per dollar each time it is placed.

The expected value of a bet is a useful concept, but keep in mind the following:

• Bets with positive expected values can lose just as often as bets with negative expected values. For the examples just given, the winning frequencies are the same. A bet that is "good" in a mathematical sense might lose most of the time.

- Conversely, bets with negative expected values can win just as frequently as bets with positive expected values. Bets that are "bad" in a mathematical sense do win a certain fraction of the time.

- For a bet to have a positive expected value, the payoff must be greater than the odds against success.

- The expected value is an average of many repetitions; it is not the outcome of a single event. For each hand, usually you either win or you lose. Fractional outcomes, such as split pots, are rare.

- To win over the long-run at poker, you must consistently place bets with positive expected values and avoid ones with negative expected values.

- The expression "on average" does not mean that if the odds against success are 4 to 1, every five bets placed will always include one success. If poker were that predictable, no one would play the game.

## Your Cards

To succeed at Hold'em, you must have the ability to judge the winning potential of the first two cards you are dealt (your pocket cards). There are exactly 1326 equally probable combinations for two cards dealt from a deck of 52. However, because the suits are all equally ranked, the number of unique starting hands is reduced to 169. Not all 169 starting hands occur with the same frequency because the number of combinations required to produce each unique starting hand differs. For example, of the 1326 combinations, six result in AA, four result in AK suited, and 12 result in AK unsuited. In terms of percent, this means the chance for AA is 0.45%, AK suited is 0.30%, and AK unsuited is 0.90%.

To compute probabilities, it is useful to divide the 169 starting hands into five distinct groups. The groups and the number of hands in each group are *pairs* (13), *straight-flush-draws* (46), *straight-draws* (46), *flush-draws* (32), and *no-draws* (32). Each group is based on what type of hand can be built when initial cards are combined with favorable community cards. The chart below summarizes the five groups and their frequencies.

## Frequencies of Starting Hands

| Starting Hand | Frequency | Description |
|---|---|---|
| Pairs | 5.9% | Two cards of the same rank. |
| Straight-Flush-Draws (SFD) | 13.9% | Two suited cards that are also part of a straight. The hand 10♥ 8♥ is a straight-flush draw (the flop could come up J♥ 9♥ Q♥). |
| Straight-Draws (SD) | 41.6% | Two cards that form part of a straight, but not a flush. With 10♥ 8♣ only a straight is possible after the flop. |
| Flush-Draws (FD) | 9.7% | Two suited cards that cannot form a straight. |
| No-Draws (ND) | 28.9% | Two cards that cannot be used as part of a straight or flush. For example Q♥ 4♣. |

Subcategories of starting hands can be identified within these five groups. For example, a hand that contains two of the top five cards, such as Ace, K, Q, J, or 10, is an Ace-high straight draw. The subcategories of starting hands can be grouped into roughly four categories of strength. The strength of a starting hand, identified in the next table, is described as premium, strong, drawing, or garbage.

## Strength Categories of Starting Hands

| Strength | Description | Examples |
|---|---|---|
| Premium | Hands that can win on their own. | Big pairs—AA, KK, QQ, JJ, 10 10; straight draws with aces such as A♣K♣, A♥ K♦. |
| Strong | Hands that will probably need improvement to win. | Medium pairs—99, 88, 77; Ace-high straight draws such as K♥Q♦; Royal Draws such as K♥J♥. |
| Drawing | Hands that will need help from the board to win. | Little pairs—66, 55, 44, 33, 22; connected straight-flush draws such as 5♦6♦; Ace-high flush draws such as A♥7♥. |
| Garbage | Should not be played. | All other hands not listed above. |

Patience is required to play Hold'em, because you rarely receive premium and strong starting cards. The next table summarizes the frequencies of selected premium and strong starting cards and the odds against occurrence.

## Frequencies of Selected Starting Hands

| Starting Hand | Frequency (%) | Odds |
|---|---|---|
| AA | 0.45 | 220-1 |
| KK | 0.45 | 220-1 |
| AK (mixed or suited) | 1.2 | 82-1 |
| Any Premium Pair A A-10 10 | 2.3 | 43-1 |
| Any Royal Draw | 3.0 | 32-1 |
| Any Ace-Face Combination | 3.6 | 27-1 |
| Any Ace-High Flush-Draw (Including Royals) | 3.6 | 27-1 |
| Any Ace-High Straight-Draw | 14.3 | 6.0-1 |
| Any Hand with an Ace (Including AA) | 15.4 | 5.5-1 |

A sense of the relative strength of the 169 starting possibilities can be obtained by examining expected value statistics compiled by the online cardroom—PokerRoom.com. Statistics for 122,031,244 pairs of pocket cards dealt at real-money tables were compiled and published on their Website. The next chart lists all 169 hands along with the expected value that resulted expressed in units of "big bets." For example, the expected value for pocket Aces was 2.32. That means that at a $5-10 table where the big bet is $10, the average profit from pocket Aces was $10 times 2.32, or $23.20. An "s" designation means suited.

## Expected Values of Starting Hands*

| Cards | E. V. | Cards | E. V. | Cards | E. V. |
|-------|-------|-------|-------|-------|-------|
| AA | 2.32 | A5 s | 0.08 | 97 s | -0.04 |
| KK | 1.67 | A7 s | 0.08 | K6 s | -0.04 |
| QQ | 1.22 | 66 | 0.07 | K5 s | -0.05 |
| JJ | 0.86 | KJ | 0.07 | K4 s | -0.05 |
| AK s | 0.77 | A4 s | 0.06 | T7 s | -0.05 |
| AQ s | 0.59 | Q9 s | 0.06 | Q7 s | -0.06 |
| TT | 0.58 | T9 s | 0.05 | K9 | -0.07 |
| AK | 0.51 | J9 s | 0.04 | 65 s | -0.07 |
| AJ s | 0.43 | QJ | 0.03 | 86 s | -0.07 |
| KQ s | 0.39 | A6 s | 0.03 | A8 | -0.07 |
| 99 | 0.38 | 55 | 0.02 | J7 s | -0.07 |
| AT s | 0.33 | A3 s | 0.02 | 33 | -0.07 |
| AQ | 0.31 | K8 s | 0.01 | J9 | -0.08 |
| KJ s | 0.29 | KT | 0.01 | T9 | -0.08 |
| 88 | 0.25 | 98 s | 0 | 54 s | -0.08 |
| QJ s | 0.23 | T8 s | 0 | Q6 s | -0.08 |
| KT s | 0.2 | K7 s | 0 | K3 s | -0.08 |
| AJ | 0.19 | A2 s | 0 | K2 s | -0.08 |
| A9 s | 0.18 | 87 s | -0.02 | Q9 | -0.08 |
| QT s | 0.17 | QT | -0.02 | 75 s | -0.09 |
| KQ | 0.16 | Q8 s | -0.02 | 22 | -0.09 |
| 77 | 0.16 | 44 | -0.03 | 64 s | -0.09 |
| JT s | 0.15 | A9 | -0.03 | T8 | -0.09 |
| A8 s | 0.1 | J8 s | -0.03 | Q5 s | -0.09 |
| K9 s | 0.09 | 76 s | -0.03 | 96 s | -0.09 |
| AT | 0.08 | JT | -0.03 | J8 | -0.1 |

| Cards | E. V. | Cards | E. V. | Cards | E. V. |
|-------|-------|-------|-------|-------|-------|
| 98 | -0.1 | T5 | -0.12 | K4 | -0.13 |
| 97 | -0.1 | 87 | -0.12 | J4 | -0.13 |
| A7 | -0.1 | 83 | -0.12 | T4 s | -0.13 |
| T7 | -0.1 | 65 | -0.12 | 54 | -0.13 |
| Q4 s | -0.1 | Q2 s | -0.12 | Q6 | -0.13 |
| Q8 | -0.11 | 94 | -0.12 | Q2 | -0.13 |
| J5 s | -0.11 | 74 | -0.12 | J3 s | -0.13 |
| T6 | -0.11 | A4 | -0.12 | J3 | -0.13 |
| Q3 s | -0.11 | T4 | -0.12 | T3 s | -0.13 |
| 75 | -0.11 | 82 | -0.12 | A3 | -0.13 |
| J4 s | -0.11 | 64 | -0.12 | Q5 | -0.13 |
| 74 s | -0.11 | 42 | -0.12 | J2 | -0.13 |
| K8 | -0.11 | J7 | -0.12 | 84 s | -0.13 |
| 86 | -0.11 | 93 | -0.12 | 82 s | -0.14 |
| 53 s | -0.11 | 73 | -0.12 | 42 s | -0.14 |
| K7 | -0.11 | 53 | -0.12 | 93 s | -0.14 |
| 85 s | -0.11 | T3 | -0.12 | 73 s | -0.14 |
| 63 s | -0.11 | 63 | -0.12 | K3 | -0.14 |
| J6 s | -0.11 | K6 | -0.12 | J2 s | -0.14 |
| 85 | -0.11 | J6 | -0.12 | 92 s | -0.14 |
| T6 s | -0.11 | 96 | -0.12 | 52 s | -0.14 |
| 76 | -0.11 | 92 | -0.12 | K2 | -0.14 |
| A6 | -0.12 | 72 | -0.12 | T2 s | -0.14 |
| T2 | -0.12 | 52 | -0.12 | 62 s | -0.14 |
| 95 s | -0.12 | Q4 | -0.13 | 32 | -0.14 |
| 84 | -0.12 | K5 | -0.13 | A2 | -0.15 |
| 62 | -0.12 | J5 | -0.13 | 83 s | -0.15 |
| T5 s | -0.12 | 43 s | -0.13 | 94 s | -0.15 |
| 95 | -0.12 | Q3 | -0.13 | 72 s | -0.15 |
| A5 | -0.12 | 43 | -0.13 | 32 s | -0.16 |
| Q7 | -0.12 | | | | |

* Data reprinted with permission of PokerRoom.com and originally published at *http://www.PokerRoom.com*. Expected values determined from the analysis of 122, 031, 244 actual hands played.

These statistics are not the result of a simulation or mathematical computation. The expected value averages are based on the actual outcomes of all 122,031,244 hands analyzed. An examination of this table confirms some common beliefs, but also reveals some surprises.

*Confirmations*

- Premium pairs play best—AA, KK, QQ, JJ, in that order, are the top four hands in terms of expected value.

- Any Ace with a face card—AK, AQ, AJ, has a positive expected value, whether the cards are suited or not.

- Most hands should not be played. Only 40 of the 169 possible starting hands have produced a positive expected value.

*Surprises*

- Any hand AX unsuited, in which X is 9 or less, had a negative expected value.

- J-10 and Q-10 unsuited had negative expected values.

Real-world poker plays differently than poker theory. The so-called worst starting hand—7-2 unsuited—because these are the lowest cards you can hold, with no possibility of a straight or flush after the flop, has done better in practice than 37 other starting hands, including many that contain Aces, Kings, Queens, and Jacks. This is evidence that players routinely overplay hands with Aces and face cards and lose more money than they should. This is also my explanation for why 7-2 suited and 3-2 suited end up at the bottom, in places 168 and 169 respectively, of the list.

*Dominated Hands*

The problem with playing high cards paired with low cards (A 3, K 5, etc.) is that these hands are frequently "dominated." You might pair the Ace or King and have a winning hand, but if you get any action, it will be from another player who at a minimum has paired the Ace or King and has a higher hole card (stronger kicker). It is costly to routinely play cards that only get action when the hand is second best. It is not enough to just have the winning hand. To profit, you must get paid when *your* hand is the best. If a hand with a weak kicker holds up, it usually will not be paid.

## Your Position

You must play starting cards appropriate for your position. In an early position, you are forced throughout the hand to make decisions with the least amount of information. For example, if before the flop, you call the blind with a drawing hand, you could be faced with a raise from one or more players with premium pairs. Since you don't know what raises you will be faced with, don't play cards from an early position that are too weak to justify calling a raise.

Compared to Seven-Card Stud, the importance of position in Hold'em is one of the key differences between the games. Position changes throughout the hand in Stud. The critical factor in determining a playable stud hand isn't position, but rather, whether the hand is "live." If your first three cards in Seven-Card Stud are A, J, J, and you look at the board and see the other two Jacks and one other Ace, you have a "dead" hand. The Jacks with Ace-kicker may look pretty, but your action should be to fold.

However, in Hold'em, only three cards initially appear on the board and they are your cards. To know when your hand is "dead" is more difficult in Hold'em because fewer cards are exposed. To judge if your Hold'em hand is "live," you must observe the bets from the other players. Therefore, position matters, and since your position stays fixed throughout the hand, you know ahead of time the betting order for the entire hand.

Prior to the flop, the person to the left of the big blind is said to be "under the gun" and must act first. That player is not allowed to check; he or she must fold, call, or raise. The small blind will act next to last and the big blind last. Both the big blind and small blind have the option of raising. Pre-flop, the big blind is the only player with the option to check, and that is only if the pot has not been raised.

After the flop and for all subsequent betting rounds, the small blind acts first, the big blind second, and the action continues in turn with the player on the button acting last. That means the blinds will be "out of position" for the remainder of the hand and the player closest to the button will have the advantage of acting last. A player's position allows some hands that are usually unplayable to become profitable if played when acting last.

To understand the effect of position, the expected value data from PokerRoom.com can be further broken down and sorted by both pocket cards and position. Three-dimensional plots showing expected value on the vertical axis versus both pocket cards and position can be constructed. In the plots that follow the seat number refers to the player position shown in the diagram in Chapter 2. The role of each seat number is listed below.

## Playing Positions

| | |
|---|---|
| Seat 1 – Small blind | Acts first for all rounds after the flop. |
| Seat 2 – Big Blind | Acts last prior to the flop. |
| Seat 3 – "Under the gun" | Acts first prior to the flop. |
| Seat 4 – Early Position | |
| Seat 5 – Mid position | |
| Seat 6 – Mid position | |
| Seat 7 – Mid position | |
| Seat 8 – Late position | |
| Seat 9 – Late position | |
| Seat 10 – "button*" | Acts last for all rounds after the flop. |

* The button position is also referred to as the dealer position because it marks the position of the player who would theoretically deal in a player-dealt game.

The three-dimensional plots constructed show three categories of pocket cards—pairs, Ace-face, and suited-connectors. The three plots show that position matters more for some categories of pocket cards than others.

*The effect of position on pairs*

The expected value of pocket pairs depends strongly on the rank of the pair and is roughly independent of position. Pocket pairs of rank 66 and below do poorly from almost any position, while premium pairs rank JJ and above do well from all positions. The plot shows that the decrease in the expected value of pairs as rank falls is substantial. A pair of Aces is 50% more profitable than a pair of Kings. A pair of Kings is 50% more profitable than a pair of Queens.

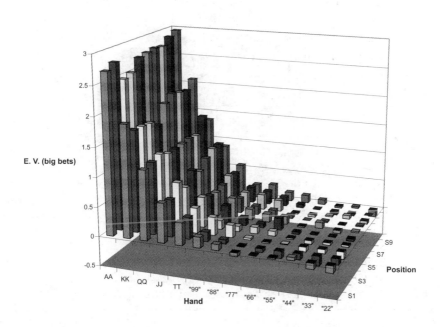

*The effect of position on "Ace-face"*

Hands containing "Ace-face" —meaning an Ace with a King, Queen or Jack—have a positive expected value from *all* positions. Like pocket pairs, the effect of position on expected value is small. Not surprisingly, the higher the face card, the higher the expected value, and suited combinations do better than unsuited. The one exception is that Ace-King unsuited does slightly better than Ace-Jack suited. Ace-face combinations, in general, do better than small pocket pairs from any position.

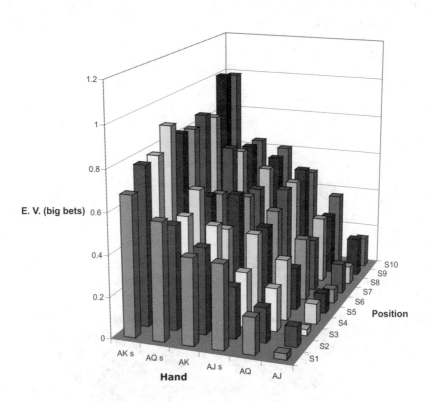

## The effect of position on suited-connectors

The expected value of suited-connectors is strongly dependent on both the rank of the cards and the seat position. These effects can be seen on the chart by looking at the increase in expected values of Jack-10 suited as the seat number increases (position becomes later), and of the expected value increase for seat 10 (last position) as the rank of cards increase. The peak of this three-dimensional plot is for Jack-10 suited in seat 9. Suited-connectors that do not contain a card of at least rank 10 have done poorly from all but the last three seat positions. The one anomaly is 8-7 suited, which has done well for players "under-the-gun." It has a negative or zero expected value for all other positions. I have no explanation for this anomaly.

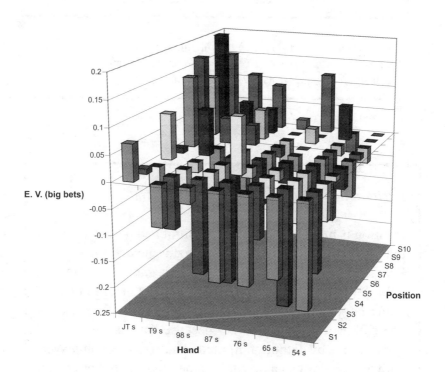

The results of this position analysis are summarized in the chart below. What the position chart tells you is that the later your position, the more types of hands are potentially playable. Drawing hands, such as suited-connectors, increase in value with later positions, because more information (number of players, potential pot size) is available. The chart does not mean you should always play a drawing hand from a late position. It means that if other decision factors are favorable—factors that are only known from having a late position—a drawing hand is playable.

## Position Recommendations for Starting Hands

| Position | Seat | Playable Hands |
|---|---|---|
| Early-position | (seats 1-3) | premium hands |
| Mid-position | (seats 4-6) | premium and strong hands |
| Late-position | (seats 6-9) | premium, strong and drawing hands |

### Position in pot-limit and no-limit Hold'em

Position is more of a factor in pot-limit and no-limit games than it is in limit. The charts analyzing position using the PokerRoom.com statistics are for limit games and are not valid for pot-limit or no-limit play. Players in a limit game with a good drawing hand can often get away with checking and calling a last position bet because the cost to see one more card is by definition limited. An early-position player with a good draw in a no-limit game often cannot afford to put his or her entire stack at risk if a late-position player makes a big bet.

## Number of Players

It is a general truth that for all premium starting cards, the more players dealt in the hand, the more likely it is someone else will have at least as good a starting hand. The effect of the number of players dealt in the hand on the probabilities is most clearly seen by calculating the occurrences of high-ranked pocket pairs. If you hold a pocket pair, the chart below summarizes the odds against one or more players at the table holding a higher-ranked pocket pair.*

The chart shows that in short-handed games, premium pocket pairs increase in value. If you hold JJ and are up against two opponents (a deal of 3), the odds against one or both of them having a higher pocket pair are 33-1. These are the same odds against KK competing with AA in a deal of seven hands.

The pattern shown in the previous chart, of premium cards being less likely to hold up as the number of players increases, is also true as the hand progresses. The more players that compete for the pot, the more likely it is that the best hand will be out-drawn. The best starting hand in Hold'em, AA, is always more likely to win than any other starting hand. However, the absolute probability of AA winning decreases as the number of players in the hand increases.

### Odds for Multiple Pocket Pairs

| | Number of Players Dealt in the Hand (Including You) | | | | | | | | |
|---|---|---|---|---|---|---|---|---|---|
| *Your Hand* | 2 | 3 | 4 | 5 | 6 | 7 | 8 | 9 | 10 |
| **KK** | 200-1 | 100-1 | 67-1 | 50-1 | 40-1 | 33-1 | 29-1 | 25-1 | 22-1 |
| **QQ** | 100-1 | 50-1 | 33-1 | 25-1 | 20-1 | 16-1 | 14-1 | 12-1 | 11-1 |
| **JJ** | 67-1 | 33-1 | 22-1 | 16-1 | 13-1 | 11-1 | 9-1 | 7.8-1 | 6.9-1 |
| **10, 10** | 50-1 | 25-1 | 16-1 | 12-1 | 9.5-1 | 7.9-1 | 6.7-1 | 5.8-1 | 5.1-1 |
| **9, 9** | 40-1 | 20-1 | 13-1 | 9.5-1 | 7.5-1 | 6.2-1 | 5.2-1 | 4.5-1 | 3.9-1 |

* Computations performed using the methods of Brian Alspach, described in his paper on "Multiple Pocket Pairs" at *http://www.math.sfu.ca/~alspach/comp35.* and published in *Poker Digest*, Vol. 5, No. 2, January 2002.

*Short-handed Hold'em*

Short-handed play requires much more aggression than a full table. At a full table with a board that has straight and flush possibilities, the chances are good that a premium pocket pair will not hold up at the end, especially if it is a multi-way pot with a good deal of action. But, in a short-handed game, players are more likely to "back" into straights and flushes than to play for them. That means you must play high cards and premium pairs more aggressively than in a full game, even when the board appears threatening.

## Pot Odds

Pot odds are the ratio of the amount of money in the pot to the amount it costs to stay in the hand. For example, when you bet $10 to contest a $100 pot, your bet is paid off 10:1 if you win. That ratio (the pot odds) should be greater than the odds against winning. For a flush-draw with one card to come, the odds are 4:1 against making the flush. Calling when you are on a flush draw and the pot odds are 10:1 is a good bet. Calling in the same situation when the pot odds are 2:1 is a bad bet. Your odds of winning the hand haven't changed, but the payoff has, and that should determine the decision. *Poker is about winning money, not about winning hands.*

The tables and graphs that follow provide the statistical data you need to compute the pot odds both before and after the flop. The tables and graphs communicate three main points. The points are:

- Straights and flushes are rare after the flop. Unless there are a large number of players entering the hand, you rarely will have the correct pot odds to play only for a straight or flush.

- Unless you have a 10 or higher in your hand, you rarely will have the best hand after the flop. You are not getting good pot odds to enter a hand with low cards.

- The person with the best hand after the flop is a favorite to win. For almost all common drawing situations, odds of improvement on the draw are less than 50%.

## Probabilities on the flop

The tables on the next page show the probabilities of having a particular ranked hand after the flop. The first table presents probabilities for starting hands in the pairs, flush-draw, and no-draw groups. Straights and straight-flushes are not possible after the flop for starting hands in these groups. Of course any two cards could improve to a straight or straight-flush later on in the hand if the right cards appear.

For starting hands in the straight-draw and straight-flush-draw groups, the probabilities on the flop are more complicated to summarize. Connected starting cards, such as 9-8, are more likely to flop a straight than gapped cards, such as 9-7. To summarize the probabilities, straight-draws and straight-flush-draws must be separated into four groups: connected (such as 9-8), one-gap (such as 9-7), two-gap (such as 9-6), and three-gap (such as 9-5). A three-gap straight-draw, such as 9-5, can only make one straight on the flop (9 high). Connected cards such as 9-8 have four straight possibilities on the flop (Q - high, J - high, 10 - high, 9 - high). Each straight possibility has a 0.3265% chance of occurring. Therefore 0.3265% times the number of straight possibilities gives the chance of a straight on the flop. The second table on the next page shows the probabilities after the flop for the different straight draw categories.

The third table shows the probabilities for starting cards that are straight-flush-draws. In this case, the probabilities for straights are slightly reduced when compared to straight-draws, and the probabilities for flushes slightly reduced when compared to flush-draws. The reason is that a small fraction of the possible

## Probabilities on the Flop for Five-Card Hands

*NO STRAIGHT POSSIBLE*

| After the Flop the Probability (in percent) of Having: | | | | | | | | |
|---|---|---|---|---|---|---|---|---|
| Starting Hand | Straight Flush | Four of Kind | Full House | Flush | Straight | Three of Kind | Two Pair | One Pair |
| Pair | — | 0.245 | 0.980 | — | — | 10.77 | 16.16 | 71.84 |
| FD | — | 0.010 | 0.092 | 0.842 | — | 1.571 | 4.041 | 40.41 |
| ND | — | 0.010 | 0.092 | —- | — | 1.571 | 4.041 | 40.41 |

*STRAIGHT–DRAWS*

| After the Flop the Probability (in percent) of Having: | | | | | | | | |
|---|---|---|---|---|---|---|---|---|
| Starting Hand | Straight Flush | Four of Kind | Full House | Flush | Straight | Three of Kind | Two Pair | One Pair |
| Connected | — | 0.010 | 0.092 | — | 1.306 | 1.571 | 4.041 | 40.41 |
| One-gap | — | 0.010 | 0.092 | — | 0.980 | 1.571 | 4.041 | 40.41 |
| Two-gap | — | 0.010 | 0.092 | — | 0.653 | 1.571 | 4.041 | 40.41 |
| Three-gap | — | 0.010 | 0.092 | — | 0.327 | 1.571 | 4.041 | 40.41 |

*STRAIGHT–FLUSH DRAWS*

| After the Flop the Probability (in percent) of Having: | | | | | | | | |
|---|---|---|---|---|---|---|---|---|
| Starting Hand | Straight Flush | Four of Kind | Full House | Flush | Straight | Three of Kind | Two Pair | One Pair |
| Connected | 0.020 | 0.010 | .092 | 0.821 | 1.286 | 1.571 | 4.041 | 40.41 |
| One-gap | 0.015 | 0.010 | .092 | 0.827 | 0.964 | 1.571 | 4.041 | 40.41 |
| Two-gap | 0.010 | 0.010 | .092 | 0.832 | 0.643 | 1.571 | 4.041 | 40.41 |
| Three-gap | 0.005 | 0.010 | .092 | 0.837 | 0.321 | 1.571 | 4.041 | 40.41 |

*Important:* *All straight draw starting hands with an Ace fall in the three-gap category because only one straight is possible. The hands AK, AQ, AJ, AT, A5, A4, A3, A2 all require three specific ranked cards to make the straight, the same as the hand 9-5. The hands KQ, KJ, 4-2, and 3-2, fall into the two-gap category because they cannot form straights higher than Ace-high or lower than Ace-low. For the same reason the hands QJ and 4-3 are in the one-gap category.*

straights and flushes will be straight-flushes.

Note that even when they are possible, straights and flushes on the flop occur, at most, about 1% of the time, usually less. Also, pay attention to the note at the bottom of the page, on Ace-high and Ace-low straight-draws. The hand AK, for example, is a three-gap straight-draw. Only one straight (Ace-high) is possible after the flop.

*Importance of high cards*

The figure below shows the probability that at least one overcard—a card on the board higher than either card in your starting hand—will appear after the flop. The probabilities range from 100% (if the highest card in the starting hand is a 2) to 0% (for an Ace in the starting hand). The figure demonstrates that holding an 8 as a high card is not much different than holding a 2. Since straights and flushes are rare, pairing pocket cards with cards in the flop is much more likely than any other event. To win over the long-run, you must play high cards, because that decreases the chance that an opponent will pair with an overcard.

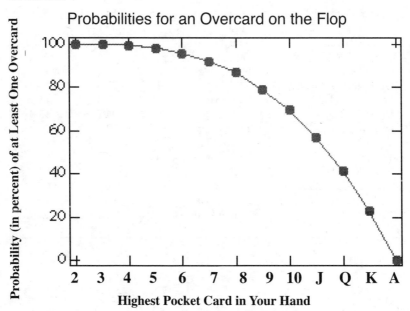

Probabilities for an Overcard on the Flop

*Common Draws*

After the flop, it is the number of unseen cards that can improve a hand (*outs*), which determine the probability of improvement on the turn or river. For example, if you have an open-ended straight-draw, eight cards are out that will improve your hand to a straight (four of each rank on each end). With two cards to come, you have a 31.5% chance of making the straight, but with one card to come, the chance drops to 17.4%. Next is a tabulation of common draws and the chances of improvement. Knowing these probabilities is essential for computing the pot odds when betting on the turn and river cards. For situations not listed in the table, count the number of outs to make the hand and read the percentage next to the number of outs.

## Probabilities for Improving a Hand

**Probabilities in Percentages for Improving a Hand After the Flop**

| Situation | Improve to | Outs | Two cards to come | One card to come |
|---|---|---|---|---|
| Open ended straight-flush-draw | Straight or Flush | 15 | 54.1 | 32.6 |
| Inside straight | Straight or one pair | 10 | 38.4 | 21.7 |
| Four Flush | Flush | 9 | 35.0 | 19.6 |
| Open ended straight draw | Straight | 8 | 31.5 | 17.4 |
| Three of kind | Full House | 7 | 27.8 | 15.2 |
| Unmatched pocket cards | One pair | 6 | 24.1 | 13.0 |
| One matched pocket card | Two pair or Three of kind | 5 | 20.4 | 10.9 |
| Two Pair | Full House | 4 | 16.5 | 8.7 |
| Inside Straight | Straight | 4 | 16.5 | 8.7 |
| One matched pocket card | Two pair | 3 | 12.5 | 6.5 |
| Pocket Pair | Three of kind | 2 | 8.4 | 4.3 |
| Three of kind | Four of kind | 1 | 4.3 | 2.2 |

A more useful way to think about drawing hands is to examine the minimum amount of winnings needed to justify the cost of continued play. The tables that follow show for the number of available outs, the minimum pot size that must be won to justify the cost. If you cannot win the minimum amount shown in the table under the cost column, your bet is not getting the correct pot odds.

There are two tables, one for two cards to come and the other when there is one card to come. For example, playing $3-6 Hold'em, you are on a flush-draw (9 outs) with two cards to come. There is a $6 bet to call and you expect to spend $12 total to get to the river. In the table for two cards to come, the intersection of the $12 column and 9-out row shows $34. You must win at least $34 to justify spending $12, because in this situation, you will have about two failures for every success.

For higher betting limits, multiply the dollar amounts by 10. Example: In a $5-10 game, you are on an inside-straight-draw (4 outs) and must call a raise ($20) to see the last card. In the table for one card to come, think of the $2 column as the column for $20. The value in the row for 4 outs is multiplied by 10 to give $230. You must win at least $230 to justify a $20 bet on an inside-straight-draw. These tables are especially useful for Internet competition, because pot sizes are precisely displayed on your screen and the table can be in front of you for reference.

---

### Counterfeit Outs

In games with community cards, such as Hold'em, not all the outs that you have are real. Some are said to be "counterfeit." Suppose you hold Jack, 9, and the community cards are Queen, Jack, 10. You hold a pair of Jacks that could improve to three Jacks if another Jack appeared, and an open-ended straight-draw that could become a King-high-straight if a King appeared or a Queen-high-straight if an 8 appeared. A naïve count of outs would give 10: two

## Minimum Pot Size for Correct Pot Odds

*For your bets (costs for additional cards) to have correct pot odds, you must win at least the amount shown under the cost column, in the row with the number of outs available to make your hand.*

ONE CARD TO COME

| | Cost of Final Card | | | | | | | | | |
|---|---|---|---|---|---|---|---|---|---|---|
| Outs | $1 | $2 | $3 | $4 | $5 | $6 | $8 | $10 | $12 | $15 |
| 1 | $46 | $92 | $138 | $184 | $230 | $276 | $368 | $460 | $552 | $690 |
| 2 | $23 | $46 | $69 | $92 | $115 | $138 | $184 | $230 | $276 | $345 |
| 3 | $15 | $31 | $46 | $61 | $77 | $92 | $123 | $153 | $184 | $230 |
| 4 | $12 | $23 | $35 | $46 | $58 | $69 | $92 | $115 | $138 | $173 |
| 5 | $9 | $18 | $28 | $37 | $46 | $55 | $74 | $92 | $110 | $138 |
| 6 | $8 | $15 | $23 | $31 | $38 | $46 | $61 | $77 | $92 | $115 |
| 7 | $7 | $13 | $20 | $26 | $33 | $39 | $53 | $66 | $79 | $99 |
| 8 | $6 | $12 | $17 | $23 | $29 | $35 | $46 | $58 | $69 | $86 |
| 9 | $5 | $10 | $15 | $20 | $26 | $31 | $41 | $51 | $61 | $77 |
| 10 | $5 | $9 | $14 | $18 | $23 | $28 | $37 | $46 | $55 | $69 |

TWO CARDS TO COME

| | Cost of Final Two Cards | | | | | | | | | |
|---|---|---|---|---|---|---|---|---|---|---|
| **Outs** | **$1** | **$2** | **$3** | **$4** | **$5** | **$6** | **$8** | **$10** | **$12** | **$15** |
| **1** | $23 | $47 | $70 | $93 | $116 | $140 | $186 | $233 | $279 | $349 |
| **2** | $12 | $24 | $36 | $48 | $60 | $71 | $95 | $119 | $143 | $179 |
| **3** | $8 | $16 | $24 | $32 | $40 | $48 | $64 | $80 | $96 | $120 |
| **4** | $6 | $12 | $18 | $24 | $30 | $36 | $48 | $61 | $73 | $91 |
| **5** | $5 | $10 | $15 | $20 | $25 | $29 | $39 | $49 | $59 | $74 |
| **6** | $4 | $8 | $12 | $17 | $21 | $25 | $33 | $41 | $50 | $62 |
| **7** | $4 | $7 | $11 | $14 | $18 | $22 | $29 | $36 | $43 | $54 |
| **8** | $3 | $6 | $10 | $13 | $16 | $19 | $25 | $32 | $38 | $48 |
| **9** | $3 | $6 | $9 | $11 | $14 | $17 | $23 | $29 | $34 | $43 |
| **10** | $3 | $5 | $8 | $10 | $13 | $16 | $21 | $26 | $31 | $39 |

remaining Jacks, four remaining Kings, and four remaining 8s. But the four remaining Kings are counterfeit, because if a King appeared, your King-high-straight would lose to anyone holding a single Ace, because that person would have an Ace-high-straight. In reality, you only have 6 outs in this situation. Always beware of counterfeit outs. Cards that improve your hand might improve someone else's even more.

## Opponents' Playing Styles

Playing styles have a big influence on how each player will choose to act in a hand. Playing styles generally fall into one of the following four categories:

**Loose-passive** players are free with their money, but their actions tend to follow the other players. Loose-passive players enter most hands and call just about every bet, but they rarely bet or raise on their own. Generally, these players are the most profitable people to play against. Beware though, since they play every hand, potentially, they can have any hand. It's difficult to know the cards they are playing. While most of their hands are weak, they can surprise you.

**Loose-aggressive** players are also free with money, but they thrive on action and want to be the center of attention. Loose-aggressive players raise often, even with weak cards. If they act after you, make sure you have a strong hand that justifies calling their expected raise. It's not their hand you have to worry about beating, but other players with strong cards who call their raises. Loose-aggressive players lose a lot of money, but if too many of them are at a table, the entire game becomes loose-aggressive. In such a game, there are many pre-flop raises and large pots contested by many players with the flimsiest of hands. Only play with strong starting cards that justify a large pre-flop expense. Against these players, you'll have large swings in your bankroll, but you don't have to win many pots to come out ahead.

**Tight-passive** players are followers at the table, but very careful with their money. Tight-passive players typically buy-in for a small amount of money and guard it. They seldom bet, rarely raise, and call bets only when they have a great hand. You won't lose money at a table full of these kinds of players, but it's difficult to make much, either. When tight-passive players dominate the table, pots are smaller because few players enter each hand and there are few showdowns. To win money, you need to win many small pots by being aggressive. Bet and raise with marginal cards to intimidate these players out of the hand.

**Tight-aggressive** players are careful with their money, but when they do play, they seize the initiative. Tight-aggressive players enter few hands, but when they do, they have strong cards. They bet and raise aggressively, forcing the other players to pay dearly if they decide to chase. If you find yourself at a table filled with tight-aggressive players, you should consider switching to another table, especially if you are new to poker. It is easy to find yourself outplayed and your money quickly gone in this kind of game. Study the play of tight-aggressive players since you should aspire to be one.

The playing style of each person at the table influences the personality of the table as a whole. The personality of the table is important early in a hand, especially when deciding whether or not to see the flop. As the hand progresses and fewer players remain, individual personalities become more important. You need to note both the group personality (when entering a hand) and the personality of the individuals (when you go up against opponents one-on-one).

Being sensitive to playing styles and how they can change is critical. Group dynamics change as players come and go, and sometimes change for no reason at all. Tight-passive tables can suddenly become loose-aggressive tables for no apparent reason. Learning to adjust your play based on your opponents' playing styles and the group dynamics is the essence of the poker strategy described in Chapter 6.

---

### *Match the game to your personality*

Certain kinds of poker games reward some personality types more than others. It is often easier to find a game that fits your personality than to change your personality to fit the game. For example, if you are a naturally cautious person with a lot of patience, Texas Hold'em with a full table (10 players) might be your most profitable game. A willingness to wait for the best cards, not play too many hands, and not overplay your cards is essential for making money at a full table. But when a Hold'em table is short-handed (5 or fewer players), cautious players run into problems. Always waiting for the best cards eats up too much money in the form of blinds and leaves you out of the action for too long. Short-handed games reward aggression. That means a naturally aggressive player who has to be in the action and can't stand waiting will often do well in a short-handed game. If you are the impatient kind of player who hates to wait and can't restrain yourself from betting, try short-handed games. Your style might be a profitable fit.

---

**For more information poker math** see the poker odds calculator on the Intelligent Poker.com Website (*http://www. IntelligentPoker.com*). It is a useful tool for testing scenarios. One feature of online play is that your hands are recorded and you can review the hand history after play. You can check out with the calculator how your play matched the mathematical expectations.

# Chapter 6. Tactics

This chapter presents tactical plays for each stage of a hand, and provides scenarios that illustrate tactical plays for commonly encountered situations. While working though each scenario:

- Reference the earlier chapters as needed. Each scenario uses information and terminology that has been introduced throughout the book.
- Get a deck of cards and lay out each play. The ability to visualize the potential hand that you have—and the hands that your opponents may have—is important.

## Entering the Hand

After receiving pocket cards, you are immediately faced with a choice: play your cards and either raise or call the blinds, or fold. In making this choice, discipline yourself to:

- Play high cards.
- Play cards appropriate for your position.

As shown in the previous chapter, the majority of starting hands should be folded. Because premium and strong hands are rare and unevenly distributed, patience is required. You may play for two hours receiving garbage or you may get several premium hands in a row. It is important to develop the discipline to play the best cards, which at times requires long periods of waiting. Be wary of playing hands that seem stronger than they are. Having suited cards adds strength to your starting hand, but not as much as you might think. Flushes are rare hands, even when you start with two suited cards. Much of the money won in Hold'em comes from matching a high pocket card with a high card on the board to form a high pair, in combination with a high kicker.

Remember that before the flop, checking is not an option. To see the flop, you must call at least the big blind. Calling raises before the flop adds to your cost and usually indicates that the raiser has a strong hand. Only call raises before the flop if you have a strong or premium hand, and in most of these cases, you should re-raise.

When you have a premium hand, you should usually raise regardless of your position at the table. With AA and KK, you should re-raise. Raising from an early position tends to narrow the field and makes it more likely that your premium starting cards will win. Raising from a late position tends to build the pot since players who already called are less likely to fold. Your premium cards are less likely to hold up against many players, but you will win more money when they do. In either case, you benefit from raising.

With many players in the hand, you can play weaker starting cards. Drawing hands face long odds on winning, but if enough players contribute to the pot, the potential winnings make it worthwhile to enter with a drawing hand. For example, if you are in the last position and you have a connected straight-flush-draw like 5♣ 6♣, and all the other players have called, but not raised the blind, entering is worthwhile. If the flop comes up 4♠ 7♦ 8♣, you have a well-disguised straight and could win big if the people holding high cards bet heavily. But the odds of hitting a flop that favorable are low. Therefore, if there are bets from the early-position players and folds from the mid-position player (which leaves only 3 or 4 players), you should fold, as well. The people who called in an early-position have good cards and you will not win enough money in this situation to justify playing for a long-shot draw.

When more players stay in the hand, or when there are more bets and raises, the pot gets large early in the hand. Large pots tend to protect themselves since players are less likely to fold when a great amount of money is on the table. When the pot is large, you should have premium starting cards or a draw to a straight or Ace-high flush. Again, for small pots, drawing hands should not be played since they don't win often.

Consider the following scenarios:

**Scenario 1**—You are dealt 2♦ 5♣ and fold the hand following the advice to play only high cards. The flop is 2♣ 5♥ 5 ♦. Betting is heavy after the turn and river cards (10♣ J♦), and a large pot is awarded to someone holding pocket Queens. Your 5's full would have beat Queens and fives if you had stayed in the hand.

Don't regret your choice to fold a hand that would have been a full house: you made the correct decision. A miracle flop does not override the fact that over the long-run, playing low cards will cost you more money than you will win. Even your miracle flop is vulnerable to overcards on the turn or river. Had a Queen hit, the person with pocket Queens would beat you. You would also lose to opponents holding Jacks, 10's, or even 10, 5. While it is true that any two cards can win, to play profitable Hold'em, you must play high cards and fold low ones.

**Scenario 2**—You are dealt 10♣ J♣ and you are in an early position. You call, and the player to your left raises. The next five people fold, and the player in the dealer position calls the raise. Then the blinds fold. Not wanting to fold after putting money in the pot, you call the raise. The flop is A♦ 2♥ 7♠. There is a bet after the flop and you fold since your hand is now worthless. You need to catch two perfect cards to make the straight and it is likely that at least one of your opponents has paired the Ace.

You should have folded after the first raise. It costs too much to play for a straight or a flush in an early position, and against so few people, little money is won even if you hit your draw. The person who raised probably has a pocket pair or overcards, so you are an underdog from the start. Had you known about the raise and the small number of players, you would not have called the blind. From an early position, you can't know, so don't call.

**Scenario 3**—In last position, you are dealt K♣ K♦. There are two callers ahead of you. You call, the small blind calls, and the big blind checks. The flop is 3♦ 9♣ 7♠. The small blind bets after the flop and you raise. The small blind calls the raise and then bets again after a turn card of 10♦. You call and then call again at the river to find the small blind takes the pot with a 9♦ 7♥ for two pair.

You should have raised pre-flop with KK. It is much less likely that the small blind would have called a raise with 9-7 off suit than call half a small bet to see the flop. If you do not raise with premium hands prior to the flop, the blinds can limp in with weak holdings. That means a flop of innocent looking garbage cards might be trouble for your KK. When you have hands like KK prior to the flop, raise and force your opponents to make decisions.

*Summary of Pre-flop Play*

These scenarios illustrate wishful thinking that you need to avoid. In short:

- Play premium hands from all positions. Raise, and call raises to stay in the game until the flop. With AA and KK, re-raise.
- Play strong hands from middle and late positions. Call the big blind, but use your judgment on calling raises.
- Play drawing hands from late positions. Only call the big blind if a large number of players remain (5 or more).

- Use judgment on calling raises, and remember that if many people also call the raise, it is correct to stay in the hand.
- Fold all other hands.

## After the Flop

After the flop, you know five of the seven cards that will form your hand. Because three of these five are community cards, the person holding the best hand after the flop is a heavy favorite to win. It is much harder to out-draw someone in Hold'em than in other forms of poker. The cards that follow the flop may improve your hand, but often, they will improve the strongest hand even more. Immediately after the flop, the questions you should ask are:

- Do I have the best hand so far?
- What cards are needed to make my hand the best?
- Why are my opponents still playing?
- What cards are my opponents looking for?

Answering these questions requires the skill of "reading the flop." Consider the following categories of flops:

**Flops with scare cards (Aces and face cards).** A face card is a King, Queen, or Jack. Because people play Aces and face cards in Hold'em, a flop with these cards often means someone has at least one pair; thus the term "scare" card, when an Ace or face card appears on the board. A person who raised before the flop might well have a big pair or Ace-face in the pocket. After a flop with scare cards, that player might have trips or two pair. To continue playing after such a flop, you should have at least the top pair and a high kicker. For example, with a flop of Q♣ J♠ 7♦, you should hold a Queen with another Ace or face card to keep playing.

**Flops with garbage cards.** A flop with low cards is less likely to have paired someone. When the flop is 2♣ 5♥ 7♦, people holding high pairs and high cards in the pocket have a great advantage since it is unlikely the flop has helped anyone. Beware, though, of players in the blind who have not called a raise to see the flop. The blind's two cards could be anything since at this point, because the blind is not in the hand by choice. If a blind gets excited by a flop of little cards, his or her hand could be two pair or better. Don't underestimate the blind's strength.

**Flops with pairs.** To win when this type of flop appears, you usually need to form another pair higher than the one on the board. If the flop is 10♥ 10♣ 3♠, and you hold A♣ 3♣, your two pair is unlikely to win without improvement. You need to pair your Ace. Everyone has a pair of tens so anyone with another pair higher than your threes beats you. Also, any time there is a pair on the flop, it is possible for someone to have a full house. This becomes more likely when there are high cards on the board. A flop of Q♣ Q♠ J♥ is more likely to have made a full house for someone than 5♣ 5♥ 8♦.

**Drawing flops.** Contain matched suits and cards in (or close to) sequence. This type of flop allows for the creation of straights and flushes. Learn to recognize when they're present and when they're not. Any flop containing two cards of the same suit will attract players holding two cards of that suit since they have a 33% chance of making the flush by the end. Flops with connected cards attract people looking to draw to a straight.

**Flops that allow pat hands.** Flops such as three of the same suit or three connected cards should not to be played against unless you can make the flush or the high end of the straight. If there is substantial betting and raising, someone already has the hand or a good draw, and you should fold.

**Combination flops.** These flops allow the formation of a variety of monster hands. Consider K♦ K♠ Q♦. If many players are holding face cards, many monster hands could result from later cards. An Ace-high or King-high-straight, Diamond flush, Kings-full, Queens-full, or even a royal flush could occur in this case. If you are holding Q♠ J♣, and there is substantial betting, get out. Your two pair has little chance of improving and many ways to lose.

With practice and observation, you will learn to read flops and to judge the kinds of hands your opponents are playing. Consider these scenarios:

**Scenario 4** — You hold A♦ Q♥ and are in a late position. The flop is Q♣ 7♦ 3♠ and the action is checked around the table to you. You are hesitant to bet since you only have a pair of Queens.

Your pair of Queens with an Ace kicker is probably the best hand at this point and should be bet. Additional cards stand a better chance of improving your hand more than your opponents' hands. For example, if an Ace appears, an opponent holding A, K has a pair of Aces, but you'll have Aces and Queens. Another Queen gives you trip-Queens. If a 7 appears, an opponent holding a pair of Jacks has Jacks and 7's, but you still win with Queen's and 7's. There are ways for you to lose: someone might have a pair of 7's in the pocket, but that person usually would have bet them ahead of you. Most likely, you have the best hand, and you should bet accordingly.

**Scenario 5** — You hold 6♦ 7♦ and are in a late position. You and six other players are competing for the pot. The flop comes 8♥ 9♥ 10♠. There is a bet ahead of you, a raise, and someone calls that raise. Excited about your straight, you call the raise.

You should have folded. With this many players betting and raising, someone already has a higher straight (like a Jack-Queen), and the players that call are on a flush-draw or holding King-Queen and hoping for a Jack on the board to make a King-high-straight. Your hand is already second best and can never improve. Remember that people play the high cards in Hold'em. Time to get out.

**Scenario 6** — You hold A♦ K♦ and from a late position, raise pre-flop. You and two other players who call the raise are competing for the pot. The flop comes Q♠ 9♠ 10♣. There is a bet ahead of you, and a raise. You decide to fold to the raise.

Folding is the correct play. Despite your strong pre-flop holding, all you have at this point are two overcards and a draw to an inside straight. Your flush possibility is gone. Investing money to continue play with overcards is generally a mistake. In this situation, someone has at least a pair and there is a possibility someone holds a Jack for the open-ended straight draw. If someone holds a Jack, that reduces the chance that a Jack will fall on the board to complete your straight, and pairing your King will actually give that person a straight. As difficult as it is, you must learn to release premium hands when the flop appears to benefit everyone else but you.

*Summary of Post-flop Play*

- Unless you have the best hand, or a draw to the best hand, you should not invest additional money after the flop.
- Knowing when a mediocre hand is the best and should be bet, and knowing when a strong hand is second best and needs to be folded, is the hallmark of a good poker player.

## After the Turn

After the turn, bets double. Your judgment of opponents and the pot odds dictate when you should stay in the hand.

- Learn to put your opponents on a hand and play accordingly.
- Invest your money in proportion to the size of the pot.

When your opponents are on a draw against you, betting to protect your hand is necessary, even when they have the correct pot odds to call your bets. Many beginning poker players fall into the trap of not betting their good hands (thinking that this would alert their opponents that they have a good hand) and calling with weak hands in hopes of catching a winning card. This is the exact opposite of what should be done. When you have the best hand, you must bet and force the other players to pay to draw out on you. Letting them see additional cards without calling a bet is giving them free cards—the equivalent of giving them infinite pot odds. You must force opponents to make decisions. Don't worry about concealing the strength of your hand. You win more money betting with good cards because opponents learn to respect your bets and fold their marginal hands. You might win a showdown with a strong hand, but you always win when your opponents fold, no matter what your cards are.

Sometimes, when many players are contesting the pot, the best hand after the turn is not a favorite to win. If you have the best hand, but many people are on a draw to beat you, the odds are that at least one of them will. This situation is known as *implied collusion*. If, for practical purposes, your opponents are colluding against you, it is better to stay in the hand as cheaply as possible. Implied collusion occurs most often when the pot is large from the beginning (many people called pre-flop raises) and everyone has the correct pot odds to stay, no matter how great the odds against their draw.

When you are on a draw, there are cases when it is correct to call bets when the pot is small, provided that the size of the pot you expect to win is large enough to justify calling the bet. In this case, you are basing your decision to play on *implied pot odds*—the ratio of the expected money in the pot against the cost to play. Estimating the implied odds requires you to judge your opponents' behavior and intentions. For example, in a small-pot game when you expect additional callers later on, or in an additional round of betting, it is correct for you to call, as well.

These following scenarios illustrate the importance of playing pot odds to your advantage.

**Scenario 7**—You hold A♣ J♠ and the flop is A♦ J♦ 3♣. You bet and everyone folds, except for one player who you suspect is on a flush-draw. The turn card is 5♠, and she checks to you. Worried that the last card might be the Diamond she needs, you check. The last card is indeed a Diamond. She bets; you call. A showdown confirms her to have a flush.

You saved money on this hand by not betting your two pair at the turn, but you made a terrible play. Your opponent paid nothing to draw to her flush. She got a free card since she had nothing to lose by staying in the hand. Four out of five times (80%), she will not hit the flush and you win the hand. You must make her pay to beat you. Over the long-run, you will win much more money than you lose.

**Scenario 8**—You hold A♣ 9♣ in a late position and the flop is 5♣ 8♣ K♦. There is a bet and seven callers, including you. At the turn, a Q♠ appears. A bet is followed by a raise that six people call. The pot is now over $100, and you need to call a $12 bet to stay in. You hesitate, knowing that 80% of the time, you will not make your flush.

Because of the large pot, you must call this bet. In this situation, you may win only one out of five tries, but the one $100 win is greater than the $60 cost of making this play five times. Over the long-run, you will come out ahead. Your opponents are correct in making you pay to beat them, but you are correct in calling.

**Scenario 9**— In a $4-8 game, you are in the big blind with K♦ 5♦ and you checked your option to raise against one other caller. The small blind folded, leaving you heads-up with a pot of only $12. The flop is 10♥ 9♠ 2♦, and after you each check, the turn card is an A♦. You check and your opponent bets $8. Should you call the bet in the hope that the river is another Diamond, giving you the nut flush?

You should fold. Many players feel compelled to play on any time a flush-draw exists, but it is rarely correct to play heads-up with a flush-draw. You are investing $8 to win $12 + $8, or $20 minimum. If the flush hits and your opponent calls your river bet, you will get an additional $8, but either way, the approximate 4 to 1 odds against your flush-draw succeeding means that you must gain at least $32 for your $8 call to have a positive expected value.

*Summary of Play After the Turn*

- If you have the best hand, make people pay to beat you.
- If you are on a draw, make sure the pot size justifies the cost.

## At the River

All the cards are out. At this point, you want to:

• Get the maximum value from your winning hands.
• Minimize your losses to opponents who have outdrawn you.

If you led throughout the hand, meaning you always bet and the others called, keep betting unless a scare card appears (an overcard to your hand or a card that appears to complete someone else's straight or flush). If this happens, check. You do not want your bet raised by someone who has outdrawn you. Use your judgment on calling bets. If your opponent only bets on the end with the best hand, don't throw money away to "keep him honest." Remember, money saved is money won. Sometimes in the last round of betting, you know exactly how you stand. If you have the nuts, bet, or if possible, raise. If you missed a draw, cut your losses and fold.

An inevitable part of poker is the *bad beat*. You have the best hand all the way. Only one or two cards in the deck can beat you and at the river, one of them appears. Most often, this happens when someone keeps a little pair in the pocket (such as 3, 3) and calls all your bets and raises on your top two pair (even though they do not have the correct pot odds). At the river, a 3 appears, a card that looks harmless, but beats you. Nothing can be done about bad beats. You cannot hesitate to bet when you have a strong hand, nor can you start playing for improbable draws yourself. Bad beats are part of the normal statistical fluctuations in the game. Your play must be geared towards the long-term trends, not the fluctuations.

**Scenario 10**—You are in an early position holding A♥ 10♦, and the board is K♣ Q♠ J♥ 3♦ 7♣. You hold the nuts. Your Ace-high-straight cannot lose because no flushes or full houses can be formed from this board. Not wanting to scare people out of the pot, you check and then everyone else checks as well. You win at showdown.

It is rarely correct to check with the nuts. You should usually bet. If no one calls, it is the same result as everyone checking. By betting, you force your opponents to make decisions. Give your opponents opportunities to make mistakes.

**Scenario 11** — You are in an early position, holding Q♣ J♦, and at the turn, the board is 3♣ Q♦ J♠ 3♠. You bet and one player calls. The river card is an A♠. You bet again, but this time your opponent raises. You call the raise and find that your opponent held A♦ K♣. Your Queens and Jacks lose to Aces and threes.

The appearance of an overcard on the river should make you cautious, especially when the card is an Ace or King. People tend to hold on to Aces and Kings. In this situation, anyone holding an Ace beats you. Always ask yourself why your opponent is staying for the river card. For this board, the A♦ K♣ hand had ten outs. If any of the three remaining Aces, three remaining Kings, or four remaining 10's appears at the river, you lose.

**Scenario 12** — You are in a late position, holding A♦ Q♥, and raise pre-flop. One player who called earlier calls your raise and everyone else folds. The board is 2♣ K♥ J♣. The player before you checks; you bet; he calls. The turn is a 3♦. Again, he checks, you bet, and he calls. You believe that he is on a draw for a flush or straight because this player usually bets if he has a pair. The river is 7♦, leaving your hand unimproved, but not completing any straight or flush possibilities for your opponent. He checks. Should you check or bet?

You should bet because you have led this hand all the way and there is no evidence that your opponent had a better hand or improved. Because you raised pre-flop and continued to bet, your opponent has to regard the King or Jack on the board as a threat. If you check, there is a risk that the 3 or 5 paired your opponent, because many players will play suited Ace-little cards because of the nut-flush possibilities. If you bet, your opponent is not likely to call with a small pair when you have been representing a big pair. Remember, this particular opponent would bet a pair of Kings, so that is not a threat to you.

*Summary of Play at the River*

- If you have the best hand, bet. Make your opponents pay.
- If you missed a draw or know your opponent made his or her draw, fold. Money saved is money won.

## Raising

Aggression is a key element of winning Hold'em and that includes raising in many situations. It also means learning what to do when your opponents raise.

*Reasons to Raise*

**Force opponents out:** This is one of the most common reasons to raise, especially pre-flop. Premium pocket pairs, and even high cards such as AK, will do better against fewer people. Against one opponent, a hand such as AK might win without improvement. Against six or seven players, AK almost always must improve in order to win. AA is a heavy favorite in heads-up play with an expectation of winning at least 75% of the time. But with five or more players, the winning expectation for AA can drop to 50% or less, depending on what the other players hold. A pre-flop raise also forces the blind bets to pay to see the flop and shakes out blinds with weak holdings. Remember that blinds can hold anything. If there was no pre-flop raise and the flop comes up with low cards, the blinds might have benefited from the flop.

**Get more money in the pot:** If you have the best hand, you should charge your opponents the maximum possible to play against it. Raising with best hand after the last card is out should be done if possible. If you hit your flush or straight-draw on the river, raise if someone bets into you. Raising to get more money in the pot also works throughout the hand in tandem with forcing people out. If you raise pre-flop with AA and get one caller, that is the same amount of money as getting two callers if you did not raise. But your chances of winning against one caller are substantially greater than against two callers.

**Get a "free card":** Raising after the flop with a drawing hand is a common money-saving play. The idea is to induce the original bettor to check to the raiser after the turn card; then the raiser can check back and see the river card for free. This saves money because bets double after the turn. To understand how this works, imagine playing with $5-$10 stakes and flopping four-cards to a flush. With two cards to come, your chances of making the flush are about 35%, which means you are still about a 2-to-1 underdog to win the hand. An opponent with a top pair after the flop, is the favorite and by betting, is forcing you to pay to draw to the flush. If you raise after the flop, it costs you an extra $5, but if that raise induces the bettor to check to you after the turn, you can check back and save the $10 cost of seeing the river card. If every time this play succeeds, you spend $5 after the flop, to save $10 after the turn, the savings will add up.

**Obtain information:** Raising will reveal how committed your opponents are to their hand. An opponent who does not respect your raise probably has a strong hand. If you raise to get a "free card" and your opponent still bets after the turn, you could be "drawing dead," meaning that it is impossible for your hand to improve to win. For example, suppose you hold J♠ 10♠ and the flop comes up with A♣ 9♠ 3♠. The player who raised pre-flop, bets and you read him for an Ace with another unknown card and decide to raise his pair of Aces, hoping to get a free card on the turn. He calls and then comes out betting after a 5♠ falls on the turn. Because he shows no fear over the flush, you must seriously consider the possibility that his cards are both Spades, and that while you hit your flush, he hit the nuts. Had you not raised after the flop, his hand would be much harder to read.

**Seize the initiative:** Raising establishes an aggressive table image and forces your opponents to make uncomfortable decisions. Suppose you raise pre-flop with A♦ Q♦ and the flop is K♣ 9♠ 5♥. If everyone checks to you, a bet might win the pot uncontested even though your hand has not improved. The other players need to consider the possibility that you now have a pair of Kings or a pocket pair, and if the flop has not improved their hands, they are unlikely to play on.

**"Steal" the blinds:** If you occupy a late position and everyone else ahead of you has folded, a pre-flop raise can sometimes pick up the blinds uncontested. The idea is to force blinds with weak holdings to fold. Even if the blinds call the raise, often the blinds will fold to a bet from a raiser if their hands do not improve after the flop. The raise also gains information if the blinds do not fold after the flop. It often means the blinds hit a good hand, or a good draw and the raiser should proceed with caution.

**"Steal" the pot:** Sometimes raising is used as a bluff. If you establish yourself as a tight-aggressive player by betting and raising with your good hands, the players will learn to respect your bets. If you sense that your opponents have weak holdings, a raise can sometimes pick up the pot uncontested.

**Scenario 13**— You hold A♥ J♠ in an early-position and call the blind bet, and then call a late-position raise. The flop is K♣ Q♣ 10♦, giving you the nut-straight. You bet and everyone folds except the late-position raiser who fires off another raise. The late position player could have flopped a set of Kings or Queens, and in that case, if the board pairs later on, you would lose to a full house. He could also be on a flush-draw so you decide to just call his raise.

Calling is a terrible play. You need to re-raise in this situation. If your opponent has a set of Kings or Queens, the chances are 27.8% that you will lose to a full house. That means you will win in this situation about 3 out of every 4 times. With the odds so heavily in your favor, you must charge your opponent the maximum to draw out on you. That means raising and re-raising as many times as you can. Do not hold back unless the board actually does pair.

**Scenario 14** — You hold A♥ J♦ in an early-position and call the blind bet. There is one additional caller from mid-position and the big blind checks. The flop comes up A♠ 3♠ 6♠. The blind leads with a bet. You raise, the mid-position player folds, and the blind folds, giving you the pot uncontested. Should you have called and hoped to get more money by not scaring the others?

Raising is correct in this situation. If you know your big blind opponent well enough to know that he would not bet without the flush, folding is an option. The worst play is to call. The problem with a call is that you gain no knowledge and force no decisions by your opponents. The big blind will see the next card, and for the cost of one small bet, the mid-position player can see another card, too. Either player could have a flush, or a flush-draw (it only takes one spade for this board to have a flush-draw). The big blind could be betting on a flush, a flush-draw, or could have paired any one of the board cards. Remember, the big blind paid nothing extra to see the flop. That means he could hold a 3-6 in this situation, an unlikely holding for the mid-position player who did pay for the flop.

All you have is the top pair with a strong kicker, and the most you can reasonably improve to is three Aces. If you call, no matter what card falls on the turn, you will be in a bad position if the big blind bets again. Do you call all the way to the end and risk losing to a flush? You must force the issue after the flop, with a raise. Then your opponents must decide how committed they are to their hands. If they do not have flushes, often they will make quick exits.

**Scenario 15**—You hold K♥ Q♠ against one other opponent who acts before you do. The flop is 6♠ K♦ 8♣. Your opponent bets and you raise. Your opponent responds with a re-raise, that you call, and then comes out betting again after an 8♥ falls on the turn. You call on the turn and again on river after a 2♦ appears. You lose to a full house when your opponent shows a 6♣ 6♦ for pocket cards.

This is a common mistake—obtaining information through a raise and then not acting on that information. If your opponent is that fearless in the face of your raise, this is a good indication that simply pairing your King is not going to win the hand. In heads-up play, you are not getting the correct pot odds to call the turn bet.

*Drawbacks to Raising*

Raising is an important tactic, but it can also be over used. Too much aggression becomes predictable aggression. There are tactics your opponents can use to punish frequent raising. You also need to use these tactics to punish opponents who raise frequently. Here are some drawbacks to raising.

**Exposure to a re-raise:** Any time you raise, you give your opponent the option of re-raising. The cost to play out the hand can become very expensive if this happens and you need to carefully consider if that cost is worth it. Players who are overly aggressive and raise frequently invite re-raises. For example, players who *always* opens pre-flop betting with a raise are setting themselves up to be re-raised. The other players will simply wait for premium hands and then re-raise the aggressive player. Also, be careful about raising on the end if you think the nuts might be out there and you do not have them. You might be paying three bets instead of one to see them.

**Reduces the pot odds:** When you raise, you are putting more money in relation to the size of the pot than calling would. For example, if the pot contains $40 and you raise a $5 bet to $10, the pot odds are now 4 to 1, compared to 8 to 1 if you call. If you get into the habit of raising with drawing hands in order to build a bigger pot in the event you hit the draw, you might find that the reduced pot odds make the draw unplayable. This is especially true if you are confronted with re-raises. There are many draws that can be profitably played when the pot odds are 8 to 1. If the pot odds are to 4 to 1 because you raised or reduced to 2 to 1 by a re-raise, the same draw might not be profitable.

**Can induce the opposite of the desired behavior:** In some circumstances, players will not participate in the hand unless the pot is big. If you call with your AA, you might face one or two opponents, but if you raise, it could spur everyone on and suddenly five or six players are calling the raise and intend to stay to the bitter end no matter how much of a longshot their draws are. Keep in mind that a pre-flop raise before anyone has called the blind bet will force players out, but a pre-flop raise after several players have called will not force players out. As the pot grows in size because of a late raise, paying one extra bet to see the flop is not a bad investment for anyone. Also, if the goal is to get more money into the pot, raising might not be the way to go. If you hit a monster hand on the turn, like a full house, and there are many players competing for the pot, it might be more profitable to simply call, as a way of inducing the other players to call too.

**Better hands will let you bet for them:** It is common behavior for others to check to the raiser and let the raiser bet. Players with better hands, especially hands that are hard to read, will be more than happy to let the raiser bet for them. The most difficult hands to read in Hold'em are trips formed with a pocket pair, and pocket cards that fill the gaps in straights. For example, a player holding 9, 8 with a flop of 10, 7, 6 is extremely difficult to read. If you raised pre-flop with a premium pair, such as AA,

KK, QQ etc, you will feel safe with a flop like this and will keep betting. There is no need for the player holding the straight to ever alert you or anyone else with a bet. Instead, a nasty check-raise will be waiting for you on the end.

**Set yourself up for a check-raise later on:** If you are too aggressive and raise more often than your cards justify, other players will notice. They will sit on their good hands by calling your raises in early betting rounds and then check-raising you in the later more expensive betting rounds. Opponents will only give you action when they have better cards and trap you with your own aggressive behavior.

**Scenario 16**—You hold A♥ Q♥ and raise pre-flop from a late-position, and two players who originally limped in call your raise. After the flop of 5♠ 7♥ 10♦, both players check; you bet, and both call. The turn card is a Q♦. Both players check; you bet and the first player raises; the second folds, and you call. The river is a 2♣. The first player bets; you call and are shown pocket 5s to make trip 5s.

One danger of always raising pre-flop with high cards is that if the flop contains low cards, the other players will know that you missed the flop. Because pre-flop raisers almost always bet post-flop when checked to, the player who flopped a set of 5s can wait before signaling strength. Had you not raised pre-flop, the player with the set of 5s might have bet immediately, and you would then have had to decide whether to play on with just two overcards against an opponent who clearly had something to bet on.

**Scenario 17**—You hold K♦ J♦ against three players and the flop is A♦ 9♦ 3♣. The player acting first bets; you raise; the other two players fold. The initial bettor re-raises; you call, and the turn card is 9♥. Your opponent leads again with a bet, and you call. The 2♣ falls for the final card and you fold to a bet.

Raising in an attempt to get a free card did not work. You ended up paying three small bets to see the turn card instead of one, and you still had to pay to see the river card. It is also unlikely that pairing your King or Jack would have won, because your opponent either had a pair of Aces or three nines. There was also the possibility that your opponent held A, 9, and in that case you were drawing dead. Your raise had the effect of driving out potential callers who might have been contributing to the pot if you did hit the flush. This is a risk of the raising to get a free card tactic. It can backfire and cost you more, not less, to get to the river.

**Scenario 18** — You raised pre-flop with A♥A♠ and the flop is A♣ K♥ Q♠. You are heads-up against the big blind who called your raise. He checks; you bet; he calls. The actions of check, bet, call continue after the turn card 3♦. After the river card of a 5♣, he checks; you bet; he raises. You call, to find that he holds J♣10♦ for an Ace-high straight.

You need to think about why your opponent would continue playing after you raised pre-flop and then the flop contained all high cards. Your opponent must have expected you to have a high pair, two pair, or most likely trips if you raised only with premium pairs. If your opponent continued playing, he must have thought he could beat those kinds of hands. You must assume that your opponent knew the contents of your hand and ask yourself why he continued playing. I have seen this scenario many times — when the hand the bettor holds is obvious to all at the table, and that means it is also obvious what hand the person calling the bets holds.

*Responding to a Raise*

There is a big difference between making a raise and responding to a raise, even if your cards and position are the same. You have four possible responses when faced with a raise: cold-call, call, re-raise, or fold. When someone raises, you need to run through the previous list of reasons to raise and think about which of these apply to your opponent before deciding on a response. Here are some considerations for each possible response:

**Cold-calling:** This option exists if the raise comes before any action on your part. When you put the entire amount of the raise in the pot all at once, you cold-call. As a general rule, routinely cold-calling raises, even with strong hands, is a sure way to burn through your bankroll in a hurry. You are rarely getting the correct pot odds to cold-call a raise.

**Calling:** If you have bet, or called a bet before the raise, you need to decide if you should call. The big difference between calling and cold-calling is the pot odds. If you call, you are paying one additional bet to continue playing, not two, because the money you put into the pot for the initial call is no longer yours. A common situation is calling pre-flop with a low-pair, such as 5-5 and then confronting a raise from someone in a later position. If two or more players call that raise you have the correct pot odds to throw one extra bet into the pot. The probability of another 5 appearing on the flop is about 10%, and there might already be ten bets in the pot. A set of 5s would be a hard-to-read hand that stands a good chance of picking up more action. Calling the raise is an acceptable play in this situation. Contrast this call with a pair of 5s to cold-calling a raise with a pair of 5s before others have acted. You are putting two bets into a pot that might only contain four or five bets. You are not getting the correct pot odds to cold-call because you will be folding this hand the majority of the times that a 5 does not appear on the flop.

**Re-raise:** In any situation when an opponent confronts you with a raise, re-raising is an option. A re-raise can have a number of uses. If you make it to the end with the nuts and are fortunate enough to have someone raise your bet, a re-raise risks nothing. A re-raise is also useful for isolating opponents. If you want to go head-to-head with the raiser, a re-raise will often chase all the other players away. A re-raise can also be used to shut down overly aggressive opponents. If you face a player who *always* opens the pre-flop betting with a raise from any position, with any holdings, a re-raise is a good counter. Opponents who make frequent use of the "raise to get a free card" tactic described earlier should also be shut down with re-raises. If they cannot get a free card they might stop the use of that tactic. Sometimes you re-raise after first calling a bet, an action known as a "limp-raise." This is a deceptive play often used when holding premium pairs in an early position before the flop. If you hold AA in first position in a tight game, an immediate raise might chase everyone out. Call first, and wait for a late-position raiser to try to steal the pot. Then jump on that player with a re-raise.

**Fold:** If you are not in a situation in which you can re-raise, folding is usually the best thing to do. The vast majority of the time, a raise represents the best hand. If you do not have the best hand, you should fold. Do not worry that by folding, you are setting yourself up to be bullied out of pots. In fact, folding to a raise can be profitable later on. An opponent who sees you fold to a raise might try to raise later on when you do have the best hand.

**Scenario 19** — You hold 3♥ 3♣ in last position. There is an early position raise and everyone else ahead of you folds to you. You cold-call the raise and the blinds fold. The flop is K♥ Q♠ 8♣. The raiser leads with a bet. You must decide how to respond.

At this point, you should either raise or fold. Calling is a poor option because it gains no information. But this situation illustrates the problem of cold-calling a pre-flop raise with a small pair. There will be overcards on the board after the flop and unless you flop a set (get a third 3, in this case), the chances are your opponent will have a higher pair. (Your opponent's raise might already represent a higher pair.) Because the probability of flopping a set is about 10%, you are not getting the correct pot odds to cold-call a raise just to go head-to-head against one opponent.

**Scenario 20** — You hold 3♥ 3♣ in the big blind. There is an early position raise and two others call the raise. The small blind folds and the action returns to you. You must decide whether to pay one additional small bet to see the flop.

There are already seven small bets in the pot and because you are the big blind, you only need to add one small bet (not two like the other callers). The pot is already paying 7 to 1, and that payoff will increase in later betting rounds. The implied pot odds justify a call in this situation. In the 90% of the hands in which you do not see a third 3 on the flop, just fold. But when this play succeeds, it promises to pay big. The payoff in the 10% of the hands that succeed should compensate for your losses when it fails.

**Scenario 21** — You hold A♦ K♣ and must respond to a pre-flop raise from a person who you know only raises with AA, KK or AK. How should you respond?

You should fold. Hard as it is to fold AK pre-flop, a flop that helps you will be hard to come by. If an Ace appears on the flop, your pair of Aces could lose to trip Aces and a worse situation occurs if a King appears on the flop (then your pair of Kings could lose to trip Kings or a pair of Aces). If an Ace or King does not appear on the flop, then at best you split the pot (if your opponent also has AK) or lose to the higher pair (in cases of AA and KK). Be thankful that your opponent is predictable when it comes to raises and save your money for another hand.

*Check-raising*

The tactic of checking and then raising a bet from a player who acts later is known as a *check-raise*. The purpose of a check-raise is to reduce the advantage that players acting last have over those who act first. If you employ a check-raise on occasion, your opponents cannot automatically assume that a check from you is a sign of weakness. It might be a sign of strength. Here is a summary of reasons for check-raising.

**Trapping aggressive players:** Some players will routinely bet no matter what their holdings if there are no bets ahead of them. They will win many small pots with that kind of play because frequently, players with marginal holdings will not challenge them. You can trap players who become predictably aggressive by check-raising them. If you know a certain player is going to bet for you, let her place the bet. Not only will a check-raise help isolate that player in the hand by forcing the others out, it will make that player think twice about betting every time there is an opportunity.

**Reducing the advantage of position:** Opponents who act after you have the advantage of position. Judicious use of the check-raise can negate some of that advantage because it puts them on notice that a check from you might be a sign of strength. A player on the end who intends to scoop up the pot with a single bet just because everyone else checked must think twice about doing that if she does not have the cards.

**Slow-playing big hands:** Players with big pairs, especially in the pocket, tend to play them aggressively if only low cards appear on the flop. If you flop a big hand against an opponent who clearly wants to keep betting, let that opponent bet. Wait until all the players have dropped out and then check-raise on a later betting round. Consider holding 7♥ 8♥ against someone who raised pre-flop with KK. The flop is 5♠ 6♥ 9♣. You have a very difficult to read straight. The player with KK will bet confidently because none of the cards on the board appear threatening. In this kind of situation, a check-raise can often make more money than an immediate bet.

*Drawbacks of check-raising*

Check-raising is not without drawbacks. Here are some possibilities to consider before attempting a check-raise:

**Gives your opponents free cards:** Any time you check, you risk the action being checked all around and no money going into the pot. Opponents who have draws then get to see the next card for free. Suppose you have 8♠ 8♦ and the flop is 8♣ 9♣ J♥. You need to bet this immediately because there are too many drawing possibilities (flushes and straights) to risk going for a check-raise. You cannot allow the possibility of your opponents seeing the next card for free. But if the flop is 8♣ 6♦ 2♥, instead you can risk checking. For this flop, you might not get any action on your set of 8s unless you give your opponents a chance to improve their hands or think they can steal the pot.

**Does not get full value for your hands:** Many players make the costly mistake of not betting on the end when the river card made their draw. The plan is to check-raise the player who bet each round, but that player alertly saw that a draw might have hit and checked back. Players who lead each betting round rarely fold on the end, but they do check back if they suspect they have been outdrawn. If you routinely try for a check-raise in this situation, it could cost you a bet. You need to be certain your opponent will actually bet on the end before you try for a check-raise.

*Defense against the check-raise*

It is important to protect yourself from check-raises. Here are some defensive acts:

**Learn to take free cards:** Do not routinely bet marginal holdings, such as low pairs or high cards after the flop, especially from last position. If the others always see you do this, they will sit on better hands and check-raise. If you take the free card, a player acting ahead of you with a strong hand will be forced to bet after the turn or risk getting nothing for the hand. Also, remember that bluffs and semi-bluffs work better after the turn when players who do not have made hands have to pay two bets to see only one additional card, and the pot is relatively small.

**Check back on the river:** If you think an opponent who checks to you might have hit a draw on the river, it usually costs nothing to check back. If that player did not hit a draw he is not going to call your bet. To know when checking back is appropriate, you need to consider earlier behavior. A player who raised pre-flop and raised again after the flop probably has a big pair and is trying to drive opponents out. If a flush or straight possibility appears on the river, his check might indicate fear that you have the flush or straight. In this circumstance, you can bet without fear of losing to a flush or straight. But, if you were the aggressor in each betting round and another player simply called, that behavior indicates being on a draw. In this circumstance, a check-raise is a possibility.

**Scenario 22 —** You hold A♣ 10♠ in the small blind and everyone folds. The big blind is an aggressive player who you know will raise in this situation if you call, regardless of what she holds. You call and then call her predictable raise. The flop is A♦ 5♦ 8♦. You check; she bets; you raise. Her response to your check-raise is to fold. Should you have check-raised or bet the pair of Aces immediately?

A check-raise in this situation provided valuable information that would have been difficult to get had you bet the pair of Aces immediately. Because you do not have a Diamond, you can never make the flush. But your opponent does not know that. You need to know if your opponent has a Diamond. If you bet and your opponent calls, she could be on a flush draw, or have a made flush. Your opponent is predictable enough for you to know that she will follow-up her pre-flop raise with a post-flop bet. By check-raising, it forces your opponent to consider the possibility that you have one or more Diamonds. Unless she has at least one Diamond, it is unlikely she will continue play with this board.

**Scenario 23**—You hold A♠ 5♠ in the big blind. The flop is 10♠ 9♠ Q♥. You check; an opponent bets and gets one other caller before you call. The turn is a 5♦. Again you check, the same person bets and the same players call. On the river, an 8♠ completes your flush. You decide to check again with the intention of check-raising. Instead, the other two players check. Your flush beats the original bettor who holds K♦ Q♣ for the top pair and the other caller, who holds A♣, J♦ for the straight.

Attempting a check-raise in this situation cost you money. Because you checked each round but then called, many players will correctly read you for a flush-draw in this situation and not bet when the third spade falls. But had you bet, at least one person would have called. The player with the straight is not going to fold and even the player with the Queens might stick around since he initiated all the betting.

**Scenario 24**—In mid-position, you hold 2♦ 2♥ and are the first to call the blind bet. Everyone else folds and the big blind checks. The flop is A♣ 4♠ 8♦. The blind checks; you bet; the blind calls. The turn card is a 10♥. The blind checks, but you fear the blind has paired one of his cards so you check back. The last card is a 2♣. This time, the blind bets and you raise. The blind calls and shows a A♥ 4♣ for two pair. Your trip 2s take the pot.

Clearly the blind meant to check-raise on the turn and this example shows how to defend against that. You know your hand is in trouble because it is unlikely that the blind would have called your post-flop bet if he did not pair at least one of his cards. That means your pair of 2s is the low pair and you must get another 2 in order to win. In heads-up play such as this, you are not getting the correct pot odds to call a bet or raise after the turn in hopes of a third 2. Had the blind led with a bet after the turn, or been able to execute a check-raise, you would have had to fold. By checking back, you got a free peak at the last card and it was one that saved you. This example also illustrates the dangers inherent in attempting a check-raise. While flopping two-pair in heads-up play appears to be a safe hand that you can play any way you want to, allowing opponents free cards, even when it is an innocuous looking 2, can be costly. Had the blind not tried to be fancy and simply bet on the turn, he would have won.

## Deception

**Pure *bluffing*.** Betting heavily with a garbage hand all the way to the river rarely works in poker. To get away with a pure bluff, you need to establish yourself as a tight-aggressive player and play opponents who, observing that, respect your bets. Even then, pure bluffing won't work against someone with the nuts. Of course, one reason for bluffing is to get caught occasionally, which deceives opponents into calling your future bets on strong hands. However, in low-limit Hold'em games, which are mostly populated by loose-passive players, you will have callers whether you bluff or not. That makes excessive use of bluffing costly since you will lose when you bluff, and it is not necessary to deceive people since your strong hands will be called anyway. Even without pure bluffing, there are many ways to practice deception. Consider these scenarios.

**Scenario 25**—You hold A♣ 9♣ in a late position and the flop is Q♣ Q♥ 10♣. There is an early position bet; three people call and you raise. Everyone after you folds except the players already in the hand, who call the raise. The turn card is A♦; everyone checks to you and you check. The river card is an 8♣ completing your flush. Everyone again checks; you bet and there is one caller—the player who first bet who holds K♥ Q♦. Your flush beats the trip Queens.

Your raise was a *semi-bluff* since your hand was not the best, but had a good chance of improving. The raise did several things. It bought a free card since the player with the best hand after the flop (trip Queens), fearing your raise, never bet them again. By inducing your opponents to check, you saw the river card for free. Since bets double after the turn, your raise was only half the amount required to call a bet after the turn card (a significant savings). Your raise also provided information. Your opponent could have flopped a full house and you could be *drawing dead*—that is, even if you hit the flush, you still lose. Not re-raising, and checking to you later on, is a signal that your opponent does not have a full house or four of a kind.

**Scenario 26**—You hold K♣ Q♦ in a mid-position. The flop is J♣ 10♥ 7♠ and the action is checked to you. With an open-ended straight-draw, but nothing else, you bet. The next player raises, one other player calls the raise, everyone else folds, and you call the raise. The turn card is a 9♠, giving you the nut straight. It is your turn, but you check, feigning fear over the raise and the straight possibility on the board. The player who raised previously bets and is called by the remaining player and then yourself. The river card is a 3♣, giving you the nuts. You check again; there is a bet; the other player folds; then you raise. Your opponent, the original raiser, who holds J♥ J♣, feels obliged to call.

Your deceptive play in this hand won a great deal of money. Had you checked your straight draw, and bet when the straight possibility appeared on the board, your opponent with the trip Jacks would have been more careful at the end. By doing the reverse, you trained your opponent to bet for you and were able to execute a successful check-raise on the end. Your opponents will also be wary in the future and not automatically take a check as a sign of weakness. It is usually a bad play to check with the nuts on the river, but this play worked because your opponent had a strong hand (as indicated by the raise) and you deceived him into believing it to be the best hand.

**Scenario 27**—You hold J♣ 10♥ in last position and the flop is 9♣ 7♠ 2♦. The action is checked all the way around and you check as well. The turn card is a K♦. The action is checked around the table to you again, but this time you bet. One person calls; the others fold. The river is a 5♥. Your opponent checks; you bet and your opponent exposes a pocket pair of 3s before throwing them away.

By waiting until the turn to bet, you were able to convince the others that the King helped your hand. That convinced the person with the small pair that his hand was lost when it didn't improve to trip 3s. Had you bet immediately after the flop, it would have looked like you were using your position to steal the pot and you might have had more callers. It is also likely that the person with the pair of 3s would have called you down. He did not call you because your turn-bet convinced him that you paired the King.

It is not correct to always play drawing hands in a deceptive manner. Often you will check when drawing, and bet when you hit the draw. However, these are ways to vary your play, and keep opponents off balance. Making intentionally misleading plays does assume your opponents are skilled and think about their actions. Opponents who don't think cannot be deceived. Against opponents who call, no matter what, don't make fancy deceptive plays—they won't notice. When your opponents call all the time, the only way to win is to have the best cards at the end.

# 7. Strategies

For successful play, it is necessary to have knowledge of the mathematical facts and tactical plays described in the previous sections. That knowledge alone will not make you successful. Your play must have an underlying strategy: a broad plan that provides a context for each action. This section discusses strategic considerations. Interwoven throughout this discussion are what I call "life analogies," which are a series of behavioral examples from life that illustrate poker concepts. In his book *Serious Poker*, Dan Kimberg makes the astute observation that while most sports professionals believe their sport is a metaphor for life, "poker players believe the converse—that life is a metaphor for poker."*

It helps to first consider why there is no magic formula for winning at poker. Imagine a formula exists that does win at poker. A formula means a pre-determined set of actions for all situations encountered. In situation 1, do A, in situation 2, do B, and so on. Once the formula is known, it would immediately become useless because poker is a zero-sum game. One person's loss is another one's gain. If everybody plays the exact same way, over time, the cards are evenly distributed so all the situations encountered become equally distributed. The result is that no one has an advantage; money flows back and forth without accumulating for any one person.

* Dan Kimberg, *Serious Poker,* 2nd Edition (ConJelCo, Pittsburgh, PA, 2002) p. 2.

> *To win at poker, your actions must be different from those of the other players; different in a way that gives you the edge.*

Clearly, a winning poker strategy must be a dynamic one; that is, a strategy that continually adjusts to conditions. The strategy outlined is based on the five decision factors described in Chapter 5: your cards, position, cost, number of players, and opponents' playing styles, combined with a classification of game conditions that are described next. The premise of the strategy is that the weight given to each decision factor depends on the game conditions. For example, your position under some game conditions is not an important factor. With a different set of game conditions, position becomes the most important factor.

To classify game conditions, four extreme cases are identified and the strategic considerations appropriate for each is discussed. A given poker game usually does not precisely match one of the extremes, but often a game will have enough elements of one of the extreme cases so that knowing what to do in the extreme provides a good strategic starting point.

---

### Life Analogy – Investing

Over the long-run, investing in the market is not a zero-sum game. Historically, wealth and the living standards that go with wealth tend to increase over time. By investing in funds that track the general market, it is possible to have a share in the expanding economy and accumulate money over time.

However, the dream of most investors is to "beat the market"—that is, to make more money than the market as a whole by buying and selling securities from other investors in such a way that money flows from them to us. Can there be a magic formula for beating the market? Obviously not or we would all apply the formula and be multi-millionaires overnight. That cannot happen because in the short term, investing is a zero-sum game: over a short period of time, there is only a finite amount of money available.

To beat the market, it is necessary to become educated about the securities being traded. Over the last decade, the Internet has made it possible for all investors to know more about the securities they trade. With a computer and Internet access, a click of a mouse makes it possible to know company financials, breaking news, real-time prices, and make immediate purchases. However, all this information has not made it easier to beat the market. When everyone has access to the same information, any change that occurs is reflected immediately in the price. Prices moved in an orderly fashion a few decades ago as information on a company slowly filtered to investors. Today, prices move abruptly overnight or in minutes, when thousands of investors respond to breaking news posted on the Internet.

Has the explosion of information, fast-trade executions, and technical stock charts made it easier to beat the market? No, it has not. Many people may claim otherwise, but look around. How many people do you know who are quitting their jobs to become securities traders? Today, investors are more knowledgeable, but beating the market is still as difficult as ever because for the most part, everyone has equal access to the same information. No matter how much information is available, when it is equally shared, no one has an edge.

There are people who do beat the market because they make better decisions. But the adjective "better" means their decisions are also different from the majority. Their decisions cannot be part of a formula, but must adjust to changes in the market before the change happens. Usually, people who are successful at beating the market have a talent for making adjustments ahead of time. They anticipate the next big trend before the crowd starts the stampede.

## Classifying Game Characteristics

In Chapter 5, individual playing styles were classified into four broad groups: loose-passive, loose-aggressive, tight-passive, and tight-aggressive. Poker games themselves also fit into these categories. In attaching an adjective to a poker game, it is the general behavior of the group being described. How does a group of people playing a game together take on a style of its own? It happens in much the same way that the individuals acquire their playing styles: it depends on the underlying reasons for the game.

The object of poker is to win money, but that is not the only reason for the game. Often, winning money isn't even the most important reason. In Alan N. Schoonmaker's book, *The Psychology of Poker,* he explains that we are kidding ourselves if we think poker is only about money. For all but a few professionals, poker is a game, not a job.

People play games for many reasons: competition, socializing, entertainment, mental challenge, etc. Money is rarely the primary motive. In fact, compared to the expense of some games, such as golf or yacht racing, a person could lose money consistently in low-limit poker games, have a good time, and still be better off financially. Some people have this view of poker—that they are paying for entertainment.

To formulate a correct strategy, you need to examine the underlying reasons for the game in which you choose to play. Two reasons must be considered in the most detail. (1) Money is a meaningful component to a poker game. It is how the game is scored, but the relative importance of money to the players must be weighed. In many situations, no one cares that much about the money. (2) Just as important as money is the social question—are people playing for friendly entertainment or for hard-nosed competition?

Imagine a two-dimensional grid where on the horizontal scale, the importance of money is plotted, and on the vertical scale is the degree of competitiveness. The next figure illustrates the grid. As games increase in competitiveness, their character changes from passive to aggressive. As money increases in importance, the game changes from loose to tight. The four corners of the grid are the extremes. The four poker situations that best exemplify the four extremes and the appropriate strategy for each case are discussed. Each quadrant of the grid represents games that are closest to one of the extremes. A different one of the five decision factors becomes most critical as the nature of the game moves to different quadrants. The critical factor is the one you need to weigh the most when making decisions on your hands. The nature of the game often means that safe assumptions can be made on the other decision factors. The recommended strategy will incorporate the safe assumptions and give careful consideration to the critical factor. Also described are the common frustrations and mistakes associated with each extreme.

## THE STRATEGIC GRID

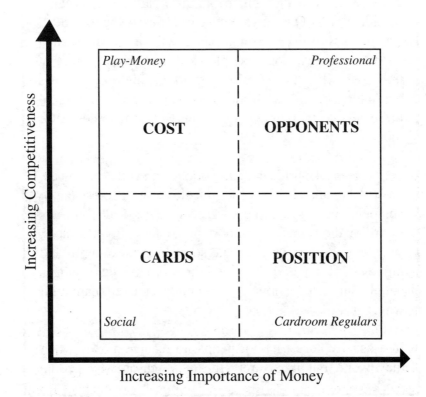

### *Life Analogy – Why do people work?*

For the money, right? No paycheck equals no food, no housing, no clothes and none of the other necessities and luxuries that sustain our lives. At least that's the answer we give our kids who are always laying claim to our paycheck. However, money is only part of the reason we or anyone else works. Examples abound of people whose work cannot be motivated by money. There are people who work even though they don't need the money. Does Bill Gates go to work because he needs money? Most heads of large companies have plenty of money and could retire early, yet they still work.

Politicians work for power, influence and a place in history. The President of the United States is paid far less than a president or CEO in private industry. Clearly the President, usually a well-off person to start with, is not motivated by the paycheck. Some people work low-paying jobs that they love when they could be working high-paying jobs that interest them less. Many artists and musicians fall into this category; their urge to create outweighs their desire for money.

People also take pride in their work. Along with a paycheck, most of us want recognition for our efforts and expressions of appreciation. We want our boss, co-workers, and customers to say we did something important for them. Book authors, such as myself, hope to create something meaningful and influential. I hope this book will be a product that changes people, and adds enjoyment to their lives in a meaningful way.

It is usually necessary for people to receive money when they work, but it is rarely the only reason why people work.

## The Four Extreme Poker Games

**Social**—a loose-passive game. A game played for entertainment.

**Play-money**—a loose-aggressive game. A game played for competition.

**Cardroom regulars**—a tight-passive game. A game played for money and entertainment.

**Professional**—a tight-aggressive game. A game played for money and competition.

## Loose-Passive Games
## (Social Poker)

Once a month, I get together with the same group of friends for a night of poker. We play unstructured "dealer's choice" games. Each chip is worth a dime and bets are rarely more than 50 cents. We do not play table stakes so we are constantly fishing green out of our pockets when our chip pile runs low. However, there is an "understanding" that if your hand is a monster, you won't be throwing down 10 and 20-dollar bills. We drink beer, munch salty snacks; at the half point, eat a meal of cold-cut sandwiches, talk about sports, work, the stock market, and generally have a good time. On a really bad night, I might loose $30 and on a good night, I make that amount. Of course, it always feels better to win than to lose, but if you are the loser that night, where else could you have had such a good time for so little money?

On "poker night," we play Hold'em and Seven-Card Stud, but we also play many junk poker games with wild cards and antes high in relation to the final pot size. In high-ante games, when most of money in the pot has gone in before anyone sees their cards, it is impossible to gain an edge. Since the game consists of the same seven people, playing month after month, year after year, money just flows around the circle. Over time, no one wins or loses—a perfect social situation.

The social game I play with my friends is an extreme example of a loose-passive game. The defining features of these games are few raises and everyone plays until the end. There is always a showdown. If you go to a casino cardroom on a weekend, at the lower betting limits you will find games that are close to fitting the loose-passive definition. Tourists, beginners, and people out to have a good time populate these games. Money is not the main issue—entertainment is the attraction. The stakes are small compared with the costs of most entertainment/social activities. Loose-passive games are actually the easiest ones to beat. To win money, you must become anti-social: that is, not play every hand through to the end.

## Strategic Considerations for Loose-passive Games

**Primary reasons for the game**—entertainment, socializing.
**Money**—no one cares.
**Competitiveness**—low.

*Safe Assumptions:*

**Position** is unimportant since everyone will call with every hand. There is little information to be gained from having an advantageous position.

**Cost** will be small in relation to the pot. Just about every drawing hand will have decent pot odds.

**Number** of players equals the number in the group. Everyone plays every hand.

**Playing styles** are passive. People rarely raise, even with the nuts.

*Most Important Factor:*

**Your Cards**. The only way to get an edge is to do what the others will not: fold unproductive hands.

*Frustrating Features of Loose-passive Games:*

**Bad beats.** After a long session of play when you end up just about even, you will be thinking about the several hundred dollars sitting on the table that you still consider yours. Of course, the money is not yours because of that one last improbable card on the end that beat you. With so many people staying to the end in each hand, implied collusion is rampant. Bad beats are an unavoidable cost of play.

**Putting people on hands.** When there are six hands up against you, how do you figure out what they all are? Someone is on a straight draw; someone is on a flush draw; someone flopped two-pair; someone has a small pocket pair and is waiting for a set. But which one of your opponents is in each of these situations?

*A Common Mistake:*

**Over aggression**, particularly raising after the flop. You flop a flush draw; a person in front of you bets. How strong is his hand? You raise to find out and expect that you will also get a free card. Three players after you call your raise and so does the original bettor. You have learned nothing, and with this many players, odds are that you will not get your free card. Often, it is better to get your flush-draw as cheaply as possible and worry about raising if you do hit the flush because someone will still call at the end.

*Strategy:*

**Fold frequently.** If you watch the game and see ten hands in a row ending with a showdown, will that change with your presence? If no one's bets are respected, yours will not be either. To claim the pot, you must have the best cards at showdown. Forget about bluffing—it won't work. In these games, you can loosen up on the position requirement for your starting cards. You can play drawing hands from an early position because you can safely assume that the requirements for playing a drawing hand—large pot, no pre-flop raise— will always be present.

However, don't start playing garbage for starting cards and think that, because when there are always many callers, anything is playable. Playing garbage is a seductive trap in loose-passive games because any two starting cards can hit the flop and win a big pot. All the pots are big, so don't compete unless you have an edge at the beginning. One way to think about loose-passive games is to imagine a poker player's dream, in which every hand has a large pot and you are always dealt the best starting cards. Want to realize that dream? Then fold every garbage hand that comes your way. With correct strategy, loose-passive games are the most profitable to play in.

## Loose-Aggressive Games
## (Play-money Poker)

Go onto the Internet and join one of the play-money games. You will find poker play at its most aggressive—raising wars with raises frequently capped, people betting heavily on the flimsiest of cards, and no caution shown when scary cards appear on the board. Of course, everyone can afford to be aggressive because the money is truly meaningless—there isn't any. Play-money poker is an extreme example of a loose-aggressive game. The defining features are a lot of betting and raising with little consideration of the cards. Loose-aggressive players are there for the competition. They are also the people who like to gamble.

Play-money poker is a good approximation of loose-aggressive games, because for loose-aggressive players, money is something they *play* with. Part of the thrill is unnerving the other players with their lack of caution towards money. Often, it only takes one or two loose-aggressive players to turn an entire table into loose-aggressive play. Everyone starts throwing money around to show that the aggressive player does not intimidate them. Soon the whole table is on a tilt.

### Strategic Considerations for Loose-aggressive Games

**Primary reasons for the game**—entertainment, competition.
**Money**—no one cares.
**Competitiveness**—high.

*Safe Assumptions:*

**Your Cards.** You will always pay dearly to get to the river in loose-aggressive games. Often, you will pay dearly just to see the flop. Make sure your cards are worth it. If you wouldn't raise with the cards you have, don't call, because you should assume that someone will raise later on.

**Position** is important, but in a different way. What counts is your seat in relation to the aggressive players. Many poker books will advise you to sit so that aggressive players are on your right, meaning that they act before you do. By acting after an aggressive player, you have better knowledge of the cost to play your cards. If the aggressive player stays in the hand, fold all but your strongest cards because it will cost too much to play speculative hands. While this is true, in my experience, there are also advantages to having loose-aggressive players on your left and having them act after you. Assume from the beginning that the aggressive player will bet, and only play your strong cards. But only bet those strong cards if you have to. In most cases, hold back and let the aggressive player bet for you. Check when it's your turn and either call or raise the bet when the action comes back. The other players will often pay to chase a loose-aggressive player when they would not pay to chase you.

**Number of players.** Usually, more than half the players will see the flop no matter how many pre-flop raises there are. Frequently, raises will goad loose-aggressive players into staying in the hand rather than drive them out. The more action, the more they feel compelled to play. They hate being left out.

**Playing styles** are aggressive. Plan on calling raises before and after the flop. Seeing the river card will always be expensive. Big money will be wagered by the other players on marginal and speculative hands.

*Most Important Factor:*

**Cost.** Make sure you are getting the correct pot odds when you throw your money out. There will be a constant temptation to gamble. In some situations, it will be correct to gamble because there will be so much money on the table that any draw is playable. Other times, the same draw should be folded because the money at stake is too small.

*Frustrating Features of Loose-aggressive Games:*

**Making sense of your opponents.** There may not be any rationale behind their play, so don't think too hard about their thought processes.

**Wild swings in your bankroll.** Loose games always result in bad beats. Add aggression to the mix and you get costly bad beats. When you do win, the pot is large, but it takes painful losses along the way to the winnings. The result is wild swings in your bankroll. It becomes tempting to not want to leave the table unless you've had an upswing, and then you still don't want to leave because it is an upswing. Loose-aggressive games require disciplined play.

*A Common Mistake:*

**Getting caught up in pre-flop raising wars while holding mediocre pocket cards.** This is especially seductive when you are one of the blinds. Any time someone is in a blind position, he feels that he already paid to see the flop and should do so no matter what. Blinds are a cost of play and yes, occasionally, you get lucky, and with a pair of garbage cards for a blind, hit a great flop. But don't call one or two raises in the blind when, with those same two cards, you would not pay anything to see the flop. Learn to let your blind money go, and don't feel you have to chase it.

*Strategy:*

**Pay close attention to the pot odds.** The pot size varies greatly from hand to hand in loose-aggressive games. For a large pot, it may be correct to call two raises if you are on a draw, especially if four or five others call, too. However, for the exact same draw and a small pot, calling raises could cost too much. It requires great discipline to know when the same situation with the cards is a different betting situation because of the pot odds. There is a tendency for people to play the same cards the same way.

Consider an inside straight-draw. You might adhere to the adage "never draw to an inside straight" and always fold, or you might be a player who never folds any kind of draw, including one to an inside straight. However, correct strategy requires a cold mathematical evaluation of the pot odds. The chart in Chapter 5 shows that with one card to come on a draw with four outs, such as an inside straight, there is an 8.7% chance of success. In a $3–6 game, if every time you draw to an inside straight, it costs $6 to see the final card, you will spend an average of $70 for each success. That means every time you try this play, there must be at least $70 in the pot or over the long-run, you will not turn a profit. In a tight $3–6 game, there rarely is this much money in the pot and folding is almost always the correct play. But in a loose-aggressive $3–6 game, pots will easily exceed

$70 if all the players at the table call a pre-flop raise. When the pot is that large and you have an inside straight-draw, you *must* make the call.

Maintaining cost discipline is psychologically difficult, because of normal statistical fluctuations and the fact that in Hold'em, unlike other forms of poker, you get to see what your last card would have been if you had not folded. What this means is that there will be times when folded hands would have won and hands you stayed with lose, and you will know in each case. Don't change your strategy because of these normal statistical fluctuations. Over the long-run, it will cost you money if you leave big pots on the table unchallenged because you refuse to draw to an inside straight, or insist on always drawing, even with small pots, just in case the right card comes up.

## Tight-Passive Games
## (Cardroom Regulars)

Visit a St. Louis Riverboat or a cardroom in suburban Seattle in the middle of the day, in the middle of the week, and you will encounter tables filled with "regulars." A "regular" means someone who plays in the same cardroom several times a week, each week. These people are easy to recognize. The employees greet them by name when they arrive and even comment on their arrival time as being either late, on-time, or early. The regulars chat with dealers and each other in a manner that assumes a shared history. You would have to know about cardroom events from the last month to understand half the conversations. At the table, there are five sets of eyes sizing up you and your play. They are clearly studying you and not each other. The scrutiny can be unnerving, although it means that they don't know you at first (an advantage) and learning about them is easier since the familiar ways in which they treat each other conveys information.

Games filled with regulars have much in common with social home games. The players are there to pass the time, playing a game they all love, in a relaxed, friendly atmosphere. The key difference is that the money is meaningful. It has to be, otherwise they would not be regulars. Unlike a home poker club, where the same $20 gets passed around the same group of people, the stakes in these games are higher and the house gets a cut of each hand dealt. If the players are equally matched, over time the house will accumulate all the money as it gets passed back and forth. These are not zero-sum games.

### Strategic Considerations for Tight-passive Games

**Primary reasons for the game**—entertainment, money.
**Money**—little is available to win.
**Competitiveness**—low.

*Safe Assumptions:*

**Cards.** Players don't compete unless they have good cards. Expect that people paying to see the flop will have Aces, face cards, and pairs.

**Cost.** High in relation to the pot size. You rarely have the correct pot odds to chase. Chasing is a common and costly mistake in these games.

**Number of players.** 3–4: the two blinds and maybe one or two callers. With few hands dealt, high cards and high pairs increase in value.

**Opponents' playing styles.** Predictable and passive. Pre-flop raises are rare and usually mean a high pair or AK. Bluffing is rare. If you are going head-to-head against someone at the end hoping they've bluffed, you are going to lose.

*Most Important Factor:*

**Position**. Since players are predictable in these games, there is a lot of information available when you have an advantageous position. Acting after a solid player, who only bets strong cards, means that you know the strength of her cards before making a decision on your hand.

*Frustrating Features of Tight-passive Games*

**No action on your best hands.** You flop a monster boat and get no callers. Your highest ranked hands of the playing session may generate little income.

**Blinds can whittle away your chip pile.** Pots are so small they often don't generate enough income to replenish your blinds. A big win to get yourself firmly in the black is hard to come by. Worse, if you fall behind, it is hard to catch up.

*A Common Mistake:*

**Becoming too tight yourself.** With so little money in each pot, there is a temptation not to bet your moderate hands. It is common in these games to see head-to-head play in which no bets are made. The two players check to each other while the dealer runs the rest of the cards. Their thinking is, why risk anything for such a small pot? The problem is, you will not make money with this kind of passive play. If you have a decent hand, bet.

*Strategy :*

**Make little wins add up.** The key is to counter the general passivity with careful aggression. "Careful" is a strange adjective for aggression, but you need a good poker sense to know when to be aggressive. Because the players only play good cards, unrestrained aggression will not necessarily intimidate them. But if you establish yourself as a tight player by being in few hands and showing good cards early on, whenever you sense weakness or hesitation from the opposition, go for the pot, even if it is small. You have to steal a few small pots in these kinds of games or you will never cover your blinds. Knowing how to play your position is key. It is risky to bet ahead of tight players when you have marginal cards. If you act first and bet a marginal hand, and a rock-solid player calls or raises, it's time to fold. However, if you hold the same marginal hand in last position and the rock solid players check to you, a bet often wins the pot outright. In both these cases, your cards may be the same, but your position determines which play is profitable.

Typically in tight-passive games, there is not much money on the table. An extreme tight-passive player buys-in for the table minimum and guards the chips, putting money in the pot only when they have a lock. You cannot win money that is not in play and you certainly can't win more money than is on the table. If you see three or more players at a table behaving in this manner, consider finding another game. Your profit potential is limited and if you do fall behind, you have no hope of catching up.

## Tight-Aggressive Games
## (Professional Poker)

For people who make a living from poker, low-limit games are not going to generate enough income. There isn't enough money on a low-limit table to live on, and you cannot win more than the available amount of money. You might think that the only difference between $2–4 Hold'em and $20–40 is the additional zero, but that is not the case. As the stakes are raised, money increases in meaning because attitudes towards money do not scale. Consider asking a middle-class person earning $50,000 per year to give you $10 and you are likely to get it. Ask a Fortune 500 CEO earning $50 million per year for the same fraction of his income, $10,000, and it is very unlikely to be given to you. The greater the dollar amount, the tighter people are. That attitude change carries over into high-limit games.

While many players pay to see the flop when it is only a dollar or two, behavior changes when it's a twenty-dollar bill.

## Strategic Considerations for Tight-aggressive Games

**Primary reasons for the game**—competition, money.
**Money**—people play to win.
**Competitiveness**—high.

*Safe Assumptions:*

**Cards.** Players usually have good cards, but be careful. They will mix things up and you should, too.

**Position**. You must play your position correctly and expect that others are doing the same.

**Cost.** High in relation to the pot size. Tight-aggressive players bet and raise to protect their hands. You are not allowed to limp in with mediocre cards when they have strong hands.

**Number of players.** 3–4: the two blinds and maybe one or two callers. Just as in tight-passive games, the fact that fewer hands are played means that high cards and high pairs stand up more often.

*Most Important Factor:*

**Opponents' playing styles.** To gain an edge, you must pay close attention to the people. Tight-aggressive players have underlying reasons for their actions, which on a rational level make sense. These people are not governed by their emotion of the moment like loose-aggressive players often are. If you can discern their plans and strategies, it is possible for you to gain an edge by anticipating their actions.

*Frustrating Features of Tight-aggressive Games:*

**Players are good. It is easy to find yourself outplayed.** Experience counts in tight-aggressive games. You are studying your opponents, but they are also studying you, and they might be better at discerning your actions than you are at discerning theirs.

**Little room for error.** A single mistake on your part can make the difference between a winning and losing session. Tight-aggressive players don't make the kind of fundamental mistakes (such as playing too many marginal hands for too long) that loose players make. There is much less money going into the pot from players who have almost no chance of winning. That means it is harder to recoup losses.

*A Common Mistake:*

**Passivity.** It is easy in these types of games to be intimidated into folding hands with which you should have stayed the course. Hands that are nearly worthless in loose-passive games because so many players are on a draw, are valuable in tight-aggressive games. Suppose you hold A, Q and the flop is Q, 5, 4, of different suits. If the next two cards match one of the suits on the board, the flush possibility might discourage you from betting in a loose-passive game with six players vying for the pot. Loose players actually play these kinds of draws. But in a tight-aggressive game, no one stays just because they are hoping for two matching cards to make a flush. If you have a top pair and top kicker in this situation, place a bet.

*Strategy:*

**You must rethink what it means to have a good flop in a tight-aggressive game.** The best flop for your cards may not be the best flop for your wallet. To illustrate this paradox, consider a time I had AK in a loose-aggressive game and the flop came up with three Aces. I got action on this hand because a loose-aggressive player in front of me thought he could bluff. The other players didn't believe him because he always bluffed and called his bets. I was in last position so all I had to do was quietly call to blend in with the unbelievers. This kind of play would never happen in a tight-aggressive game. If I held AK, and the flop came up three Aces, I would have a worthless hand. No one would give me any action. To get action in a tight-aggressive game, it would be better if the flop didn't contain an Ace. A flop of K, 7, 3, would generate more action and I would still be in a good position. I would not have the lock of all the Aces, but if someone bet into me with a King, I would have the top kicker. An Ace could still fall later on and it is less likely that the 7 or the 3 are a threat, which they might be in a loose-aggressive game where people play any two cards.

Not only must you rethink what it means to have a good flop, you must also rethink what it means to have a good hand. You may get away with stealing pots by betting marginal cards, and then lose with strong cards. The difference is that your opponents won't challenge you unless they have strong cards. When your opponents are weak, they will back down. The attitude, "I'll call to keep him honest," that pervades loose games doesn't exist in tight-aggressive games. If your opponents call or raise, don't become confident just because your cards are good this hand, and in a prior hand that you won, your cards were weaker. Your strong hands may be losers if tight-aggressive players are not respecting your bets.

*Life Analogy – Investment Scams*

In recent years, the news has been full of investment scams. All scams have a common element: to induce herd behavior and then run in the opposite direction. What makes something a scam is the element of dishonesty. Scam artists say things they know to be false for the purpose of profit. The direction of the stampede does not matter so long as the scam artist goes the opposite way. For example:

**Pump and dump.** The now-classic example is Enron. By use of phony accounting, the top executives created huge demand for their company's stock into which they sold their shares. By the time the public realized that their shares of Enron were worthless, the top executives had cashed out hundreds of millions of dollars.

**Trash and stash.** This is the same basic idea as a "pump and dump scam," but it is done in reverse. A notable example occurred on August 25, 2000, when a college student concocted a phony press release distributed over the Internet, stating that Emulex would not meet earnings expectations. In less than an hour, the company's share price fell 62%, wiping away $2.5 billion of market capitalization. Of course the scam artist shorted shares of Emulex prior to his hoax and covered his short position with cheap shares purchased while the sellers stampeded.

While these are extreme examples of herd behavior brought on by dishonesty, they illustrate a truth that applies to honest investment decisions. The truth is that you will never make money when you are part of a stampede. To profit, you must be standing apart from the crowd.

## Analyzing Game Characteristics

To think about poker strategically is difficult. Most people play the game by looking for the right cards. They hope that their starting cards are good, that the flop hits them, that they will outdraw the other players, and that the other players will not outdraw them. Thinking never progresses beyond what cards will improve my hand, and what cards I should fear.

To go beyond the superficial analysis of cards, you need to develop the mental discipline to analyze the kind of game you are in, both before, during, and after play. While your name is on the waiting list, scope the games you might enter. During the game, think about whether the table dynamics have changed. After play, think about the key decisions you made. Keep a poker diary and analyze which plays worked and which did not.

To orient your approach to the game in terms of the strategic grid figure, here is a list of questions you should ask yourself while observing games:

- Are raises frequent or rare?
- Are showdowns frequent or rare?
- On average, do many players pay to see the flop, or just a few?
- On average, how large are the pots in relation to the final bet size?
- Are common drawing hands getting the correct pot odds?
- Are players showing good starting cards at showdown, or just about anything?
- What is the demeanor of each player?
- Are people relaxed and socializing or serious and intense?
- What are the sizes of the chip piles?
- Does a large chip pile represent a large buy-in or a winning player?
- Does a small chip pile represent a small buy-in or a losing player?
- Do raises scare players out of the hand or egg them on?
- Are there obviously aggressive players?
- Are there obviously tight players?

Extreme behavior is particularly revealing about the nature of the game. Does every hand end in a showdown? Are there never any pre-flop raises? Answer yes to those two questions and it is a loose-passive game. By mentally asking yourself the kinds of questions listed, you will be able to orient yourself on the strategic grid and know the critical factors in your decision-making.

## Summary

Poker is an exquisitely balanced game. For every action, there is a counteraction; for every strategy a counter strategy. Much like a martial art that depends on balance and timing, your approach to poker must be dynamic and adjustable. In his book *The Theory of Poker,* Sklansky provides a table of common poker mistakes and corresponding strategies for exploiting each mistake.* All the mistakes are described in terms of extremes, such as "bluffs too much," "bluffs too little," "never bluffs," "never slow plays." Each mistake requires a counter strategy tailored to turn your opponents' excesses against them. The lesson I take from Sklansky's table is that poker is not a game about strength and aggression; rather, it is a game about balance and self-control. *You do not control your opponents in a poker game. You control yourself and adjust your play so that your opponents' excesses become their own undoing.*

---

* David Sklansky, *Theory of Poker,* 3rd Edition (Two Plus Two, Las Vegas, NV, 1994) pages 254-255.

# 8. Online Poker

Online poker is still poker. The same mathematical facts apply and the same tactics are employed. But online play is substantially different than face-to-face play in brick-and-mortar cardrooms. Success requires tactical and strategic adjustments to the new conditions.

## Differences of Online Poker

Online play differs from face-to-face play in four substantial respects:

- Play is faster
- Play is less social
- Less information on your opponents' play is immediately available
- Less overhead is involved

On the surface these appear to be trite observations, but the effects of these differences are profound. You need to adjust how you play. First consider the effects of each of these changes.

*Effects of Faster Play*

- Two to three times more hands per hour are dealt
- Hourly win/loss rates are magnified

Online poker games typically deal more hands per hour than a human dealer in a brick-and-mortar cardroom. The reason is that the software automates dealer actions such as shuffling the cards, determining the best hand, and awarding the pot. These actions, that take a human dealer a noticeable amount of time, happen instantaneously in the online world. Texas Hold'em in a brick-and-mortar cardroom typically proceeds at a rate of 30 to 40 hands per hour, but the online counterpart is often twice as fast—60 to 80 hands per hour.

Because so many more hands per hour are played, time is effectively compressed when you play online. Your expectations based on in-person play of a "typical" poker session are distorted. When playing online, your sense is that rare events—quads, straight flushes, bad beats, and multiple players holding pocket pairs—are happening with alarming frequency. Many online players become convinced that the increased frequency of rare events means that the deal is not random. When an opposing player goes on a *rush*, meaning receives a streak of winning hands, the rush will play out in 10 to 15 minutes and leave the others believing that the game is rigged.

Faster play also means that hourly win/loss rates are magnified and so are the swings in a bankroll. A reasonably tight, knowledgeable player can sit down in a brick-and-mortar cardroom with $100 to play limit $3-6 Hold'em and even with bad luck, expect that money to last for two to three hours. A string of bad luck in online play can burn up $100 at a $3-6 Hold'em table in 30 to 45 minutes. You can lose money that fast while making correct decisions. Because time is so compressed online, winning players win more money per hour and losing players loose more money per hour in comparison to their play for equivalent stakes in a brick-and-mortar cardroom. If you are an experienced player in brick-and-mortar cardrooms and decide to try to play online, plan on having a buy-in that is larger than your normal amount. Also, consider starting at lower limits than you normally play until you adjust to the greater volatility.

Online players also have the option of participating in more than one game at a time. On a computer screen, multiple windows can be opened for play, each at a different table. It is not an activity that I recommend for novices, but some experienced players do play simultaneously at more than one table, a feat that is only possible in the online world. Again, the differences between winning and losing players will be magnified by simultaneous play. On a per hour basis, more hands will be dealt and more money will be put in play.

*Effects of Less Social Interaction*

- Non-verbal cues are absent
- People behave differently when their identity is concealed

When players compete face-to-face, plenty of non-verbal interactions take place that have an outcome on the game. But, in an online environment there is no information on sudden changes in posture or eye movements that can telegraph an intended action before it is a player's turn to act. It is not possible to see someone reach for his or her chips. While less information is available, it also means you don't have to spend mental energy observing the other player's mannerisms. Even better, you don't have to worry about your own mannerisms and the information you might be giving away. The proverbial "poker face" is not a component of online poker.

Anonymity also leads people to employ more aggressive tactics. You will see check-raises and bluff-raises much more frequently in online play than you will in-person. People are less afraid both of looking foolish and making the other players look foolish. The result is that many more online games fall into the loose-aggressive category than games in brick-and-mortar cardrooms. If you are used to typical low-limit games in public cardrooms that are loose-passive, with many of the players checking and calling, the online experience will require an adjustment. You must be prepared for frequent raises, re-raises, and check-raises—tactics that are not as frequent in "friendly" brick-and-mortar cardrooms.

*Social Differences*

In my experience bluff-raises are rare in low-limit games played in-person. Recently, with so many new poker players who believe that unrestrained aggression is the key to winning, bluff-raises have become more frequent, but still, it is not a widely used tactic. But, online play is peppered with bluff-raises and that fact, I believe, indicates a key difference between the way people behave when face-to-face versus the anonymous remote interactions of the Internet. That difference became clear to me when I unintentionally executed a bluff-raise in a brick-and-mortar cardroom. Acting last in a three-player pot, I misread the board and mistakenly believed that I had a straight. At the river, a player with one-pair bet, a player with two-pair called, and I put in a raise.

Bluffs can be very convincing when you genuinely believe that you are not bluffing. Unfortunately, I only convinced the player with the best hand to fold; the other player called. When in my moment of mental confusion, I tried to claim the pot, the dealer politely pointed out that my "straight" did not connect. At that point, the player who folded the two-pair became furious with me and started cursing. "I sure wish you knew what you were doing," he said. "You just cost me an entire pot." I don't know if his anger would have been lessened had my bluff-raise been intentional. Somehow, I think not. What this incident illustrates is that in face-to-face play, the other players expect you to behave a certain way and apply social pressure when you do not. Even though I did not violate any rules, I was berated for my play. In an online environment, these kinds of social inhibitions are not in place.

*Effects of Less Information Immediately Available*

• Opponents' tactics are difficult to know
• Opponents' starting hands are difficult to know

One of the biggest differences in the conduct of online games is the showdown. In a brick-and-mortar cardroom at showdown, the players often turn their cards face-up on the table for all to see. The dealer inspects the cards and awards the pot to the best hand. But the rules of poker only require the cards of a "called" hand to be shown. A player with a hand that was not called is allowed to toss the cards into the muck without showing them to anyone. But in brick-and-mortar cardrooms, players show cards far more often than the rules require. Exceptionally good hands—quads, straight flushes—are often shown off when there are no callers. Bad beats are frequently shown to make the point that the hand was played correctly even though it lost. In the social setting of a brick-and-mortar cardroom, everyone wants his or her play to look good to the others. The result is that everyone has the chance to observe the kinds of cards people play and the reasoning behind the plays.

Because the "dealer" in an online game is a computer program that is both infallible and all-knowing, it is not necessary for everyone to show their cards at showdown. In an online cardroom, the option to show your cards at the end of a hand exists in the form of a check box or pop-up menu in the software interface. Most players do not select that option. At showdown, only the called hands and the winning hands that called are displayed. The software instantly mucks losing uncalled hands. Players who do show their hands are usually selective about it and do not show every hand. You could be set up if you take what you are shown too seriously. What this means is that it is much more difficult to know your opponents' tactics.

Knowing your opponents' starting hands is even more difficult online than understanding their tactics. Few starting hands are ever revealed online, and a loose-aggressive playing style has come into vogue in which players enter hands and raise with just about anything.

However, I have a reason for use of the qualifier "immediately" for available information. Unlike brick-and-mortar play, computer programs record every action taken in a hand and compile vast databases that can be analyzed. The cardrooms do this to look for suspicious betting patterns that might indicate cheating. But, the software that allows players to participate in the game also records hand histories on their computers. Players can go back and review the hands and decisions made. Most software also has a "players notes" feature that allows users to record observations about opponents for use the next time that opponent is encountered.

In recent years, third-party software has proliferated that performs sophisticated statistical analysis of hand histories. Many of these programs will work in "real-time," meaning the user can have analysis performed and updated while playing, and the software provides advice on decisions during the hand. With the software currently available, it has become possible for players to achieve mathematically perfect play.

For example, a third-party software package, *Poker Office,* works alongside the player interface for dozens of online poker rooms. It computes the probabilities, pot odds, and hand rankings as each hand is played and overlays that statistical information onto the graphical interface used to play. It models the playing styles of all the game participants and provides statistical summaries and player icons to represent each style. All of this is done in real-time so that much of the guesswork for the mathematical aspects of decision-making is eliminated. You can learn more about software packages like *Poker Office* at *http://www.IntelligentPoker.com.*

Some players question the ethics of using third-party software for these purposes. However, there is no practical way that online poker rooms can police the use of any assistance during play, whether it is computer aided or another person. Players need to be mindful that their actions during play can be monitored, recorded, and analyzed by sophisticated computer software.

*Effects of Less Overhead*

- You do not need to win as much to turn a profit
- You can be extremely selective about the games you play

The biggest advantage to online play is that aside from the rake, there is almost no overhead involved. What I mean by overhead is the costs associated with going to the cardroom. You do not have to free up an entire afternoon or evening to travel. There are no expenses incurred for driving, parking, and eating. Not having a real dealer to tip is a significant savings over the long-run.

In fact, the absence of real dealers means that online cardrooms can spread games with much lower stakes than in the brick-and-mortar world. Finding stakes lower than $2-4 is rare when a real dealer must be paid to run the game. Cardrooms cannot afford to pay a dealer if the stakes are too low. But online, you can find an extremely wide variety of stakes for low-limit games. There are $0.02-0.04, $0.05-0.10, $0.25-$0.50, $0.50-$1.00 and $1-$2 games found online as well as the more familiar $2-4, $3-6, $5-10, and $10-20.

The absence of overhead also means that you can afford to be much more selective in game choice and table choice. This is the single biggest advantage to playing online. Long-run success in poker requires finding games that are both within the limits of your bankroll and your abilities as a player. If you consistently play at stakes too high in relation to your bankroll, there will never be a "long-run" because a run of bad beats will wipe you out. If you consistently play at tables with tough tight-aggressive opponents, it will be difficult to win enough to cover the rake.

The availability online of small-stakes games means that a modest bankroll of a few hundred dollars can support poker play over an extended period of time. Online play also allows the simultaneous observation of dozens of tables before deciding to take a seat. There are even third-party software packages that will assist in table and seat selection. For example, *Poker Wiser* is an online search service that monitors the current action at the tables for dozens of online cardrooms. A subscriber to the service provides table selection parameters—cardrooms, games, stakes, styles of opponents, etc.—and a list is shown of current tables matching the criteria. It also tracks individual players and alerts users when and where a specific desirable opponent becomes available.

## Tactical Considerations Online

The tactics described in Chapter 6, of course, apply online. But, there are some tactical considerations unique to the online environment.

*Online Tells*

A "tell" is an action or mannerism by another player that inadvertently tips the strength of his or her hand. Tells are more important in face-to-face play in brick-and-mortar cardrooms than in online games in which it is impossible to see the other players. However, there are certain online tells to observe. The most common tell is the player's response time. A long response time can occur when a player misses a flop or a draw and is unsure of how to proceed. However, some players will take a long time with a strong hand to feign hesitation. Other players will bet a strong hand instantly. Some players will bet instantly when bluffing to feign strength. Pay attention to the response times of the players you are up against and note if there are any patterns.

Be alert to your own patterns, especially if you use the "predetermined action" button on the interface because an instantaneous response signals that you decided before knowing the others' actions. That is good when folding because it speeds up the game. But, for all other actions, you should manually click the button when it is your turn. For example, don't use the "check/fold" button when in the blind. If no one raises, your instant check alerts the others that you would have folded to a raise. It is better to keep your response times consistent to avoid inadvertently tipping information about your own hand.

*Online Tactical Patterns*

Poker in any environment is about spotting patterns in the behaviors and decisions made by opponents. Patterns in response times can be telling, but patterns in tactical usage are even more important to observe. Online, because of the faster play and no other distracting behaviors, patterns are easier to spot. Here are some examples of common patterns in the way opponents play their hands:

- Does a player always open-raise?
- Does a player always raise on the button when everyone ahead folds?
- Does a player always call after the flop, but fold unimproved hands after the turn?
- Does a player frequently raise for free cards?
- Does a player check-raise frequently when in an early position?
- Does a player raise with any pocket pair from any position?
- Does a player who raised pre-flop always make a continuation bet?
- Does a player who raised pre-flop always raise post-flop?
- Is the breaking of an established pattern by a player a sign of strength or weakness?

Once you spot a pattern, it is easy to adjust your own tactics to take advantage of the additional information. Just don't fall into the trap of thinking that a player who always performs a certain action never has good cards. For example, a player who, given the chance, always open-raises regardless of his or her holding, will still be dealt a share of quality cards.

---

### Common Patterns and Responses

Blinds who always call a pre-flop raise and either fold to a continuation bet if they don't hit the flop, or call and check-raise on the turn if they do. If you think a blind who hit the flop has you beat, check back on the turn and take the free river card. Don't pay two bets to see the last card if you are behind.

A player who raises with high cards and always follows with a continuation bet can sometimes be bluffed off the pot if no high cards appear on the flop. From the blind you can check-raise to feign connecting with low cards on the flop. If the player continues after the check-raise, with either a call or a re-raise, that is often a good indication of a pocket pair.

A player who always follows a pre-flop raise with a continuation bet post- flop, suddenly decides to check. The break in this pattern could signal that he or she flopped a monster and is trying to set a trap. Proceed with caution.

---

*Online Aggression*

As a general rule, players online are looser and more aggressive. It is easy to bet money when all that is required is a mouse click, so people think less about putting money in the pot. Not being seen means you can check-raise, bluff, and bluff-raise without having to look at your opponent. Body language is not a factor in online games. The result is that everyone plays more aggressively. That affects the tactics in the following ways.

**Position matters more online.** In a typical low-limit brick-and-mortar game, many players simply call before the flop and that allows the play of more speculative hands from early positions. But in an aggressive online game, capped betting before the flop is not uncommon. You don't want to get caught having to pay three-bets to see the flop with a speculative hand. If you decide to play speculative hands from an early position, it is often better to raise and represent them as premium hands.

**Betting and raising has greater fold-equity online.** Not only is aggression more common online, it is also more respected. Raising in a passive brick-and-mortar game rarely induces players to fold. You will get more fold equity with raises online and you need to capitalize on that fact. In online play, if you consistently wait for the best hand before raising, you will get run over by the other players' aggression. In low-limit brick-and-mortar games there is little point to raising unless you have the best hand.

**More free cards should be taken online.** To defend against frequent use of the check-raise online, you should take more free cards after the turn from players who check. Be especially aware of strong opponents who check to you after thinking it over. That moment of indecision is often a sign that the player is torn between betting immediately or attempting a check-raise.

**Defense against the bluff-raise is necessary online.** The bluff-raise is a rarely-used tactic in low-limit brick-and-mortar games, in part because it rarely works in that environment. But online, where aggression is more respected the bluff raise is a frequent play. Watch for overly aggressive opponents and the use of the "pre-determined action" buttons for raising. These are often signs of bluff-raising. You often can set up players who bluff-raise frequently by backing down in the face of their first raise. Then, in a situation when you have the cards, hit them with re-raises.

*Online Player Turnover*

Frequent player turnover is more of a factor in online games because many players enter and leave online games quickly—5 to 10 minutes is not uncommon. It is rare to see players sit down at a table in a brick-and-mortar cardroom for a few minutes. Sessions of a few hours are more the norm in brick-and-mortar environments.

There are important effects of rapid player turnover. One is that you must learn to adjust quickly to changes in playing conditions. An aggressive player will suddenly vanish and a passive player takes the seat. A game with frequent pre-flop raises that narrowed the field to two or three players might change to a game in which most players call pre-flop and hands have five to six players. The change at the table means you have to change your strategy. There will also be periods when the game is short-handed. For just three hands, two players sit out while two others leave the table. When a game is shorthanded, even temporarily, starting hand requirements change. High cards go up in value and drawing hands go down. You need to be alert to when this happens.

Always ask yourself if the reasons you chose a particular table still apply. Suppose you are winning because of the presence of one or two passive players who call with anything. If those players leave and are replaced by tight players, your winnings will decrease no matter how well you play. Consider scouting for another table with passive players present.

Another effect of frequent player turnover is that your "table image" matters less. In a brick-and-mortar cardroom, over a period of hours, you can build an image that others will notice. You can still establish a table image online, but it is trickier. It is important to pay attention to the players entering and leaving your game because a carefully cultivated table image will not mean anything if the game consists of all new players. If you have cultivated an image as a tight player and trained the others to fold to your bets, it becomes profitable to bluff more. But, that assumes you have shown good cards to the other players when called. If everyone at the table has recently joined the game, your tight player image will be in someone else's memory, not in the minds of your current opponents. If the entire table has changed over in the past 30 minutes, your image no longer matters. No one has seen your play.

The advice about online table image assumes that you play sporadically and compete against different people each time. If you are a regular, and more importantly, are seeing the same opponents on a regular basis, your table image always matters. The others could have extensive notes and even a computer analysis of your play. You should also be taking notes on frequent opponents.

---

### Small Samples Can Distort Perceptions

It is common in poker to have runs of bad cards lasting for hours. When this happens and you have to fold hand after hand, it becomes difficult to get action when a good hand does arrive. The other players read you as being extremely tight-passive (a rock) and will only bet their best hands against you. It becomes necessary to relax your starting requirements and bet mediocre hands just to insure action later on. But in an online environment, there is an easy solution to the problem of only getting action when your good cards are second best — switch tables. Then you won't need to invest money on bad cards to keep from being seen as a rock.

If you sit down at a table and a run of great cards occurs that allows you to bet aggressively, you might be seen as a maniac (extremely loose-aggressive). This is a great image to have when your cards are running good and should be exploited to the fullest.

Conversely, what this means is that a half hour of observing an opponent's playing patterns might not be enough to tell how he or she falls on the loose-tight and passive-aggressive scales. A player who always bets aggressively, but then shows good cards, might be a very tight player on a good run of cards. A player who appears extremely passive because she has done nothing for an hour might be an extremely aggressive player on a bad run of cards.

In studying your opponent's play for patterns, pay more attention to the kinds of tactics employed, what the tactic means, and how you might counter or respond to a frequently used tactic. A half hour of observing an opponent's online play is often enough time to get a sense of tactical play, but might not be enough time to draw accurate conclusions about overall playing style.

## Strategic Considerations Online

When you play online, you give up much of the social interaction that takes place in a brick-and-mortar cardroom and the opportunity to study your opponents in person. In exchange, you get a much greater selection of tables to choose from with much faster games and instant availability any time of day or night. The first strategic consideration when playing online are the stakes. These can be roughly separated into four tiers.

**Tier 1:** Micro-stake games: $0.02-0.04, $0.05-0.10, $0.25-$0.50. Games such as these, played for pennies, nickels and dimes, are good games to teach you the mechanics of online play, or the mechanics of a new game. You can experiment without risking much of your bankroll. For example, if you know Hold'em and want to try Omaha, these would be good games to start the learning process.

**Tier 2:** Low-limit games: $0.50-$1.00, $1-$2, $2-4. These are the most popular stakes and easiest to find. On the strategic grid, these games are generally loose-passive to loose-aggressive. Look for loose-passive tables that are characterized by relatively large, average-sized pots that result from many callers rather than a few raisers. Poker is most profitable when the table has passive players who call frequently, but rarely raise.

**Tier 3:** Mid-limit games: $3-6, $5-10, $10-$20 $15-30. These are serious games populated by players who might be deriving a significant portion of their income from online poker. You need to have a significant bankroll (at least $1000 to $2000) to compete over the long-run in these games. A bankroll of a few hundred dollars will not support apparently modest $3-6 play. Normal runs of bad luck will wipe it out.

**Tier 4:** High-limit games: $20-40 and up. It is possible to find no-limit games online with $1000-2000 blinds and players seated with stacks in excess of $100,000. Anyone can observe these games, and often the players include professionals well-known from television.

Once you determine the stakes that best suit your ability, bankroll, and goals, the critical strategic skills for long-term success are money management and game selection.

**Money management:** You will need more money than you think. Plan on having a bankroll of at least 200 big bets for whatever stakes you play. For pot-limit and no-limit play, never have more than 10% of your bankroll on the table. It sounds like a large bankroll—$800 for $2-4 play, $1200 for $3-6 play—but the aggressive play online results in large swings in bankrolls. Resist the urge to play at higher stakes after a loss to recover the money faster. Instead, move to lower stakes so that you lower the risk of going broke. As soon as you start playing at stakes higher than your bankroll can support, poker ceases to become a game of skill and crosses over to gambling.

**Game selection:** Simply put, you should remain in games when you are winning and quit games when you are losing. That advice sounds trite, but many players find it difficult to follow. When behind there is a natural human desire to "get even" before moving on to a different game. The irony is that switching tables to a softer game will often result in getting even faster. Staying at a table when you are losing often results in digging a deeper hole. There is a tendency to blame losses on bad luck, but you will experience more "bad luck" against good players. The reason is that good players are rarely drawing dead, while bad players often stay too long in pots with almost no chance of winning. If you are frustrated by frequent bad beats, it's not because the deal is rigged, it's because more bad beats are possible from the beginning. Good players simply will not give action without a reasonable chance of winning. The ability to effortlessly switch tables is a tremendous advantage online. Make use of that ability to avoid compounding losses.

## Summary

Switching between online and brick-and-mortar play requires adjustment. Experienced online players often find in-person play incredibly slow and are careless about tells. Experienced brick-and-mortar players often find online play a difficult environment for reading opponents and the added aggression overwhelming. But, with appropriate adjustments, it is possible to enjoy and succeed at both forms of poker.

The advantages to playing online are easy availability, no expenses beyond the rake, and choice from a large selection of ongoing games. To make the most of those advantages, be very selective about the tables you play. It costs nothing to wait for a better time, or to switch tables. You can easily avoid playing in games in which you are not a favorite.

The disadvantages to online play are larger fluctuations in bankrolls and difficulty in reading other players. Disciplined money management is required to survive online. Avoid the temptation to play at stakes higher than your bankroll can support.

Reading players is necessary for a psychological game like Hold'em. While that is more difficult in an online environment the first time you play someone, you have a better ability to track and profile frequent opponents.

# Part III

# Putting It All Together

So far this book has provided a systematic outline of the principles for success at Texas Hold'em poker. What follows is a series of five essays on poker, and gambling, in general. The purpose of these essays is to discuss some counter-intuitive mathematical ideas and their relationship to human behavior that must be understood to succeed over the long-run at any gambling endeavor.

The first three essays (Chapter 9) address probability theory. In my many years teaching math, I have found that probability concepts are among the most difficult for students to grasp. Part of the problem is our human tendency to believe that everything happens for a reason. It is difficult to accept the idea of events happening for no reason. People constantly search for patterns in sequences of random events, and, in fact, find patterns. However, patterns found within random event sequences have no predictive value. You will always be able to find patterns because humans are good at finding patterns—it is how we learn. But patterns found in a sequence of past random events will not predict the outcome of future random events, which is the essential meaning of randomness.

People also have a related tendency to project personal meaning into random events. When playing lotteries, horses and roulette, for example, we pick numbers that have personal meaning, such as our birthday, child's birthday, or anniversary. Because enough people pick meaningful numbers, over time, the laws of chance dictate that some of these numbers will win on occasion. But again, accidental coincidence does not mean that these numbers are predictive in any way. It just means that people are good at finding meaning in the events that make up their lives. Few people are willing to accept the fact that a good deal of the important events in our lives happen by chance.

Part of the difficulty with accepting the unpredictability of future random events, is that mathematically, it is necessary to distinguish between two types of events—independent and conditional. Each time the deck is reshuffled and the cards dealt, all memory of the past is erased. Each starting hand is an independent event with its own unchanged probability. The first essay in Chapter 9 discusses probability concepts for independent events. Once a hand is dealt, probabilities become conditional. What is the probability of an Ace appearing on the board? If you hold two Aces, that probability is substantially reduced compared to the situation in which you hold no Aces. If you hold two Aces and you have good reason to believe your opponents hold the other two, the probability of another Ace appearing has fallen to zero. The second essay in Chapter 9 discusses these kinds of situations when probabilities are altered because of conditions. Lastly, Chapter 9 discusses the mathematical requirements for winning over the long-run. Randomness means that anything can happen in the short-run, but what happens if you play month after month, year after year?

Chapter 10 is a discussion of the psychological attributes necessary for success. Most poker books stress the need for patience. However, poker requires a different kind of patience than the kind your mother taught. Waiting for an event that can happen at any time is different from waiting for an event that will happen in a given amount of time. The first essay in Chapter 10 concerns the need for a new understanding of "patience." The second essay discusses concepts in the field of behavioral finance that apply to poker. Behavior finance is a field of study that combines psychology and economics to understand how people make financial decisions. For decisions that involve risk and uncertainty, studies have shown that people are prone to making poor decisions that are contrary to self-interest. Understanding concepts such as loss-aversion and mental accounting will help improve your poker game and business decisions.

The third Chapter 10 essay elaborates on the need for a flexible, dynamic strategy and how adjustments are made during a day of playing poker. It compares the problems of programming computers to play chess and to play poker. It is much more difficult to program a computer to play world-class poker than it is to play world-class chess. The reasons relate to the need for poker players to make many more adjustments to their strategies during play than is required of chess players.

The last essay is a discussion of the roles of luck and skill in poker. As poker has grown in popularity in the past decade, so has government hostility toward the game. Many of the arguments against poker are based on a misunderstanding of the role of luck in poker, sports in general, and in normal life events.

# 9. Mathematical Considerations

## Past, Present and Future— Do Probabilities Change?

I have a friend who believes that if you toss a coin three times, and it comes up heads each time, a greater than even chance exists for it to land tails on the fourth toss. If you question why she believes the probability changes, her answer is: "Over the long-run, the coin must land heads as often as tails, so if a streak of heads occurs, a tail becomes more probable since even numbers of each must be maintained."

This fallacious belief that the coin's past history affects its future is fun to explore with further questions. Examples:

- Suppose I flip the coin three times and it comes up three heads, then I put it away. Tomorrow I take it out again. Is the probability still greater that a tail will occur? If the probability is greater, what happens if I wait a week or a month or a year?

- If after some elapsed time interval (day, week, month), the probabilities reset to 50-50, why does this happen?

- If there is no time interval that resets the probabilities to 50-50, how do I know it wasn't due for three heads in a row? After all, I may have just received the coin, so how do I know the previous owner hadn't flipped it five times and gotten all tails?

- How exactly has the probability changed of a tail occurring after three heads in a row? What will it be if just one head has appeared, or after five heads in row?

If my friend's belief is true, all these questions should have answers. The fact that all answers to these questions would be nonsense shows the belief is false.

Of course, a more profitable exercise would be to find a betting person who believes that a past sequence of coin-flips affects the future. If this person is willing to pay better than even money on the outcome of a fourth head each time three heads appear in a row, you are assured of making money. Since past coin flips have no affect on future ones, the probabilities remain 50-50. Anyone willing to pay out better than even money on wagers against coin-flips—even selected coin-flips that occur after streaks—will lose over the long-run.

I relate the story of my friend's belief in coin-flips because it is easy to see that the belief is wrong. However, many gamblers share the same wrong belief and don't realize it. They will behave as if the past does affect the future. Examples of common behaviors:

- You have just lost seven hands in a row at blackjack. You decide to bet the table maximum on the eighth hand because it must be time for a win. After all, how often do you lose eight hands in a row?

- You have received garbage poker hands for the last hour and decide that no matter what, you will bet heavily on the next hand because it must be time for a winning hand.

- You repeatedly play the same lottery numbers, believing that if those numbers haven't won yet, their time must be coming.

Each of these behaviors results from believing that "I'm due." Claiming that "I'm due" is just another way of claiming that the past affects the future.

There are more subtle expressions of this wrong thinking, such as believing that other players in the game affect the probabilities. Examples:

- Some poker players believe that the more players there are competing for a pot, the more likely it is that they will be dealt three-of-a-kind or better. It is easy to fall into this trap, since winning hands tend to be higher when there are more players at the table. Three of a kind is much more likely to be the winning hand when seven players compete, while with two players, a high pair is often enough to win. However, winning hands are higher, only because more hands are dealt, and to win, you have to beat more people. Whatever the number of players, the probability of you, an individual, receiving three-of-a-kind is always the same. Present events, such as the number of players who decide to fold early, do not after-the-fact affect the probabilities on the past event of the deal. Just as the past doesn't affect the future, the present does not affect the past.

- Some poker players believe in betting heavily during winning streaks and advise not to leave the table. This may be sound advice if the reasons for the winning streak have to do with being at a table filled with bad players. However, if the reason is a sudden streak of great cards, there is no reason to believe this has anything to do with the table, your seat, your opponents, the dealer, the day of the week, the color of your socks, or any factor, period. Good streaks happen just like bad streaks. There are no reasons; that is just the nature of a series of random events.

Make sure that your playing decisions are grounded in correct reasons. Analyze the reasons for your decisions. If the reason comes down to believing that the past affects the future, the reason is wrong.

## Behaviors That Change the Odds

Many players understand that probabilities do not change from hand to hand. They know that an unseen card has an equal chance of being any one of the remaining unseen cards. However, they fall into the trap of treating all cards not in their hand as unseen cards. Cards held by your opponents are not unseen cards. Your opponents have seen them and their actions are a source of information. Only one card is out that beats you, but if your opponent acts like she has that one card, don't think that being beaten is unlikely. Many players make the mistake of playing only their cards and never asking the question: Why are my opponents still in the hand?

On a St. Louis riverboat a number of years ago, the following hand occurred at my table. After the deal, a player in an early position raised pre-flop. Except for one player who called the raise, everyone else folded. The player who initially raised—I will call Player 1—had played a tight game all afternoon. I had observed one other pre-flop raise from him earlier that day and it came on pocket Aces, so I took his raise as a sign of strength. He also appeared to be a regular (the casino employees all knew him by name and greeted him warmly). Players who are regulars at certain cardrooms often play tight, solid games. Otherwise, they can't afford to be regulars. The player who called his raise, Player 2, called without hesitation, so I also put him on a strong hand. The flop came up A, 10, 6. Player 1 bet; Player 2 called. The turn card was an Ace. Player 1 bet and again Player 2 called. The river card fell as a K. Player 1 bet, and Player 2 raised. Player 1 countered with a re-raise. In this cardroom, the rule was that if two players went head-to-head on the end, raises were not capped. The rule allowed players to get into a raising war as long as they had money on the table. Player 2 re-raised and the war was on. At this point, it was obvious to me what each player held. Player 1 must have had pocket Aces, and Player 2, pocket Kings. Four Aces beats Kings-full, but Player 2 seemed oblivious to that possibility. He continued to counter each re-raise with another. Finally, Player 1 decided he had taken enough of Player 2's money, put down a final re-raise and exposed his two Aces. Player 2 showed his two Kings and shook his head in disbelief.

Losing with Kings-full to four Aces is a highly improbable bad beat. I'd raise, too, if I hit Kings-full at the river, but with this board, would I completely discount the possibility of my opponent having the remaining two Aces, or even one Ace and the remaining King? Player 2 with Kings-full has seen 7 cards, which leaves 45 unseen cards, 2 of which his opponent has. Pick 2 cards from 45 unseen cards and there are 990 possibilities, only three of which (AK, AA, AK) beat Kings-full for this board. However, Player 1's cards are not two random unseen cards from 990 possible combinations. He has seen them and acted in such a way that eliminates from consideration almost all of these 990 possibilities. Player 1 would not be re-raising if he held 2, 5 or J, 7 or 4, 8, so why is he re-raising? It is not correct for Player 2 to assume that the odds of losing are remote (3 in 990), given Player 1's behavior.

Many beginners make the mistake of Player 2 above: They only play their cards and never consider why their opponents are in the hand. As a further example of how behaviors change the probabilities, consider a hand I played in the now-defunct Prince George's County Maryland cardrooms.

I was playing $5-$10 Omaha when a woman joined the game, sitting to my left, whose play immediately changed the dynamics of the table (See the Appendix for an explanation of Omaha). She played very aggressive poker and rarely called. Her actions were bet, raise, or fold, and she played in most of the hands. She raised pre-flop, regardless of her position, for almost every hand. Since I sat on her right, I knew that any bet I called would be raised, so I tightened my starting requirements for hands, folding hands I ordinarily would call with, calling with my premium hands and letting her put in the raise for me. I was the only player at the table who made this adjustment. Everyone else, seeing that her pre-flop raises conveyed little information, called her raise. Soon, almost every player at the table called her pre-flop raise every single hand. With so much money seeding the pot, no one wanted to fold before seeing the flop. The entry of this one player changed the entire table dynamics, causing an extremely loose-aggressive game to develop.

In a loose-aggressive game, so-called "bad beats" are actually highly probable. One hand, in particular, stands out as an example of how the new table dynamics distorted the probabilities. Of my four starting cards, two were Kings. I called, she put in her raise, and every single person at the table (there were eleven including me) called her raise. The three cards that came on the flop were K, A, and 8, all of different suits. I bet my set of Kings. She raised, the man to her immediate left called her raise, and everyone else dropped, returning the action back to me. Because two players were up against me after seeing the flop, I thought it likely that each had an Ace, and possibly one of them had an Ace, 8, giving them Aces-up. My three Kings had to be the top hand so I re-raised. She called, a first for her that day; he called. The turn card came, a 3 of the only suit not yet on the board (There would be no flush possible). I bet, she called, and he called. Her sudden respect for my bets and his refusal to go away convinced me they both had Aces-up.

The river card was an Ace. Had I been going against one player, I would have checked. But I knew I would not be raised since each of them had to fear the other. I bet my Kings-full (since I knew I had to call with it). If you know you are going to call, and do not fear a raise, take the initiative and bet. Your opponents might not have hit their draw and could fold. In this case, they had hit. Both of them called and each turned over an Ace, 8. As the dealer stacked the chips into two piles in order to split the pot between them, he shook his head in disbelief and said to me: "That was the *only* card that could beat you."

But how improbable was that last card being the one remaining Ace? My two opponents each have four cards and I "know" they each have an Ace. That means there is only one remaining Ace among the 36 cards that are not part of our three hands or the board. The odds appear to be 1 in 36 or 2.7%, the fact that shocked the dealer.

However, given the behavior of the players at the table, this assessment is not accurate. Think about the table dynamics. Every single person called this woman's pre-flop raise. When an Ace showed on the flop, no one holding an Ace would have dropped. Her raise pre-flop scared no one; neither would her raise after the flop have scared anyone holding an Ace. The man to her left didn't scare, and with 11 pre-flop raises ($110) in the pot, anyone with a chance to win would have stayed. When the other eight people at the table folded a total of 32 cards after the flop, *it meant none of those cards was an Ace*. When the dealer reached for the river card, only four cards remained in the deck and one of them had to be an Ace. The odds of me being beaten were 1 in 4. As the favorite, my bets and raises were correct, but my loss was not a great improbability.

In the previous section, I explained that the distribution of cards to players and the board are completely random events with no memory of the past. However, once the cards are dealt and players have seen them and acted, events cannot be considered random. The probability of a four falling on the board may be the same as an Ace, but an Ace is much more likely to have paired someone than a four. Many players keep any hand containing an Ace, but almost no one keeps every hand that contains a four. To be successful, you need to put your opponents on hands and play accordingly. Do not think only of your cards and the probability that a random unseen hand is better. Always ask yourself: "Why are my opponents acting the way they are?"

## Requirements for Success

To gamble successfully, you must:

- Have a sufficient bankroll
- Place bets with positive expectations
- Accumulate statistics

Having a sufficient bankroll means that the size of a typical bet must be small in comparison to your total bankroll so that normally occurring losses do not wipe you out. In the movie, *Rounders*, the hero, an expert Hold'em player, violates this rule when he wagers his entire bankroll on a single hand of high-stakes, no-limit Hold'em. He is dealt A♣ 9♣. The flop is A♠ 8♣ 9♠. Figuring his opponent is on a spade draw, he bets his two pair. He is thrilled with the turn card (9♥) giving him 9's full. When the river card is a 3♠, he figures his opponent has made his spade-flush and will call any bet. He goes all-in with his entire bankroll ($30,000). This is a good bet because his opponent cannot have two nines, is unlikely to have the other two Aces, and will be hesitant to fold a flush. The problem: the remaining two Aces is exactly what his opponent has. Aces-full beat nines-full and in the next scene, our hero is back to his day job. Despite his poker expertise, he is unable to buy into any games. The hero's mistake wasn't how he played; it was wagering everything he had on one hand.

Placing bets with positive expectations means that if the bet is won, the payoff is greater than the odds against winning. In other words, the pot odds must be favorable. Over the long-run, you cannot win money if you consistently place bets with unfavorable payoffs. Many poker players always draw to certain hands. If they need one card to complete a flush or a straight, they will stay in the hand no matter how much it costs or how much money is at stake. With one card to come, completing a flush or open-ended-straight happens about one out of every five tries. If the payoff isn't at least 5 to 1, you are losing money, because your one win every five tries will not be enough to pay for the inevitable four losses. Just because you will win a certain percentage of these bets, doesn't mean you should make them.

Accumulating statistics means that many, many bets must be placed. It is this third condition that most people fail to understand. Most books on gambling state the need for a sufficient bankroll and teach how to place bets with positive expectations (good bets) and avoid bets with negative expectations (bad bets). While this knowledge is necessary, it is not sufficient to be a winner. What is often glossed over is the necessity of accumulating statistics.

The reason for this omission is that accumulating statistics is work. The attraction of gambling is the possibility of wealth without work. But the truth is, *successful gamblers must work hard for their winnings*.

To illustrate why all three conditions must be present, consider one form of gambling: selling life insurance.

You start a company selling life insurance, and you sell your first policy to a 20-year old person in good health for $100. You agree to pay $100,000 if that person should die within a year. Since the odds of a person that age dying within a year are about 10,000 to 1, it is very unlikely that you will have to pay out any money. But suppose a freak accident befalls that person tomorrow. If you do not have a sufficient bankroll, you will be bankrupt before you have a chance to sell another policy.

If you do have a sufficient bankroll, the bet you placed does have a positive expectation. You are offering to pay at a rate of 1000 to 1 for an event that has 10,000 to 1 odds against occurring. Suppose your customer refuses to pay $100 for the policy, so you lower the price to $1. At this price, your customer will eagerly buy your policy, but you have just placed a bet with a negative expectation. You agreed to pay at a rate of 100,000 to 1 for an event that has 10,000 to 1 odds against occurring. However, there is a strong temptation on your part to sell the policy for $1, because the chances of the person dying have not changed. The odds are overwhelming that at the end of the year, you will be $1 richer. Your sale is much easier, and pocketing $1 is better than nothing.

The temptation to sell the policy for $1 illustrates a paradox associated with gambling. Whatever price the life insurance policy sells for, the odds are overwhelmingly in favor of you keeping the money. However $1 is a bad bet that should be avoided and $100 is a good bet that should be made.

*The difference between good and bad bets only becomes apparent when statistics are accumulated*—after you do the work of selling many life insurance policies. If you sell 10,000 policies, it becomes a certainty that at least one person will die. If you charged $1 each, the $10,000 collected does not cover one loss. Your business is headed for bankruptcy. However, if you sell 10,000 policies at $100 each, the million dollars collected covers 10 deaths. While it is almost certain that at least one customer will die, it is extremely unlikely that 10 will die. Your business has to make money.

Anything can happen to a single customer. Therefore, a good bet (the $100 policy) could lose and a bad bet (the $1 policy) could win. If you sell only one policy, knowledge of mortality rates is useless. Knowing the difference between good and bad bets pays off only when statistics are accumulated, *and it is only through the accumulation of statistics that you are assured of making money.*

The strategies for playing poker described in this book are designed to maximize your expectations for winning over the long-run, *as you accumulate statistics.* However, even when bets are correctly made and hands correctly played, the outcome of any given hand or any given playing session is uncertain.

Poker is a deceptive game because good players don't always win and bad players don't always lose. There are statistical fluctuations in the outcomes. Your goal should be to make the right decisions for the right reasons. You should not get upset or elated over outcomes of single hands. Only as time passes and trends become clear, is it possible to evaluate the quality of your decision-making.

# 10. Psychological Considerations

## Choose Your Battles

How often have you entered into a dispute, which afterwards, you judged was not worth it? It could be a price dispute at a store, an annoying action of a co-worker, or a trivial argument with a family member. In the end, winning or losing didn't matter. The most you could have hoped to gain would never compensate for the cost in time, effort, or ill-will generated. With experience, you learn to avoid confrontations that in the long-run are not worth the cost. We all have our "principles," but savvy people choose their battles. They know when it is worth taking a stand and when it is better to let things go.

In poker, learning to choose the right battles is crucial to success and it is perhaps the hardest skill to learn. Your first impulse in any confrontation is to act. You come to the poker table to compete for the pot. Watching others vie for the money feels counter to that goal. How is folding hand after hand competing? Inaction also leads to complacency. You stop paying close attention and then miss out on the opportunities that do occur. Poker is a fast-moving game and decisions must be made quickly. For these two reasons—the desire to compete and the need to stay alert—it is difficult to suppress the urge to play in most of the hands. Even if intellectually you know to fold, your emotions constantly urge you to make exceptions.

All books on poker correctly state that the number one mistake most beginners make is *to play in too many hands.* Be patient and wait for the right situation and cards is the standard advice. This advice is sound, but in my opinion, it is poorly expressed because patience is the wrong idea. Patience is what you need waiting in line at the bank, waiting for the light to turn green, waiting for an unproductive meeting to end. In all these cases, you know when your goal—banking, driving, returning to useful work—will be reached. Patience is accepting that your goal will come in its own time; that it cannot be rushed. Also, being patient means that if you pass the time daydreaming, nothing is lost.

Contrast waiting in line with waiting for a decent hand in a poker game. In poker, you never know when your goal—a favorable betting opportunity—will occur. You must be mentally alert and ready for action at all times because at any time, you might have to act. In the meantime, unfavorable betting opportunities are constantly present, tempting you to take foolish chances. Rather than patience, what you need to learn is what I call "deliberate non-action." *You must understand that not acting is one of the most important actions in poker.* You must accept the counter-intuitive idea that not taking action is an integral part of the game and essential to your long-range goal of making money.

If folding is not your most frequent action, you are playing badly. It is nice to wish for hand after hand of great cards, such as pocket Aces and pocket Kings occurring several times per hour. You fantasize about betting forcefully as both of your pocket cards pair up on the flop, while your opponents shrink back in fear. There will be times when these events happen; times when you can do no wrong and winning is easy. There also will be long hours, even long days, of hand after hand of garbage. During these times, your chip pile gets eaten away by the blinds, the few good starting hands you get don't hit on the flop, and the game seems utterly pointless and futile.

Poker encompasses both euphoria and frustration. It is impossible to have one without the other because over the long-run, statistics rule. Play in enough hands and the distribution of cards received and draws hit approaches the percentages in the charts. The trouble with poker is that you have no control over the good times and bad times. The nature of randomness means that events happen with no discernable pattern. You are never due for either a good streak or a bad streak. Whatever your thoughts are—however alert you feel; however ready you are for action—your mental state will not change the distribution of the cards.

While alertness does not change the cards, it does affect the one thing you do control: the decisions you make. Again, this is why patience is the wrong idea. Being patient means you fall into a routine of automatic decisions that dulls your thinking and causes you to lose your edge. Alertness is required at all times, and to stay alert, you must think of non-action as a deliberate action.

Consider the outcome of a hand at my table one afternoon in an Atlantic City casino. A showdown occurred between two players with a board of mediocre cards: 6♣ 2♠ 5♥ 6♦ 9♥. Expecting boring hands, none of us at the table, including the dealer, paid close attention. One of the players showed 2♦ 5♦, and having matched both his pocket cards, claimed the pot. The other player with a 5♣ 10♣ didn't object so the dealer pushed the chips to the player with 5's over 2's and set up for another hand. Only after the transaction ended, did a few of us at the table wake up and realize that the pot had been awarded to the losing hand. By then, it was too late to change the outcome.

When you first read this, did you immediately see that the 5, 10 was the winning hand? The 2's were irrelevant because the board had a pair of 6's. This meant each player's hand consists of the same two pairs—5's and 6's. The kicker (fifth card) decided the hand and since the 10♣ was higher than all other cards on the board, it beat the 9♥ on the board. (If a card higher than a 10 was on the board, say a Jack, the players would have shared the same kicker and the pot would have been split. The best five-card hand for each player in that case would have been 5's and 6's with a Jack kicker, and the 10 would not have played.) By not analyzing the situation, the player with the winning hand lost an entire pot; potentially the difference between a profitable and an unprofitable playing session.

Deliberate non-action means you don't let the routine take the edge off your play. To stay focused, analyze the actions of the players and dealers, and take breaks. Be mentally alert at all times and ready to act. Over time, small mistakes add up to big losses and small victories add up to big profits. If you are not paying attention at a crucial time, as in the example above, you lose money. But if staying focused requires you to contest every pot, you also lose money.

The concept of tight-aggressive play is to forcefully contest pots only when you have the edge. Keep mentally focused by careful observation of the other players when the odds are against you. Choose only battles in which you are the favorite, and don't feel that you have to win every time. If you select the best situations to challenge your opponents and ignore the marginal ones, you will accumulate money over time.

Alan Schoonmaker explains in his book *The Psychology of Poker** that the successful tight-aggressive style for poker is unnatural. In his observation, only in the professions of fighter pilot and police officer are there people capable of tightly controlled aggression. Tight people are naturally cautious while aggressive people tend to take chances. The combination of the two traits results only from a deliberate training process. It does not happen on its own.

## Behavioral Finance Applied to Poker

As mentioned before, a field of study has arisen known as behavioral finance. It combines psychology and economics to model and predict how people make financial decisions. Of particular interest are financial decisions that involve risk and uncertainty. A key finding from studies in behavioral finance is that people do not always act in their best interest when making financial decisions that involve risk.

Of course to make that discovery the researchers had to define "best interest." What exactly is a person's "best interest" when it is not possible to know ahead of time the outcomes for a particular course of action or its alternatives? According to behavioral finance studies, to act in your "best interest" means to choose the alternative with the greatest expected value (as defined in Chapter 5). When it comes to decisions with unknown outcomes, consistently choosing the alternatives with the greatest expected values is the best you can do. As with all events involving risk, the actual financial outcomes might be better or worse than the expected values, but it is not possible to make better decisions. Probability theory teaches that over time, the fluctuations should average out so that final outcomes are close to the expected values. Therefore it is not in a person's best interest to ever choose alternatives offering less than the maximum expected value.

It is no surprise that some people will occasionally make poor choices when it comes to financial decisions with uncertain outcomes. But researchers found that circumstances arise in which the vast majority of people will consistently and predictably make the wrong choice. The reasons are psychological and relate back to my assertion in the previous essay that money means different things to different people. In fact, for each person the psychological value of a given amount of money can vary greatly. A person does not treat all of the dollars he or she has equally. Instead, money in a person's possession is divided into different "mental accounts." Each account is treated differently, especially in regards to risk-taking behavior. Mental accounting affects decisions and it is both harmful and beneficial.

For example, consider a serious problem for investors known as loss-aversion. Investors hesitate to sell a stock for any kind of a loss, but will quickly sell for a small gain. Apparently, money that is lost goes into a different mental account than money that is gained. As a result, winning stocks never get a chance run up big gains, while losing stocks turn into large losses. Mathematically, selling winners and keeping losers is the exact opposite of what an investor should do to succeed in the market. But studies show that loss-aversion is so widespread that year after year average investors fail to keep up with market averages.

However, mental accounting can also help savers and investors. A person can set aside vacation money in a change jar, use payroll deductions to contribute to a retirement account, put cash in a drawer to buy holiday gifts, and in each case, pretend the money set aside is unavailable for any other purpose than the one intended.

This labeling of money is entirely mental because in the marketplace, all dollars are the same. But it allows the person to meet pre-planned financial goals without making everyday decisions complex to the point of paralysis. Imagine weighing the impact on your retirement of decisions made while grocery shopping. Will buying the store brand of milk as opposed to a more expensive label mean you can retire to Florida a month earlier? Better to have separate mental accounts for groceries and retirement funds than to consider the entire financial picture for every buying decision.

Because the object of poker is to make financial decisions in the face of uncertainty, it is important to understand the psychology of mental accounting. You need to avoid the errors that mental accounting induces and learn its benefits.

The psychology of loss-aversion that dogs investors is also a major problem for poker players. It is easy for a player to quit when ahead, but difficult to leave a game when behind. As a result, players who fall behind try to compensate by taking more risks and making reckless plays that they would not make if they were ahead. It is the psychology of loss-aversion that leads to a player "going on a tilt" or "steaming" after a bad beat. Nothing is more frustrating than to play, patiently waiting for the right moment; it finally arrives—a great hand, large pot, good position, correct read—then the wrong card on the river undoes all the work. In poker, this scenario happens frequently. Many players respond by ceasing to be patient, lowering their starting hand requirements, and staying in subsequent hands too long.

The problem is that the distribution of cards has no knowledge of a particular player's bad beat. Luck might average out over the long-run, but no law of probability requires luck to average out within the next few hands after a bad beat. Instead, the other players at the table will note when someone is on a tilt and exploit that for their gain. Losses for the player on a tilt become magnified even more. Gains from many hours of careful, patient, thoughtful play can evaporate in a matter of minutes.

More troubling is that it does not take bad beats for loss-aversion to cause problems. Examples:

- Many players have difficulty leaving a table when their losses result from the others playing better. Simply switching tables might lead to an immediate improvement in outcomes. But it is difficult to admit being outplayed by the others and to let go of the money lost to them.

- Many players have difficulty accepting normal fluctuations in outcomes and understanding just how large these fluctuations can be. In poker, it is possible to play perfectly—make correct reads, use the most effective tactics for each situation, place bets with only positive expected values, never tilt—and still have losing sessions. Because perfect play can still result in short-term losses, players must have a sufficiently large bankroll to absorb normally occurring losses. Many times players lose by being chronically under-funded, meaning they play at limits that are too high in relation to their bankrolls. Normally occurring short-term losses can wipe out under-funded players. It becomes impossible for the "long-run" to happen.

It is important to have a bankroll with no less than 200 big bets for whatever limit you play. This means you must step down in limits when you fall below that threshold, not up, as many players do. Moving to higher limits to recoup losses at lower limits magnifies the problem of fluctuations in outcomes.

But mental accounting can also benefit poker players, particularly in regards to bankroll management. Just like a saver or investor, a poker player should set aside money only for poker. A player's bankroll should be treated as a separate account with rules for deposits and withdrawals. The size of the bankroll, along with skill and interest, should dictate playing limits. A player can even subdivide his or her bankroll; allocating different fractions for different poker games and limits while tracking the results separately. Mentally separating a poker bankroll in this manner allows a player to uncover strengths and weaknesses and to know when a permanent move upward in limits is worthwhile.

Mental accounting can help overcome a poker player's most difficult psychological hurdle—focusing on decisions rather than outcomes. Too many players have their thinking influenced by outcomes of individual hands. But in poker, it frequently occurs that a poor decision leads to a good result and that a good decision leads to a bad result. That is because many bets with positive expected values lose most of the time. Your focus should not be on the outcomes; it should be on the decision-making process and whether or not the decisions were correct. Unless your poker bankroll is in a separate mental account it will be very difficult psychologically to focus on the decisions rather than the outcomes.

Understanding how mental accounting affects behavior will improve not only your poker game, it will also help you improve everyday buying and investment decisions.

## Adjust Your Play to Conditions

A common technique for training people to make critical decisions in real-time, under stress, is the use of computer simulations as a substitute for experience. Need to learn how to land a fully loaded 747 airliner in a thunderstorm with half its engines out? With modern computer simulators, a pilot can practice this maneuver repeatedly without risking lives. Police trainees learn how to use their weapons by practicing with life-sized videos of realistic encounters. They learn when it is correct to shoot someone and when it is a mistake, again without actual lives being at risk.

For game players, computers are programmed to simulate opponents. Without actual money or prestige on the line, students of a game can spend hours practicing under realistic conditions. Chess players, for example, routinely train with personal computers against inexpensive computer programs that play at the master level. While computers play chess differently than humans, that difference has become harder to detect. For the average chess player, it is difficult to beat a computer. Today, chess programs that run on powerful machines routinely beat grandmasters. If you want a strong opponent—with infinite patience—to teach you chess, a computer is a good substitute. Learn to play chess well against a computer and you are on your way to beating people.

But can a computer play poker well against humans? It is interesting to compare the problem of programming a computer to play chess with the problem of programming a computer to play poker. By the late 1990s, computer scientists had accomplished the goal of creating a chess-playing computer that could compete with the world's best chess players. In 1997, a team of researchers working at IBM programmed a supercomputer—*Deep Blue*—that defeated in a match the reigning World Chess Champion, Gary Kasparov. In the six-game match, *Deep Blue* won 2 games, Kasparov won 1 game, and 3 draws resulted. Not an overwhelming victory for the computer, but a victory nonetheless.

Computer scientists in the 1990s also had their sights set on building a computer that could beat the top poker players in the world. Surprisingly, that is a much more difficult problem. At the University of Alberta in Canada, the Computer Poker Research Group has for more than a decade worked on designing a computer program that can play poker at a world-class level. An early version of their poker program—*Loki*—appeared in 1997 and human opponents easily won against it.

Not until July 2007 did the research group hold its first man versus machine poker championship. The program *Polaris* took on two poker professionals, Phil Laak and Ali Eslami, in heads-up limit Texas Hold'em. The humans won, but the computer made a strong showing. Finally, in July 2008, *Polaris* defeated several top human poker players. Still, heads-up, limit-play is a highly controlled environment compared to a full table with no-limit stakes. A computer that can compete in the World Series of Poker is still in the future.

It is instructive to examine the reasons why the two games (chess and poker) present such different programming problems. Why did it take another decade for the programmers struggling to write poker-playing programs to catch up with the chess computer programmers? Understanding the reasons helps identify the knowledge and skills an expert human poker player needs. After all, the most interesting question raised by these human-versus-machine contests is: Why are the humans so difficult to beat? A person unfamiliar with the game of poker might think that the computer, with its perfect memory, total objectivity, vastly superior computational ability, and precise mathematically play, should win every time at both chess and poker. Why, despite all the innate advantages a computer possesses, do humans even have a chance?

Chess has a clearly defined object: checkmate your opponent's King. All chess moves, and the plans motivating them, have checkmate as their long-range goal. Since checkmate is easily defined mathematically, programming the computer's goal is straightforward. Chess is also a game of perfect information. At all times, both participants in a chess game have complete knowledge of the board and the location of all the pieces in play. The computer never has to deal with uncertainty. With its perfect memory and superior computation speed, in just minutes it can generate and evaluate tens of millions of possible future positions. But, human chess players, who consider about 50 possible future positions when selecting a move, can compete against a computer. It is difficult to substitute the computer's method—a brute force calculation—for the long-term strategic thinking and deep understanding of relationships between the chess pieces possessed by human grandmasters. It is simply not necessary for a human grandmaster to examine tens of millions of possibilities in order to find the best move.

Poker also has a straightforward object: to win money. But, unlike chess, it is a game of imperfect information. A brute force calculation is not possible because of all the unknowns. There is no "best move" in poker like there often is in chess. Simply playing your cards, with no consideration of the other players, will not work in poker. Humans must study their opponents and learn to anticipate and predict their future actions. To further complicate matters, the object of the game — winning money — means different things to different people, and to a computer, money means nothing. Even more confusing, money can mean different things to the same person. As I mentioned before, when I play poker on the first Friday of every month, year after year, with the same six friends, the motivation is to socialize and be entertained. The difference between a good or bad night is whether I win or lose $20. That is not a meaningful amount of money to any of us. The result is an evening when we play loose junk poker games that require no strategic thinking.

When I play in Atlantic City, I behave differently. I risk several hundred dollars with the goal of winning a few hundred. To me, that amount of money is meaningful, but not an amount so large that it will cause me financial harm if I lose. Unlike Friday night poker, the games I play in are tightly structured. My motivation is the thrill of competition. I put on a game face and think carefully about the decisions I make. I feel good when I win, frustrated when I lose.

I have told you my motivations and budget limitations. Each of my opponents has a different set of reasons for playing and a different budget. Even though we play in the same game, the meaning of the money is different for each of us. At a poker table, why people play the way they do depends not so much on the cards they are dealt, but what the money means to them and their reasons for playing. That means I must adjust my play to them.

In a 2001 paper* titled "The Challenge of Poker" by Darse Billings and his fellow researchers at the University of Alberta,

*Darse Billings, Aaron Davidson, Johnathan Schaeffer, Duane Szafron, "The Challenge of Poker," June 22, 2001, The University of Alberta Computer Poker Research Group has this paper posted on their site *http://poker.cs.ualberta.ca.*

they wrote that opponent modeling "is essential to achieving high performance in poker." Their early poker program—*Poki*— constructed statistical models of each opponent and altered its play to exploit observed patterns and tendencies." In other words, the poker program adjusted to the people as it played. However, opponent modeling is a tough problem in poker because human tendencies are rarely static. To understand the difficulty of this modeling problem consider a five-hour session I had playing poker in Atlantic City.

**1st hour (late morning):** I began at a full table and everyone played in almost every hand. Passive play ruled—no one raised pre-flop or in any other betting rounds. Mostly players called. In this environment, I played looser than otherwise. Drawing hands became profitable because I could see the flop cheaply and knew that a big pot waited for me if I hit the draw. Drawing hands were playable from almost any position since I "knew" everyone would call and no one would raise. I had to fold high pairs quickly if they didn't improve on the flop, because with so many people in the hand, someone always hit a draw. It generally took "trips" or better to win, and with the pots large, there was always a showdown, so there was no point in trying to bluff. The big pots also covered my mistakes.

**2nd hour (lunch time):** The game was frequently short-handed because players kept leaving for 20–30 minute intervals to eat. Sometimes only 5 to 6 players were present which led to confusion on blinds, since people kept missing their blind. My cost to play went up because I stayed at the table, so my blind position came up more frequently. Players remained passive. I played aggressively, especially with big pairs and premium starting cards. Drawing hands became unplayable from any position since there were so few players to contribute to the pot. Two pair, especially if one was large, often won. Fewer showdowns occurred, so I stole some pots with aggressive raising. I needed to steal pots, or the frequent blinds would eat up my chip pile.

**3rd hour (early afternoon):** The table filled with aggressive players. Almost always, a pre-flop raise occurred. Playing cards appropriate for my position became critical. I could not limp in with weak starting cards because I would be raised. I needed to have premium starting cards and be prepared to raise or call a raise to stay in a hand. Mistakes became costly since the aggressive play meant I paid dearly to chase.

**4th hour (mid-afternoon):** The action dried up and the game tightened considerably. Most players folded their starting cards. Whether my hand was mediocre or a monster didn't matter much since I couldn't attract bettors either way. With little money in play, my earnings potential dropped to near nothing. While keeping my seat, I started scouting other tables, considering a switch.

**5th hour (late afternoon):** Frustration with the lack of action set in. Someone raised pre-flop, there was a re-raise, and then someone yelled "cap it." Everyone put in three bets to see a flop. Suddenly, the entire table was on a tilt. Chips flew everywhere, even when players held the flimsiest of cards. Wild swings occurred in everyone's bankroll. To play profitably, I needed a lot of money and the very best cards. Playing with anything less than premium cards from any position wasn't worth it, because the pre-flop expenses became too high. I needed to be a heavy favorite pre-flop to justify putting up so much money.

Notice that as the day progressed, strategy that was correct one hour became incorrect later on. This is hardly ever true at chess, in which a strong move is always a strong move. Poker players must constantly adjust to the changing social dynamic. Chess players must adjust to changing situations, but not in the same way poker players do. Chess positions usually have a best plan of action and often a best move. It is the position that matters, not the opponent. Chess players are taught to always assume their opponent will make the best move and plan accordingly. If their opponent fails to make the best move, the task usually becomes easier. Mastering chess involves learning thousands of positions and the best plan of action for each of them.

However, in poker, best play depends not on the cards, but the situation. Players must make continual adjustments to their underlying strategy. For the same cards, correct strategy may change completely depending on the situation. Adjusting is something humans do well but computer programs find difficult.

The great British mathematician, Alan Turing, argued in a famous article entitled "Computer Machinery and Intelligence," published in 1950 in the philosophical journal, *Mind*, that a computer could be said to "think" if interacting with the computer proved indistinguishable from interacting with a human. Put a human and the computer in two separate rooms, and allow a human to interrogate them unseen. If the interrogator, through a series of probing questions, can't distinguish the computer's answers from the human's, the computer is said to pass the "Turing Test" and, according to Turing, is actually thinking.

Restrict interactions to the microcosm of chess, and computers today can almost pass the Turing Test. Based on chess moves alone, it is difficult for the expert to distinguish a human grandmaster from a computer. But when it comes to poker, is the Turing Test even meaningful? There is an insidious problem with programming computers to play poker, which in my opinion, raises the Turing Test to a higher level. The problem is not whether people can figure out if they are up against a computer. It is whether the computer can figure out people, especially the ever-changing social dynamics in a randomly selected group of people.

Nobody at a poker table would care whether or not the computer played poker "like a person" because human play varies so widely, it would be difficult to define what that even means. There are plenty of people who play poker in a predictable "programmed" manner that would be indistinguishable from early poker programs. Such play would have discernable patterns that more experienced poker players would exploit. To play poker at a high level, it is necessary to model your opponents' behavior and to actively thwart opponents' attempts to model your play. Strong human poker players will intentionally display patterns in their play so that their opponents will start to have expectations. Then they will obtain an advantage at an opportune time by breaking a pattern that opponents have come to expect.

Computers must deal with more than imperfect information and the need to model opponents; they must not be too predictable, themselves, and cope with opponents actively working to deceive the program. It is also necessary to model how multiple opponents interact with each other. Determining best play in a multi-way pot is a different problem than a heads-up pot. How the different players model each other will influence the actions each takes and a human poker player must take that into consideration. Winning at poker often depends on who can adjust faster to changing circumstances. Humans are extremely good at discerning change and adjusting.

So should you practice poker against a computer simulation? It is a great way to learn the mechanics of the game and to receive real-time coaching on the math. Many computer simulations have a coaching feature with advice and updated pot odds and probabilities while you play. One simulation is "Poker Academy Pro" *(http://www.poker-academy.com/)* in which you can play against "bots" that will model your weaknesses and try to exploit them. It works on both Macintosh and Windows systems and can be purchased over the Internet and downloaded directly onto your computer. It has windows with coaching and statistics that update as the hand plays out. You can even customize the playing styles of the different "bots." The program will allow you to practice both tournament and cash-game play.

But I have found that computer simulations do not substitute for play against real people. Actual people are so much more interesting. The emotional content in human play is present even in the remote and sterile online environment. Most people are far more unpredictable and emotional than any computer simulation programmed to randomize its play or adopt different "personalities." Human unpredictability is an advantage at poker and makes it such an interesting game. Go back and study how

I adjusted each hour in my poker session. You will not find that kind of variability in a computer simulation.

## Learning to Create Luck

Poker enthusiasts have long debated the role of luck in poker. Clearly poker involves both luck and skill. If the game did not require skill, you would not see consistent life-long winners. Luck alone cannot explain multiple World Series bracelets for players such as Doyle Brunson, Phil Helmuth, and Johnny Chan. But, skill alone cannot explain players such as Chris Moneymaker who parlayed a $40 entry into an online satellite tournament to a $2.5 million payout as the 2003 World Series of Poker Champion. How much of poker is luck and how much is skill? The question is not solely philosophical, because powerful politicians and law enforcement agencies have worked to ban poker on the grounds that it is entirely luck and should be subject to gambling laws.

But the crusade against poker makes me wonder why law enforcement has not gone after the organizers of chess tournaments? As in a poker tournament, each participant in a chess tournament must pay an entry fee on registration. The pool of money collected is used to pay for the cost of event, to pay the organizers for their work, and to form a prize pool to award to the winners. For decades, chess tournaments that are open to players of all ages have been funded in this manner. When I was as young as 14, I saved money from my allowance to play in chess tournaments and on more than one occasion, returned home with a substantial cash prize.

The stock answer to my seemingly absurd question is that chess is not gambling because it depends on skill. No random element exists in chess. All information about the position is exposed on the chessboard for each player to see. Each player freely makes his or her decisions with full knowledge of the position. As a result, an amateur chess player, if given a thousand tries, would not win even a single game against a grandmaster. In contrast, if the cards fell just right, an amateur poker player could, on occasion, beat a professional. All of this is true, and as a result, the importance of skill in chess presents a huge problem for chess tournament organizers. An adequately funded tournament with an attractive prize pool needs a large number of players willing to pay the entry fee. Masses of average chess players are not going to contribute their money to prize pools they have no chance of winning. After all, it is known before play begins that the handful of masters who show up will be the only ones competing for the top spots.

The chess organizer's solution to this problem originated decades ago and it involves introducing elements of luck into the awarding of prizes. Introducing luck into an outcome based on skill is actually easy. It is an obvious but little mentioned truth about any contest that involves skill—when the competitors have similar abilities, the outcome is not predictable. The reason is that when competitors have comparable skills, chance events often prove decisive.

Consider the example of baseball, a sport that requires near superhuman skill to play at the professional level. In the major leagues, the difference between a first place team and last place team is the difference between winning six out of every ten games as opposed to winning four out of every ten games. That means the predicted outcome of any major league baseball game is very close to that of a coin flip. Chance events, such as bad bounces, dropped fly balls, or questionable strike calls, are often decisive. As a result the statistically best team does not always win the World Series. But the role of chance in baseball is not a problem. In fact, the unpredictability is desirable because participants and spectators have little interest in competitions with known outcomes. Fans would not pay to see a major league team take on local high school teams.

So chess tournament organizers generate substantial prize pools with a performance rating system that groups chess players into classes with comparable abilities. Cash prizes are awarded in each class. As a result, all participants feel that they have a chance of winning money and willingly contribute to the prize pool. Anyone can win because when skills are about equal, momentary lapses of attention, sudden flashes of inspiration, or unexpected moves; in other words—chance events determine the prizewinners. As players improve, they move into higher classes and are forced to compete for prize money with higher skilled players.

Predictability is regarded as a bad thing in many competitive activities, not just chess. Organizers of golf and bowling leagues, with the consent of the contestants, devise methods to reduce the role skill in awarding prizes. Raw scores are "handicapped" so that it is possible for a novice player having a good day to "win" against a professional player having a bad day. Handicap systems allow novices and average players to set realistic goals for improvement, rather than be discouraged by the fact that playing at a professional level is not obtainable unless a player actually becomes a professional.

However, as players improve, a funny thing happens—they become luckier. In chess, strong players save more apparently hopeless positions and have opponents who make more mistakes when playing against them. As a novice, I began to think I needed to be lucky to win, but as I experienced the role of luck in chess, I learned a lesson that has served me well in life: *strong players know how to create luck.* They know how to keep up unrelenting pressure so that any lapse in attention by their opponent is decisive. No matter how dire the situation, strong players keep looking for opportunities, keep setting traps, and keep making the game as difficult as possible for their opponents. They learn to find moves that might not be the "best move," but are moves that they know will be psychologically unsettling for their opponents and induce mistakes.

The ability to create luck is useful in chess, but it is the critical skill in poker. Uncertainty is built into the game of poker so no handicap system is necessary. A poker player must study the cards, looking for opportunities. A poker player does not expect to win every hand, or come out ahead in every playing session, any more than a baseball player expects a hit in every game. But the idea of poker is to keep looking for favorable chances. Most betting opportunities are unfavorable and should be avoided, but players who keep in the game, and stay focused and alert, find betting situations that are worth the risk. Not every worthwhile bet will pay, but if enough favorable bets are placed, over time the mathematical laws governing chance dictate that a profit will accrue.

We live in a culture that is increasingly risk-averse. Elaborate laws have developed to protect us from the vagaries of chance. Consenting adults are arrested for risking their own money in a poker game because they might suffer financial harm if they lose. Never mind the financial harm from the arrest or government seizure of funds. The government snoops into our bank accounts, questioning the entities we do business with and how much we spend. To protect us from risk the government insists it is necessary that we give up personal privacy, free choice, and freedom of association.

In fact, politicians, government officials and law enforcement agencies are extremely disingenuous when they claim that citizens need to be protected from financial harm caused by poker. In public cardrooms and online, the games dealt are generally honest. The wide variety of available limits allows players with just about any budget to play responsibly. Contrast the poker industry with the financial services industry. Over the past decade, massive collusion and fraud in stocks, mortgages, and banking has resulted in financial ruin for millions of people and cost billions of dollars. But the government response to events such as the subprime mortgage crisis is to say that the homebuyers should have better understood the risks and made more responsible choices. Only after the collapse of large banks and investment firms does law enforcement question business practices. Then the officials are shocked—just shocked to discover dishonesty and outright fraud.

My goal in writing this book is to help readers understand the risks of poker and make responsible choices. I hope that no one with a gambling problem is reading or visiting the book's Website. This book is intended for adults interested in the game of poker, and who want to learn more about it. Poker is fun and enjoyable, and even if you lose money, it can be controlled so that the cost is no greater than any other form of recreation or entertainment.

The combination of luck and skill present in poker models many kinds of situations in life. Examine the life of any successful person and you will find that the success required difficult-to-acquire-skills that took years of practice to hone. You will also find that those skills would have amounted to little without some "lucky break." Every successful person has a right-place right-time kind of story to tell. We learn that in life, just as in poker, success requires both skill and luck. And if you ask successful people to recount all their efforts along the way to success, you will discover that failures occurred. Success happened because of repeated attempts, even after failures. In other words, that person learned how to create luck.

# Part IV

# Where to Go from Here

This book is intended to be both a beginning and a guide. After reading to this point, you should be able to hold your own in the typical low-limit Hold'em games found in public cardrooms and online. Of course, the real fun in poker isn't reading; it is playing. This part has information on places to play, both in person and online. Chapter 11 gives advice on how to choose an online cardroom. The advantage of online poker is that you can play any time from any where for any level of stakes.

If you want to play in-person, traveling to a public "brick-and-mortar" cardroom is often necessary. Chapter 12 has a list of over 200 hundred places to play in the United States and Canada. The list is not comprehensive and is only as up-to-date as the publication of this book, but it shows that playing opportunities exist in many locations throughout North America.

# 11. Online Poker Rooms

In the first edition of this book, I provided detailed information on 15 online poker rooms. By the time the book went to press, some of the information was out of date. Within three years, all the information was out of date. Because industry change is so rapid, I will not even attempt to give detailed information about online cardrooms. Instead, this chapter will provide general guidelines for choosing an online poker room. Up-to-date information, bonus codes, and details about current playing venues are at the book's Website: *http://www.IntelligentPoker.com*.

## How to Choose an Online Cardroom

Online poker is an extremely competitive business. Poker players seeking online action have an overwhelming amount of choice. In making that choice here are two questions to ask.

**Are you a resident of the United States?** A large fraction of the online poker venues will not serve U. S. players; so if you live in the U. S. your choices are immediately limited. If you live outside the U. S. and online poker is legal in your jurisdiction there are many more cardrooms available. But, poker is a game about money and most of the money wagered online still comes from the United States. A cardroom that welcomes all players should be seriously considered even for players outside the U. S.

**What kind of games do you like to play?** Texas Hold'em is the most popular game in the world. All online venues spread Hold'em with a wide variety of stakes and table sizes that range from heads-up to a full 10 players. At most sites an online Hold'em player is seated quickly at his or her game of choice. It is also possible for players with modest bankrolls to participate in the no-limit and pot-limit forms of Hold'em because of maximum buy-in rules. For example, a player sitting at a $1-2 no-limit table at the online site Full Tilt Poker cannot buy-in for more than $200. The rule results in a rough parity in stack size at the table so that a player who can afford a deep stack does not have a permanent advantage in a small-stakes game.

Players who want to expand their poker skills and interests beyond Hold'em must find cardrooms that spread the games they want to play. The rising popularity of Omaha, Omaha High-Low, Razz, Seven-Card Stud, and Seven-Card Stud High-Low has resulted in most online cardrooms spreading these games. It is now common for cardrooms to offer mixed tables where the deal rotates between different poker variations.

However, players who want games other than Hold'em must consider the size of the player base when choosing an online cardroom. If the site has too few players, there will not be enough interested players online at a given time to support games other than Hold'em. The problem of too few players becomes more pronounced at higher limits because as limits rise, player availability decreases. A small online venue might have an active $1-2 Seven-Card Stud High-Low table all the time, but if you want to play $5-10, that table might never run.

To get a feel for the size of a site's player base, go online as an observer and check the lobby for the number of players currently seated. For sites that routinely seat 20,000 or more at any given time, most poker variations offered will run. But for sites that seat 5000 players or fewer at any given time, game choice will be limited.

Here are additional considerations when choosing an online room:

**Longevity of the site:** There has been a great deal of consolidation in the online poker industry now that its explosive growth has curtailed and the U. S. government has made it difficult for U. S. residents to transfer money to the sites. Larger sites have absorbed many smaller ones. Look for well-established sites with a viable player base numbering in at least the tens of thousands.

**Tournament versus cash:** If you are a tournament specialist, you need to carefully study the tournament offerings for each site. While cash-games have standard structures with only small variations, there are an infinite number of ways for structuring tournaments. Many tournament players have become specialists in particular formats and should find a site with offerings that match their specialty.

**Familiarity with other players:** If you play at middle to high limits at a small site, or prefer games other than Hold'em, you will face the same opponents on a regular basis. That means you will have the ability to know and study their play and they will have the ability to track your play. This will be particularly true if you play many hours each week. If that is the case, you must be cognizant that your playing decisions are being tracked and analyzed. To be successful requires that you pay attention to the specific tendencies of regular opponents. If you play low-limit Hold'em infrequently at a large site, you might never play the same person twice. Tracking will not be an issue.

**Time of day:** Games tend to be looser on weekends and during evenings when there are more hobbyists online. Daytime poker has a greater percentage of professionals. But, daytime is not the same time everywhere. A daytime player on the east coast of the United States might want to look for sites with a heavy European base because it will be evening in Europe when he or she plays.

**Promotions:** All sites run promotions and offer deposit bonuses. But, be careful that you don't play over your limit in order to chase bonus money. See the section that follows on how online bonuses work.

**Computer operating system:** Owners of computers with the Windows operating system can play anywhere. Macintosh owners must consider compatibility issues discussed in the next section.

## Online Poker on a Macintosh

Developers of online poker software have concentrated on applications for Windows-based computers because more than 90% of the personal computers manufactured run the Windows operating system. But, people in education, graphics design, and desktop publishing use the Macintosh operating system heavily, and many Macintosh owners see no reason to ever own a Windows-based machine. While 10% is a small fraction, in absolute numbers it amounts to millions of people and many of them enjoy online poker. While Mac owners have limited choice when it comes to poker, they do have the ability to play poker online and options for expanding their choices.

*Poker interfaces*

There are two approaches to software for online poker—download and no-download. Most poker sites use the download approach in which players install an application that runs on their personal computers. Initial contact with the poker site is made through a Web browser, but once the poker application is downloaded and installed, actual play is conducted using the application. The no-download approach works completely through the Web browser, usually with the use of a Java script that provides the player's interface to the poker tables. Each approach has its advantages and disadvantages and some poker sites offer both options.

The download approach is generally preferred because it uses the full resources of the user's computer, making it possible to run faster, more elaborate software applications. The problem is that software applications must be adapted for each operating system and it is only feasible to support a limited number of operating systems. Often Macintosh and older Windows operating systems are not supported.

The no-download approach using Java only requires that the user have access to a computer with a Web browser. That means the user can play poker online from any computer with an Internet connection. It does not have to be the user's own computer because it is not necessary to install special software. The computer can have a Mac or a Windows operating system because Java is a cross-platform language. But software that runs only over the Web is more restricted in what it can do. It is also a challenge for Java programmers to write code that interacts with different Web browsers in the same way.

*Macintosh options*

Mac users have the following options if they want to play online poker.

1.  Play at sites with no-download interfaces. Most sites with this require only that a Web browser work well on Macs.

2.  Find sites that offer downloads for the Mac operating system. There are poker sites that have the option of downloading software that runs native on Macs. While these sites are fewer in number, they include some major sites and more sites are developing software for Macs.

3.  Own an Intel-based Mac, which includes any Mac purchased later than 2006. Purchase a full version of Windows to run on that Mac. It is possible to run

Windows natively on Intel-based Macs by using Bootcamp or purchasing the application Parallels *(http://www.Parallels.com)*. With Windows running natively, any Windows application can be used, including all the poker applications. While this is the most expensive option for Mac users, it provides the greatest amount of choice. It also allows the player to use many third-party software applications designed to assist real-time poker decision-making and analyze results. (See Chapter 8 for explanations of third-party poker software.)

While it might appear difficult at first, Macintosh users can play poker online, and with appropriate software adaptations, have the full range of options available to Windows users.

## How Online Bonuses Work

Most online cardrooms offer deposit bonuses when you sign up. That means the cardroom will provide matching funds for a certain percentage of your initial deposit. This allows you to get more for your money when you play. But bonus offers come with conditions and it is wise not to let meeting those conditions influence your play or money management.

There are very few cardrooms that simply add the bonus money to your account when you make your first deposit. The majority of sites require you to play and generate income for the cardroom before any bonus money is released. For example, as of this writing, Full Tilt Poker offers a 100% deposit bonus up to $600. That means if you make an initial deposit of $600, Full Tilt will match the entire amount with bonus money. But none of that match is immediate. You need to play to earn that bonus. Full Tilt awards 1 Poker Point for each $1 raked from the pot. Each point counts for $0.06 towards the bonus. That means Full Tilt must rake $10,000 from the pots you contribute to before the $600 bonus will be completely released. How many hands of play that amounts to depends on the stakes and the amount of action. The bonus comes with a four-month expiration date, but it is released in $20 increments as it accrues. It is possible to earn partial bonuses even if you don't qualify for the entire amount before the expiration date.

Bonuses are a good thing for players, but only if thought of as something extra. If you start playing for the bonus money, you can find yourself in trouble because it is easy to have your playing decisions altered by bonus considerations. The changes in behavior that bonuses induce are not always for the better. Here are the traps caused by bonuses that players need to avoid:

**Playing at too high a level in relation to your skill and/or bankroll.** The higher the stakes, the faster you will collect bonus money because the larger pots result in a greater rake. Since most bonuses come with an expiration date, speed is of the essence if you want to collect the full amount. But if you make a $500 initial deposit and then sit down at a $10-20 table to speed up the bonus award, you are asking for trouble. A $500 bankroll is not large enough to support $10-20 play. Most likely, you will lose the money before qualifying for the bonus. Do not play at limits higher than you otherwise would just to collect bonus money. Always play at limits that are within your skill level and that your bankroll can support.

**Playing more hours than you should.** For large bonuses, it usually takes a great deal of time to earn all the money. On a per hour basis, playing for bonus money is not worth it. If a rush to beat the bonus expiration date is causing you to play when you are tired, distracted, impatient, or should be tending to other matters, you might be losing more money with sub-optimum play than you will ever make from the bonus. Do not let bonus considerations cause you to play when you are not at your best.

As long as you keep to your game and do not alter it based on bonus considerations, you should take full advantage of any extras the cardroom has to offer.

# 12. Brick-and-Mortar Poker Rooms

As of this writing, legal public cardrooms that spread Texas Hold'em exist in at least 28 states and almost all the Canadian provinces. What follows is a list of almost 300 cardrooms in the United States and Canada with names, addresses, and phone and Website contact information. The list is by no means all-inclusive. Game availability changes and cardrooms come and go, so be sure to call ahead before planning a trip.

The United States list is sorted alphabetically by state and then by ZIP code. The Canadian list is sorted alphabetically by province and then alphabetically by the cardroom names. Most of the cardrooms listed offer regularly scheduled tournaments. Call or visit the Websites to find out about schedules, buy-ins and prizes.

# United States Poker Rooms
# (by state and ZIP code)

*Arizona*

**Harrah's Phoenix AK-Chin Casino**
15406 Maricopa Road
Maricopa, AZ 85239
480-802-5000
http://www.harrahsakchin.com

**Gila River Casino at Wild Horse Pass**
5550 West Wild Horse Pass
Chandler, AZ 85246
800-WIN-GILA
http://www.wingilariver.com

**Casino Arizona**
9700 E. Indian Bend
Scottsdale, AZ 85256
480-850-7777
http://www.casinoarizona.com

**Fort McDowell Casino**
10424 Noth Fort McDowell Road
Fountain Hills, AZ 85264
800-843-3678
http://www.fortmcdowellcasino.com

**Gila River Casino at Vee Quiva**
6443 Komatke Lane
Laveen, AZ 85339
800-WIN-GILA
http://www.wingilariver.com

**Bluewater Casino**
11222 Resort Drive
Parker, AZ 85344
888-243-3360
http://www.bluewaterfun.com

**Paradise Casino**
450 Quechan Drive
Yuma, AZ 85364
888-777-4946
http://www.paradise-casinos.com

**Mazatzal Casino**
Highway 87 - Mile Marker 251
Payson, AZ 85541
800-777-7529
http://www.777play.com

**Apache Gold Casino**
Old Highway 70
San Carlos, AZ 85550
800-272-2438
http://www.apachegoldcasinoresort.com

**Casino of the Sun**
7406 S. Camino de Oeste
Tucson, AZ 85746
800-344-9435
http://www.casinodelsol.com

**Desert Diamond Casino**
7350 S. Nogales Hwy
Tucson, AZ 85746
800-639-8783
http://www.desertdiamondcasino.com

**Casino del Sol**
5655 West Valencia Road
Tucson, AZ 85757
800-344-9435
http://www.casinodelsol.com

**Hon-Dah Casino**
777 Highway 260
Pinetop, AZ 85935
800-929-8744
http://www.hon-dah.com

**Bucky's Casino**
1500 Hwy 69
Prescott, AZ 86304
800-96PINES
http://www.prescottresort.com

**Cliff Castle Casino**
353 Middle Verde Road
Camp Verde, AZ 86322
800-381-7568
http://www.cliffcastlecasino.net

*California*

**Commerce Casino**
6131 East Telegraph Road
Commerce, CA 90040
323-721-2100
http://www.commercecasino.com

**Bicycle Casino**
7301 Eastern Avenue
Bell Gardens, CA 90201
800-625-7864
http://www.thebicyclecasino.com

**Club Caribe Casino**
7617 Atlantic Avenue
Cudahy, CA 90201
323-560-5995

**Crystal Park Casino**
123 East Artesia Blvd.
Compton, CA 90220
310-661-4808
http://www.thecrystalcasino.com

**Hustler Casino**
1000 West Redondo Beach Blvd.
Gardena, CA 90247
877-968-9800
http://www.hustlercasinola.com

**Normandie Casino**
1045 West Rosecrans Ave.
Gardena, CA 90247
310-352-3400
http://www.normandiecasino.com

**Hollywood Park Casino**
3883 West Century Blvd.
Inglewood, CA 90303
310-330-2800
http://www.playhpc.com

**Hawaiian Gardens Casino**
11871 Carson Street
Los Angeles, CA 90716
562-860-5887
http://www.hawaiiangardenscasino.net

**Viejas Casino**
5000 Willows Rd.
Alpine, CA 91901
800-847-6537
http://www.viejas.com

**Sycuan Casino**
5469 Casino Way
El Cajon, CA 92019
800-2-SYCUAN
http://www.sycuancasino.com

**Oceans Eleven Casino**
121 Brooks Street
Oceanside, CA 92054
888-439-6988
http://www.oceans11.com

**Casino Pauma**
777 Pauma Reservation Rd
Pauma Valley, CA 92061
760-742-2177
http://www.casinopauma.com

**Fantasy Springs Resort**
Casino 84-245 Indio Springs Pkwy.
Indio, CA 92203
800-827-2946
http://www.fantasyspringsresort.com

**Spot Light 29**
46-200 Harrison Place
Coachella, CA 92236
866-377-6829
http://www.spotlight29.com

**Casino Morongo**
49750 Seminole Drive
Cabazon, CA 92239
800-252-4499
http://www.casinomorongo.com

**Spa Resort Casino**
401 East Amado Road
Palm Springs, CA 92262
888-999-1995
http://www.sparesortcasino.com

**Sundowner Cardroom**
15638 Ave. 296
Visalia, CA 93292
559-627-9624
http://www.sundownercardroom.com

**Agua Caliente Casino**
32-250 Bob Hope Dr.
Rancho Mirage, CA 92270
888-999-1995
http://www.hotwatercasino.com

**Golden West Casino**
1001 South Union Avenue
Bakersfield, CA 93307
661-324-6936
http://www.goldenwestcasino.net

**San Manuel Casino**
777 San Manuel Blvd.
Highland, CA 92346
800-359-2464
http://www.sanmanuel.com

**Central Coast Casino**
359 W. Grand Ave.
Grover Beach, CA 93433
805-474-8500
http://www.slopoker.com

**Lake Elsinore Hotel & Casino**
20930 Malaga Road
Lake Elsinore, CA 92530
951-674-5160
http://www.lercasino.com

**Central Coast Casino**
1124 Black Oak Drive
Paso Robles, CA 93446
805-226-0500
http://www.slopoker.com

**Soboba Casino**
23333 Soboba Rd.
San Jacinto, CA 92583
866-4-SOBOBA
http://www.soboba.net

**Chumash Casino**
3400 East Highway 246
Santa Ynez, CA 93460
800-248-6274
http://www.chumashcasino.com

**Pechanga Resort & Casino**
45000 Pechanga Parkway
Temecula, CA 92592
877-711-2WIN
http://www.pechanga.com

**Paiute Palace Casino**
2742 North Sierra Highway
Bishop, CA 93514
888-3PAIUTE
http://www.paiutepalace.com

**Player's Club**
906 N Ventura Ave
Ventura, CA 93001
805-643-1392
http://www.playersclubventura.com

**Diamond Jim's Casino**
118 20th Street West
Rosamond, CA 93560
661-256-6724
http://diamondjimscasino.net

**Tachi Palace Hotel & Casino**
17225 Jersey Avenue
Lemoore, CA 93245
866-4-PALACE
http://www.tachipalace.com

**Chukchansi Gold Resort and Casino**
711 Lucky Lane
Coarsegold, CA 93614
866-7-WIN-WIN
http://www.chukchansigold.com

**Table Mountain Casino & Bingo**
8184 Table Mountain Road
Friant, CA 93626
559-822-7777
http://www.tmcasino.com

**Club One Casino**
1033 Van Ness Avenue
Fresno, CA 93721
559-497-3000
http://www.clubonecasino.com

**Lucky Chances Casino**
1700 Hillside Boulevard
Colma, CA 94014
650-758-2237
http://www.luckychances.com

**Artichoke Joe's**
659 Huntington Ave
San Bruno, CA 94066
650-589-3145
http://artichokejoes.com

**The Palace Poker Casino**
22821 Mission Blvd.
Hayward, CA 94541
510-582-1166
http://www.thepalacepokercasino.com

**Lucky Buck Cardroom**
1620 Railroad Ave
Livermore, CA 94551
925-455-6144
http://www.theluckybuck.com

**California Grand**
5867 Pacheco Boulevard
Pacheco, CA 94553
925-685-8397
http://www.calgrandcasino.com

**Napa Valley Casino**
3466 Broadway/Hwy 29
American Canyon, CA 94589
707 644 8851
http://www.napavalleycasino.net

**Oaks Card Club**
4097 San Pablo Avenue
Emeryville, CA 94608
510-653-4456
http://www.oakscardclub.com

**Casino San Pablo**
13255 San Pablo Ave
San Pablo, CA 94806
510-215-7888
http://www.sanpablolytton.com

**Bay 101**
1801 Bering Drive
San Jose, CA 95112
408-451-8888
http://www.bay101.com

**Garden City Casino**
360 South Saratoga Ave
San Jose, CA 95129
408-244-3333
http://www.gardencitycasino.com

**Cameo Club**
552 W. Benjamin Holt Drive
Stockton, CA 95207
209-474-1777
http://cameoclubcasino.com

**Casino Real**
1355 N Main St
Manteca, CA 95336
209-239-1455
http://www.thecasinoreal.com

**Turlock Poker Room**
270 W. Main St.
Turlock, CA 95380
209-668-1010
http://www.turlockpoker.com

**Robinson Rancheria Bingo and Casino**
1545 East Highway 20
Nice, CA 95464
800-809-3636
http://www.rrrc.com

**Blue Lake Casino**
777 Casino Way
Blue Lake, CA 95525
877-BLC-2WIN
http://www.bluelakecasino.com

**Elk Valley Casino**
2500 Howland Hills Road
Cresent City, CA 95531
888-574-2744
http://www.elkvalleycasino.com

**Cher-ae Heights**
27 Scenic Drive
Trinidad, CA 95570
800-684-2464
http://www.cheraeheightscasino.com

**Cache Creek Casino**
14455 Hwy 16
Brooks, CA 95606
800-452-8181
http://www.cachecreek.com

**Lucky Derby Casino**
7433 Greenback Lane
Citrus Heights, CA 95610
916-726-8946
http://www.luckyderbycasino.com

**Capitol Casino**
411 N. 16th St.
Sacramento, CA 95811
916-446-0700
http://www.capitol-casino.com

**Limelight Card Room**
1014 Alhambra Blvd
Sacramento, CA 95816
916-446-2208
http://limelightcardroom.com

**Angies Poker Club**
1414 Park Avenue
Chico, CA 95928
530-892-2282
http://www.angiespokerclub.com

**Colusa Casino**
3770 Hwy 45
Colusa, CA 95932
530-458-8844
http://www.colusacasino.com

**Feather Falls Casino & Lodge**
3 Alverda Drive
Oroville, CA 95966
877-652-4646
http://www.featherfallscasino.com

**Gold Country Casino**
4020 Olive Hwy
Oroville, CA 95966
800-334-9400
http://www.goldcountrycasino.com

**Win River Casino**
2100 Redding Rancheria Rd
Redding, CA 96001
800-280-UWIN
http://www.win-river.com

*Colorado*

**Ameristar Blackhawk**
111 Richman Street
Blackhawk, CO 80422
720-946-6673
http://www.ameristarcasinos.com

**Colorado Central Station Casino**
340 Main Street
Black Hawk, CO 80422
800-843-4753
http://www.coloradocentralstation.com

**Golden Gates Casino**
261 Main Street
Black Hawk, CO 80422
303-582-2906
http://www.goldencasinogroup.com

**Gilpin Casino**
111 Main Street
Black Hawk, CO 80422
800-538-5825
http://www.thegilpincasino.com

**The Lodge Casino**
240 Main Street
Black Hawk, CO 80422
303-582-1771
http://www.thelodgecasino.com

**Fortune Valley**
321 Gregory Street
Central City, CO 80427
800-924-6646
http://www.fortunevalleycasino.com

**Double Eagle Hotel & Casino**
400-442 East Bennet Ave.
Cripple Creek, CO 80813
800-711-7234
http://www.decasino.com

**Midnight Rose Casino**
256 East Bennett Ave
Cripple Creek, CO 80813
800-635-5825
http://www.triplecrowncasinos.com/
Midnight_Rose

**Ute Mountain Casino**
3 Weeminuche Drive
Towaoc, CO 81334
800-258-8007
http://www.utemountaincasino.com

*Connecticut*

**Foxwoods Resort Casino**
39 Norwich Westerly Rd.
Mashantucket, CT 06338
800-369-9663
http://www.foxwoods.com

**Mohegan Sun**
1 Mohegan Sun Bld
Uncasville, CT 06382
888-226-7711
http://www.mohegansun.com

*Florida*

**Sun Cruz Casino**
610 Glen Cheek Rd
Cape Canaveral, FL 32920
800-474-DICE
http://www.suncruzcasino.com

**Dania Jai-Alai Cardroom**
301 East Dania Beach Blvd
Dania Beach, FL 33004
954 920-1511
http://www.betdania.com

**Seminole Casino - Hollywood**
4150 N St Road 7
Hollywood, FL 33021
954-961-3220
http://www.seminolehollywoodcasino.
com

**The Isle Casino**
1800 SW 3rd Street
Pompano Beach, FL 33069
800-843-4753
http://www.theislepompanopark.com

**Miccosukee Hotel Resort**
500 Southwest 177 Ave
Miami, FL 33194
877-242-6464
http://www.miccosukee.com/resort.html

**Seminole Hard Rock Hotel & Casino**
1 Seminole Way
Hollywood, FL 33314
866-502-7529
http://www.seminolehardrockhollywood.
com

**Seminole Hardrock Hotel and Casino**
5223 North Orient Road
Tampa, FL 33610
866-502-7529
http://www.seminolehardrocktampa.com

**Tampa Bay Downs**
11225 race track road
Tampa, FL 33626
813-298-1798
http://www.tampabaydowns.com

**Derby Lane**
10490 Gandy Blvd
St. Petersburg, FL 33702
727-812-3339
http://www.derbylane.com

**Naples Fort Myers Greyhound Track**
10601 Bonita Beach Road
Bonita Springs, FL 34135
239-992-2411
http://www.naplesfortmyersdogs.com

**Seminole Indian Casino**
506 South 1st St.
Immokalee, FL 34143
800-218-0007
http://www.theseminolecasino.com

**Seminole Brighton Casino**
Route 6 – Hwy 721
Okeechobee, FL 34974
866-2-CASINO
http://www.seminolecasinobrighton.com

*Iowa*

**Prairie Meadows**
1 Prairie Meadows Drive
Altoona, IA 50009
800-325-9015
http://www.prairiemeadows.com

**Terrible's Lakeside Casino**
777 Casino Dr.
Osceola, IA 50213
877-477-5253

**Casinomaha**
1 Blackbird Bend
Onawa, IA 51040
800-868-UBET
http://www.casino-omaha.net

**Winnavegas Casino**
1500 330th Street
Sloan, IA 51055
800-468-9466
http://www.winnavegas.biz

**Argosy of Sioux City**
100 Larsen Park Road
Sioux City, IA 51102
800-424-0080
http://www.argosy.com/siouxcity

**Ameristar Council Bluffs**
2200 River Road
Council Bluffs, IA 51501
712-328-8888
http://www.ameristarcasinos.com

**Harrah's Council Bluffs Casino**
1 Harrah's Blvd
Council Bluffs, IA 51501
712-329-6004
http://www.harrahscouncilbluffs.com

**Horseshoe Council Bluffs Casino**
2701 23 Ave
Council Bluffs, IA 51502
712-329-6000
http://www.horseshoecouncilbluffs.com

**Meskwaki Casino**
1504 305th Street
Tama, IA 52339
800-728-4263
http://www.meskwaki.com

**Catfish Bend Casino**
3001 Winegard Drive
Burlington, IA 52601
866-792-9948
http://www.catfishbendcasino.com

**Isle of Capri Bettendorf**
1821 State Street
Bettendorf, IA 52722
800-724-5825
http://www.isleofcapricasino.com

## Illinois

**Hollywood Casino - Aurora**
49 West Galena Blvd
Aurora, IL 60506
800-888-7777
http://www.hollywoodcasinoaurora.com

**Rockford Charitable Games**
417 Preston St.
Rockford, IL 61102
800-965-7852
http://www.rockfordcharitablegames.
com

## Indiana

**Ameristar East Chicago**
777 Ameristar Blvd
East Chicago, IN 46312
866-711-GAME
http://www.ameristarcasinos.com

**Horseshoe Casino**
825 Casino Center Dr
Hammond, IN 46312
219-473-7000
http://www.horseshoehammond.com

**Majestic Star Casinos**
1 Buffington Harbor Drive
Gary, IN 46406
888-2B-LUCKY
http://www.majesticstar.com

**Horseshoe Southern Indiana**
11999 Casino Center Drive SE
Elizabeth, IN 47117
866-676-SHOE
http://www.horseshoe-indiana.com

**Casino Aztar**
421 Northwest Riverside Dr.
Evansville, IN 47708
800-342-5386
http://www.casinoaztar.com

## Kansas

**Golden Eagle Casino**
1121 Goldfinch Road
Horton, KS 66439
888-464-5825
http://www.goldeneaglecasino.com

**Prairie Band Casino**
12305 150th Road
Mayetta, KS 66509
785-966-7777
http://www.pbpgaming.com

## Louisiana

**Treasure Chest Casino**
5050 Williams Blvd
Kenner, LA 70065
800-298-0711
http://www.treasurechest.com

**Harrah's New Orleans**
512 South Peters Rd
New Orleans, LA 70130
504-533-6000
http://www.harrahsneworleans.com

**L'Auberge Hotel & Casino**
777 Avenue L'Auberge
Lake Charles, LA 70601
866-580-7444
http://www.ldlcasino.com

**Coushatta Casino Resort**
777 Coushatta Drive
Kinder, LA 70658
800-584-7263
http://www.coushattacasinoresort.com

**Isle of Capri Casino**
307 I-10 Service Road
Lake Charles, LA 70669
800-843-4753
http://www.isleofcapricasinos.com/
Lake_Charles

**Eldorado Resort Casino Shreveport**
451 Clyde Fant Parkway
Shreveport, LA 71101
877-602-0711
http://www.eldoradoshreveport.com

**Paragon Casino Resort**
711 Tunica
Marksville, LA 71351
800-946-1946
http://www.paragoncasinoresort.com

*Michigan*

**Motor City Casino**
2901 Grand River Avenue
Detroit, MI 48201
866-STAY-MCC
http://www.motorcitycasino.com

**Greektown Casino**
555 E. Lafayette
Detroit, MI 48226
888-771-4386
http://www.greektowncasino.com

**MGM Grand Detroit**
1777 Third St
Detroit, MI 48226
877-888-2121
http://www.mgmgranddetroit.com

**Soaring Eagle Casino**
6800 Soaring Eagle Boulevard
Mount Pleasant, MI 48858
888-732-4537
http://www.soaringeaglecasino.com

**Four Winds Casino Resort**
11111 Wilson Rd
New Buffalo, MI 49117
866-494-6371
http://www.fourwindscasino.com

**Little River Casino Resort**
2700 Orchard Highway
Manistee, MI 49660
888-568-2244
http://www.littlerivercasinos.com

**Leelanau Sands Casino**
2521 N West Bay Shore Dr
Peshawbestown, MI 49682
800-922-2946
http://www.casino2win.com

**Turtle Creek Casino**
7741 M-72 East
Williamsburg, MI 49690
800-922-2WIN
http://www.turtlecreekcasino.com

**Kewadin Shores Casino**
3039 Mackinac Trail
Saint Ignace, MI 49781
800-539-2346
http://500nations.com/casinos

**Kewadin Vegas Casino**
2186 Shunk Road
Sault Ste. Marie, MI 49783
800-KEWADIN
http://www.kewadinsault.com

**Chip Inn's Island Resort Casino**
W399 Highway 2 & 41
Harris, MI 49845
800-682-6040
http://www.chipincasino.com

**Lac Vieux Desert**
N5384 Highway 45
North Watersmeet, MI 49969
800-583-3599
http://www.lvdcasino.com

*Minnesota*

**Running Aces Card Room**
15201 Zurich Street NE
Columbus, MN 55025
877-RUN-ACES
http://www.runningacesharness.com

**Canterbury Park Card Club**
1100 Canturbury Rd.
Shakopee, MN 55379
866-667-6537
http://www.canterburypark.com

**Prairie's Edge Casino Resort**
5616 Prairie's Edge Lane
Granite Falls, MN 56241
866-293-2121
http://www.prairiesedgecasino.com

**Grand Casino Mille Lacs**
777 Grand Ave
Onamia, MN 56359
800-626-5825
http://www.grandcasinosmn.com

**Northern Lights Casino**
6800 Y Frontage Rd NW
Walker, MN 56484
800-252-PLAY
http://northernlightscasino.com

**Shooting Star Casino and Hotel**
777 Casino Road
Mahnomen, MN 56557
800-453-STAR
http://www.starcasino.com

*Missouri*

**President Casino Laclede's Landing**
1000 N. Leonor K. Sullivan Blvd
Saint Louis, MO 63102
800-772-3647
http://www.presidentcasino.com

**Ameristar Casino St. Charles**
One Ameristar Boulevard
Saint Charles, MO 63301
636-949-7777
http://www.ameristarcasinos.com

**Argosy Casino Hotel & Spa**
777 N.W. Argosy Casino Parkway
Riverside, MO 64150
816-746-3100
http://www.stayargosy.com

**Ameristar Casino Hotel Kansas City**
3200 North Ameristar Drive
Kansas City, MO 64161
816-414-7000
http://www.ameristarcasinos.com

*Mississippi*

**Gold Strike Casino Resort**
1010 Casino Center Drive
Robinsonville, MS 38664
888-24K-STAY
http://www.goldstrikemississippi.com

**Grand Casino Tunica**
13615 Old Highway 61 North
Robinsonville, MS 38664
662-363-2788
http://www.harrahstunica.com

**Hollywood Casino-Tunica**
1150 Casino Strip Blvd
Robinsonville, MS 38664
800-871-0711
http://hollywoodcasinotunica.com

**Horseshoe Casino Hotel**
1021 Casino Centre Drive
Robinsonville, MS 38664
800-303-7463
http://www.horseshoetunica.com/

**Sam's Town Hotel & Casino**
1477 Casino Strip Resort Blvd
Robinsonville, MS 38664
800-456-0711
http://www.samstowntunica.com

**Pearl River Resort & Casino**
Hwy 16 W.
Choctaw, MS 38664
866-44PEARL
http://www.pearlriverresort.com

**Bayou Caddy's Jubilee Casino**
211 N. Lakefront Rd.
Greenville, MS 38701
662-335-1111
http://www.bayoucaddyjubilee.com

**Ameristar Vicksburg**
4116 Washington Street
Vicksburg, MS 39180
601-638-1000
http://www.ameristarcasinos.com

**Beau Rivage Hotel & Casino**
875 Beach Boulevard
Biloxi, MS 39530
228-386-7444
http://www.beaurivage.com

**IP Hotel & Casino**
850 Bayview Avenue
Biloxi, MS 39530
888-WIN-AT-IP
http://www.ipbiloxi.com

**Palace Casino Resort**
158 Howard Ave
Biloxi, MS 39530
800-PALACE-9
http://www.palacecasinoresort.com

*Montana*

**Soda Butte Lodge**
209 Hwy 212
Cooke City, MT 59020
406-838-2251

**Locomotive Inn Casino**
216 1st Avenue South
Laurel, MT 59044
406-628-7969

**Eagle Nest Casino**
1515 4th Avenue North
Billings, MT 59101
406-259-1104

**Shooters Casino**
1600 Avenue D
Billings, MT 59105
406-252-6220

**Cassidy's Poker Room**
105 South Main
Plentywood, MT 59254
406-765-1116

**Classic 50's Casino Cardroom**
1802 14th. St. SW
Great Falls, MT 59404
406-453-0136

**Flamingo Lounge & Casino**
3028 10th Ave S.
Great Falls, MT 59405
406-727-4474

**The Brick Sportsbar & Casino**
2401 12th Avenue South
Great Falls, MT 59405
406-452-6021

**Bluff Magazine Poker Room**
700 W. Custer Ave
Helena, MT 59602
406-449-8066

**Cats Paw Card Room**
721 North Seventh Avenue
Bozeman, MT 59771
406-586-3542

**Silverstrip Casino**
680 SW Higgins Ave
Missoulia, MT 59803
406-728-5643

**Sawbuck Saloon**
1301 South Main
Kalispell, MT 59901
406-755-4778

*North Dakota*

**Dakota Magic**
16849 102nd St. SE
Hankinson, ND 58041
800-325-6825
http://www.dakotanationgaming.com

**Spirit Lake Casino**
7889 Highway 57 South
St. Michaels, ND 58370
701-766-4747
http://spiritlakecasino.com

**4 Bears Casino and Lodge**
202 Frontage Road
New Town, ND 58763
800-294-5454
http://www.4bearscasino.com

*Nebraska*

**Rosebud Casino**
HC 14
Valentine, NE 69201
800-786-ROSE
http://www.rosebudcasino.com

*New Jersey*

**Bally's Park Place**
Park Place & Boardwalk
Atlantic City, NJ 08401
609-340-2000
http://www.ballysac.com/casinos/ballys-atlantic-city/hotel-casino/property-home.shtml

**Borgata Hotel Casino & Spa**
One Borgata Way
Atlantic City, NJ 08401
609-317-1000
http://www.theborgata.com

**Caesars Atlantic City**
2100 Pacific Avenue
Atlantic City, NJ 08401
609-348-4411
http://www.caesarsac.com

**Harrah's Atlantic City**
777 Harrahs Blvd
Atlantic City, NJ 08401
609-441-5741
http://www.harrahs.com/destinations/atlantic-city/hotel-casinos/market-home.shtml

**Tropicana Casino & Resort**
Brighton Avenue & The Boardwalk
Atlantic City, NJ 08401
800-345-8767
http://www.tropicana.net

**Trump Taj Mahal**
1000 Boardwalk at Virginia Avenue
Atlantic City, NJ 08401
609-449-1000
http://www.trumptaj.com

**Atlantic City Hilton**
Boston Ave. & The Boardwalk
Atlantic City, NJ 08401
888-224-4586
http://www.hiltonac.com

**Showboat Atlantic City**
801 Boardwalk
Atlantic City, NJ 08401
609-343-4000
http://www.showboatac.com

**Trump Plaza Hotel & Casino**
2225 Boardwalk and Mississippi
Atlantic City, NJ 08401
609-441-6000
http://www.trumpplaza.com

*New Mexico*

**Santa Ana Star Casino**
54 Jemez Canyon Dam Rd
Santa Ana Pueblo, NM 87004
505-867-6540
http://www.santaanastar.com

**Sky City Casino**
I-40 Exit 102
Acoma, NM 87034
888-759-2489
http://www.skycitycasino.com

**Isleta Casino and Resort**
11000 Broadway SE
Albuquerque, NM 87105
505-869-4102
http://www.isletacasinoresort.com

**Sandia Casino**
30 Rainbow Rd NE
Albuquerque, NM 87113
800-526-9366
http://www.sandiacasino.com

**Cities of Gold Casino**
10-B City of Gold Road
Santa Fe, NM 87501
800-455-3313
http://www.citiesofgold.com

**Inn of the Mountain Gods Casino**
287 Carrizo Canyon Road
Mescalero, NM 88340
888-324-0348
http://www.innofthemountaingods.com

*Nevada*

**Sunset Station**
1301 West Sunset Road
Henderson, NV 89014
888-786-7389
http://www.sunsetstation.com

**Club Fortune Casino**
725 South Racetrack Road
Henderson, NV 89015
702-566-5555
http://www.clubfortunecasino.com

**Virgin River Hotel & Casino**
100 Pioneer Blvd.
Mesquite, NV 89027
877-GETAWAY
http://www.virginriver.com

**Eureka Casino Hotel**
275 Mesa Blvd
Mesqite, NV 89027
800-346-4611
http://eurekamesquite.com

**Colorado Belle Hotel & Casino**
2100 S Casino Drive
Laughlin, NV 89029
877-460-0777
http://www.coloradobelle.com

**Don Laughlin's Riverside Casino**
1650 Casino Drive
Laughlin, NV 89029
800-227-3849
http://www.riversideresort.com

**River Palms Casino**
2700 South Casino Drive
Laughlin, NV 89029
800-835-7904
http://www.river-palms.com

**Poker Palace**
2757 Las Vegas Blvd. North
North Las Vegas, NV 89030
702-649-3799
http://www.pokerpalace.net

**Texas Station Gambling Hall & Hotel**
2101 Texas Star Lane
North Las Vegas, NV 89032
800-654-8888
http://www.texasstation.com

**Binion's Gambling Hall**
128 East Fremont Street
Las Vegas, NV 89101
800-937-6537
http://www.binions.com

**El Cortez Hotel & Casino**
600 East Freemont Street
Las Vegas, NV 89101
800-634-6703
http://www.elcortezhotelcasino.com

**Four Queens Casino**
202 Fremont Street
Las Vegas, NV 89101
800-634-6045
http://www.fourqueens.com

**Golden Nugget**
129 E. Fremont St.
Las Vegas, NV 89101
702-385-7111
http://www.goldennugget.com

**Plaza Hotel & Casino**
One Main Street
Las Vegas, NV 89101
800-634-6575
http://www.plazahotelcasino.com

**Palace Station**
2411 West Sahara Ave
Las Vegas, NV 89102
800-634-3101
http://www.palacestation.com

**Orleans Hotel & Casino**
4500 West Tropicana Avenue
Las Vegas, NV 89103
800-675-3267
http://www.orleanscasino.com

**Palms**
4321 W. Flamingo Rd.
Las Vegas, NV 89103
866-942-7777
http://www.palms.com

**Rio All-Suite Hotel & Casino**
3700 West Flamingo Road
Las Vegas, NV 89103
866-746-7671
http://www.riolasvegas.com

**Gold Coast Casino**
4000 W. Flamingo Rd.
Las Vegas, NV 89103
800-331-5334
http://www.goldcoastcasino.com

**Stratosphere**
2000 Las Vegas Blvd. South
Las Vegas, NV 89104
702-380-7777
http://www.stratospherehotel.com

**Arizona Charlies Hotel & Casino**
740 South Decatur Boulevard
Las Vegas, NV 89107
888-236-8645
http://www.arizonacharliesdecatur.com

**Bellagio**
3600 S. Las Vegas Blvd.
Las Vegas, NV 89109
888-987-6667
http://www.bellagio.com

**Circus Circus**
2880 Las Vegas Blvd South
Las Vegas, NV 89109
800-634-3450
http://www.circuscircus.com

**Harrah's Las Vegas**
3475 Las Vegas Blvd South
Las Vegas, NV 89109
800-214-9110
http://www.harrahslasvegas.com

**Imperial Palace Hotel and Casino**
3535 Las Vegas Blvd South
Las Vegas, NV 89109
866-523-2780
http://www.imperialpalace.com

**Mirage**
3400 Las Vegas Blvd South
Las Vegas, NV 89109
702-791-7111
http://www.mirage.com

**Monte Carlo Resort & Casino**
3770 Las Vegas Blvd South
Las Vegas, NV 89109
800-311-8999
http://www.montecarlo.com

**Riviera Hotel & Casino**
2901 Las Vegas Blvd South
Las Vegas, NV 89109
800-634-3420
http://www.rivierahotel.com

**Sahara Casino**
2535 Las Vegas Blvd South
Las Vegas, NV 89109
866-382-8884
http://www.saharavegas.com

**Venetian Casino Resort**
3355 Las Vegas Blvd South
Las Vegas, NV 89109
877-883-6423
http://www.venetian.com

**Planet Hollywood Resort & Casino**
3667 Las Vegas Blvd South
Las Vegas, NV 89109
866-919-PHRC
http://www.planethollywoodresort.com

**Bally's Las Vegas**
3645 Las Vegas Blvd South
Las Vegas, NV 89109
702-967-4111
http://www.ballyslasvegas.com

**Caesars Las Vegas**
3570 Las Vegas Blvd South
Las Vegas, NV 89109
866-227-5938
http://www.caesarspalace.com

**Hooters Hotel & Casino**
115 East Tropicana Avenue
Las Vegas, NV 89109
866-LVHOOTS
http://www.hooterscasinohotel.com

**Paris Las Vegas**
3655 Las Vegas Blvd South
Las Vegas, NV 89109
877-603-4386
http://www.parislasvegas.com

**Treasure Island**
3300 Las Vegas Blvd South
Las Vegas, NV 89109
800-288-7206
http://www.treasureisland.com

**Wynn Las Vegas**
3131 Las Vegas Blvd South
Las Vegas, NV 89109
877-321-WYNN
http://www.wynnlasvegas.com

**Excalibur Hotel & Casino**
3850 Las Vegas Blvd South
Las Vegas, NV 89119
877-750-5464
http://www.excalibur.com

**Luxor Hotel & Casino**
3900 Las Vegas Blvd South
Las Vegas, NV 89119
877-386-4658
http://www.luxor.com

**Mandalay Bay Resort & Casino**
3950 Las Vegas Blvd South
Las Vegas, NV 89119
877-632-7800
http://www.mandalaybay.com

**Boulder Station**
4111 Boulder Highway
Las Vegas, NV 89121
800-683-7777
http://www.boulderstation.com

**Sam's Town**
5111 Boulder Highway
Las Vegas, NV 89122
800-897-8696
http://www.samstownlv.com

**Hard Rock Hotel & Casino**
4455 Paradise Road
Las Vegas, NV 89169
702-693-5000
http://www.hardrockhotel.com

**Ascuaga's Nugget**
1100 Nugget Ave
Sparks, NV 89431
800-648-1177
http://www.janugget.com

**Boomtown Hotel & Casino**
I -80 Exit 4
Reno, NV 89439
775-345-6000
http://www.boomtownreno.com

**Harvey's Tahoe Lake Casino**
18 Highway 50
Lake Tahoe, NV 89449
800-HARVEYS
http://www.harveystahoe.com

**Horizon Casino**
50 Highway 50
Lake Tahoe, NV 89449
800-648-3322
http://www.horizoncasino.com

**Mont Bleu Casino**
55 Hwy 50
Lake Tahoe, NV 89449
888-829-7630
http://www.montbleuresort.com

**Eldorado Hotel & Casino**
345 North Virginia Street
Reno, NV 89501
800-879-8879
http://www.eldoradoreno.com

**Atlantis Casino**
3800 South Virginia Street
Reno, NV 89502
800-723-6500
http://www.atlantiscasino.com

**Peppermill Hotel Casino**
2707 South Virginia Street
Reno, NV 89502
800-648-6992
http://www.peppermillreno.com

**Circus Circus Hotel and Casino**
500 North Sierrra Street
Reno, NV 89503
800-648-5010
http://www.circusreno.com

**Club Cal-Neva**
38 East Second Street
Reno, NV 89505
877-777-7303
http://www.clubcalneva.com

**Grand Sierra Resort & Casino**
2500 East Second Street
Reno, NV 89595
800-501-2651
http://www.grandsierraresort.com

**Red Lion Inn & Casino**
2065 Idaho Street
Elko, NV 89801
775-738-2111
http://www.redlioncasino.com

**Cactus Pete's**
1385 Highway 93
Jackpot, NV 89825
775-755-2321
http://www.ameristarcasinos.com

**Horseshu Hotel and Casino**
Highway 93 at the Idaho border
Jackpot, NV 89825
775-755-7777
http://www.ameristarcasinos.com

*New York*

**Turning Stone Casino & Resort**
5218 Patrick Road
Verona, NY 13478
800-771-7711
http://www.turning-stone.com

**Mohawk Bingo Palace**
202 Route 37
Akwesasne, NY 13655
866 452 5768
http://www.mohawkpalace.com

**Seneca Gaming And Entertainment**
11099 Rt. 5
Irving, NY 14081
800-421-2464
http://www.senecagames.com/irving

**Seneca Niagara Casino**
310 Fourth Street
Niagara Falls, NY 14303
877-873-6322
http://www.senecaniagaracasino.com

**Seneca Gaming And Entertainment**
768 Broad Street
Salamanca, NY 14779
877-860-5130
http://www.senecagames.com/salamanca

*Ohio*

**Highlands Players Club**
4059 SR 36/37
Delaware, OH 43015
740-362-ACES
http://highlandsplayersclub.com

**Eastside Players Club**
4252 Eastland Square Drive
Columbus, OH 43232
614-524-4627
http://eastsideplayersclub.com

*Oklahoma*

**WinStar Casino**
Exit 1 on I-35
Thackerville, OK 73459
800-622-6317
http://www.winstarworldcasino.com

**Cherokee Casino in Tulsa**
777 West Cherokee Street
Catoosa, OK 74015
800-760-6700
http://www.cherokeecasino.com

**Cherokee Casino West Siloam Springs**
U.S Highway 412 and State Highway 59
West Siloam Springs, OK 74438
800-754-4111
http://www.cherokeecasino.com

**Cherokee Casino Roland**
Interstate 40 and State Highway 64
Roland, OK 74954
800-256-233
http://www.cherokeecasino.com

*Oregon*

**Spirit Mountain Casino**
27100 Southwest Highway 18
Grand Ronde, OR 97347
800-760-7977
http://spiritmountain.com

**Chinook Winds Casino**
1777 NW 44th Street
Lincoln City, OR 97367
888-244-6665
http://www.chinookwindscasino.com

**Seven Feathers Casino**
146 Chief Miwaleta Lane
Canyonville, OR 97417
800-548-8461
http://www.sevenfeathers.com

**Mill Resort & Casino**
3201 Tremont Avenue
North Bend, OR 97459
800-953-4800
http://www.themillcasino.com

**Kahneeta High Desert Casino**
6823 Highway 8
Warm Springs, OR 97761
800-554-4SUN
http://www.kahneeta.com

**Wild Horse Casino & Resort**
72777 Highway 331
Pendelton, OR 97801
800-654-9453
http://www.wildhorseresort.com

*South Dakota*

**Royal River Casino Bingo & Hotel**
607 S. Veteran's Street
Flandreau, SD 57028
800-833-8666
http://www.royalrivercasino.com

**Dakota Sioux Casino**
16415 Sioux Conifer Road
Watertown, SD 57201
800-658-4717
http://www.dakotasioux.com

**Fort Randall Casino**
RR One
Wagner, SD 57380
800-362-6333
http://www.fortrandallcasino.com

**Grand River Casino**
Highway 20
Mobridge, SD 57601
800-475-3321
http://www.grandrivercasino.com

**Miss Kitty's Gaming Emporium & Casino**
649 Main Street
Deadwood, SD 57732
800-873-1876
http://www.historicbullock.com/kitty/index.php

**Old Style Saloon #10**
657 Main Street
Deadwood, SD 57732
800-952-9398
http://www.saloon10.com

**Star of the West Casino**
700 Main Street
Deadwood, SD 57732
800-688-1876

**Gold Dust Casino**
688 Main Street
Deadwood, SD 57732
800-456-0533
http://golddustgaming.com

**Lucky Nugget Card Club**
622 Main Street
Deadwood, SD 57732
605-578-1815
http://www.luckynuggetgh.com

*Texas*

**Kickapoo Lucky Eagle Casino**
Rt 1 Lucky Eagle Road
Eagle Pass, TX 78852
888-255-8259
http://www.kickapooluckyeaglecasino.com

*Washington*

**Muckleshoot Casino**
2402 Auburn Way South
Auburn, WA 98002
800-804-4944
http://www.muckleshootcasino.com

**Kenmore Lanes Cardroom**
7638 NE Bothell Way
Bothell, WA 98028
425-486-8646

**Diamond Lil's Cardroom**
361 Rainier Avenue South
Renton, WA 98055
425-255-9037
http://www.diamondlilscardcasino.com

**Freddie's Club of Renton**
111 So. 3rd Street
Renton, WA 98055
425-228-3700
http://www.freddiesclub.com

**Hideaway Cardroom**
14502 Aurora North
Seattle, WA 98133
206-362-9494

**Magic Lanes Cardroom**
10612 15th Avenue South West
Seattle, WA 98146
206-244-5060
http://www.magiclanesbowl.com

**Swinomish Casino**
12885 Casino Drive
Anacortes, WA 98221
888-288-8883
http://www.swinomishcasino.com

**Olivia's Poker Hall**
190 E Bakerview Rd
Bellingham, WA 98226
360-734-7148

**Slo-Pitch Pub and Casino**
1145 E. Sunset Drive
Bellingham, WA 98226
360-733-2255
http://www.slopitchpub.com

**Tulalip Casino & Bingo**
10200 Quil Ceda Blvd.
Tulalip, WA 98271
888-272-1111
http://www.tulalipcasino.com

**Oak Bowl**
531 SE Midway Blvd
Oak Harbor, WA 98277
360-679-2533
http://www.oakbowlcardroom.com

**Chips Casino**
1500 N.E. Rddell Road
Bremerton, WA 98310
360-377-8322
http://www.michelsgaming.com/
chipscasino/bremerton-chips.html

**Seven Cedars Casino**
270756 Highway 101
Sequim, WA 98382
800-4-LUCKY-7
http://www.7cedarscasino.com

**Suquamish Clearwater Casino**
15347 Suquamish Way NE
Suquamish, WA 98392
800-375-6073
http://www.clearwatercasino.com

**Luciano's Casino**
3327 Ruston Way
Tacoma, WA 98402
253-756-5611

**Emerald Queen Casino**
2024 E. 29th St.
Tacoma, WA 98404
888-831-7655
http://www.emeraldqueen.com

**King Solomons**
212 4th Avenue East
Olympia, WA 98501
360-357-5552

**Mac's Tavern and Cardroom**
210 E Heron
Aberdeen, WA 98520
360-533-3932

**Little Creek Casino**
91 West State Route 108
Shelton, WA 98584
800-667-7711
http://www.little-creek-casino.com

**Shoalwater casino**
4112 Highway 105
Tokeland, WA 98590
866-834-7312
http://www.shoalwaterbaycasino.com

**The New Pheonix Casino**
225 West 4th Street
La Center, WA 98629
503-281-0932
http://www.thenewphoenixcasino.com

**Yakama Legends Casino**
580 Fort Road
Toppenish, WA 98948
877-7COME11
http://www.yakamalegends.com

**Northern Quest**
100 Hayford Road North
Airway Heights, WA 99001
888-603-7051
http://www.northernquest.com

**Riverbend Casino**
2721 N Market Street
Spokane, WA 99207
509-483-9499

**Lilac Lanes & Casino**
1112 E Magnesium Rd
Spokane, WA 99208
509-467-5228
http://www.lilaclanesbowling.com

**Wisconsin**

**Menominee Casino Hotel**
N277 Hwy 47/55
Keshena, WI 54135
800-343-7778
http://www.menomineecasinoresort.com

**St Croix Casino**
777 Highway 8 & 63
Turtle Lake, WI 54889
800-U-GO-U-WIN
http://www.stcroixcasino.com

# Canadian Poker Rooms
# (by province)

*Alberta*

**Baccarat Casino**
10128 104 Avenue
Edmonton, Alberta T5J 4Y8
877-616-5695
http://www.baccaratcasino.net

**Cash Casino**
4040 Blackfoot Trail SE
Calgary, Alberta T2G 4E6
403-243-2273
http://www.cashpoker.ca

**Casino Calgary**
1420 - Meridian Road N.E.
Calgary, Alberta T2A 2N9
403-248-9467
http://www.casinoabs.com

**Casino Edmonton**
7055 Argyll Road
Edmonton, Alberta T6C 4A5
780-424-9467
http://www.casinoabs.com

**Casino Lethbridge**
3756 2nd Avenue South
Lethbridge, Alberta T1J 4Y9
403-381-9467
http://www.casinoabs.com

**Casino Yellowhead**
12464 - 153 Street
Edmonton, Alberta T5V 1S5
780-463-9467
http://www.casinoabs.com

**Elbow River Casino**
218 18th Avenue SE
Calgary, Alberta T2G 1L1
403-289-8880
http://www.elbowrivercasino.com

**The Palace Casino**
2710, 8882 - 170 street
Edmonton, Alberta T5T 4J2
780-444-2112
http://www.palacecasino.com

*British Columbia*

**Boulevard Casino**
2080 United Boulevard
Coquitlam, British Columbia V3K 6W3
604-523-6888
http://www.blvdcasino.com

**Cascades Casino & Hotel**
20393 Fraser Highway
Langley, British Columbia V3A 7N2
604-530 1500
http://www.cascadescasino.ca

**Grand Villa Casino**
4331 Dominion Street
Burnaby, British Columbia V5G 1C7
604-436-2211
http://www.grandvillacasino.com

**Lake City Casino – Kamloops**
540 Victoria Street
Kamloops, British Columbia
250-372-3336
http://www.lakecitycasinos.com

**Lake City Casino – Kelowna**
1310 Water Street
Kelowna, British Columbia
250-860-9467
http://www.lakecitycasinos.com

**Lake City Casino – Penticton**
21 Lakeshore Drive West
Penticton, British Columbia
250-487-1280
http://www.lakecitycasinos.com

**River Rock Casino Resort**
8811 River Road
Richmond, British Columbia V6X 3P8
604-247-8900
http://www.riverrock.com

**Starlight Casino**
350 Gifford Street
New Westminster, British Columbia
V3M 7A3
604-777-2946
http://www.starlightcasino.ca

*Manitoba*

**Club Regent Casino**
1425 Regent Avenue West
Winnipeg, Manitoba R2C 3B2
204-957-2500
http://www.casinosofwinnipeg.com

**McPhillips Street Station Casino**
484 McPhillips Street
Winnipeg, Manitoba R2X 2H2
204-957-2500
http://www.casinosofwinnipeg.com

*Nova Scotia*

**Casino Nova Scotia Halifax**
1983 Upper Water Street
Halifax, Nova Scotia B3J 3Y5
888-6GAMES6
http://www.casinonovascotia.com

*Ontario*

**Casino Rama**
5899 Rama Road
Rama, Ontario L0K 1T0
800-832-PLAY
https://www.casinorama.com

**Fallsview Casino Resort**
6380 Fallsview Boulevard
Niagara Falls, Ontario L2G 7X5
888-325-5788
http://fallsviewcasinoresort.com

**Great Blue Heron Charity Casino**
21777 Island Road
Port Perry, Ontario L9L 1B6
888-29 HERON
http://www.greatblueheroncasino.com

**OLG Casino**
30 Bay Street West
Sault Ste. Marie, Ontario P6A 7A6
800-826-8946
http://www.olg.ca

**OLG Casino**
40 Icomm Drive
Brantford, Ontario N3S 7S9
888-694-6946
http://www.olg.ca

**OLG Casino**
50 Cumberland Street South
Thunder Bay, Ontario P7B 5L4
877-656-4263
http://www.olg.ca

*Québec*

**Casino de Charlevoix**
183 rue Richelieu
La Malbaie, Québec G5A 1X8
800-665-2274
http://www.casinosduquebec.com/
charlevoix

*Saskatchewan*

**Casino Regina**
1880 Saskatchewan Drive
Regina, Saskatchewan S4P 0A8
800-555-3189
http://www.casinoregina.com

**Dakota Dunes Casino**
204 Dakota Dunes Way
Saskatoon, Saskatchewan S7K 3J8
306-667-6400
http://www.dakotadunescasino.com

**Gold Eagle Casino**
11902 Railway Avenue East
North Battleford, Saskatchewan S9A
3K7
306-446-3833
http://www.siga.sk.ca/gold_eagle/index.
html

**Northern Lights Casino**
44 Marquis Road West
Prince Albert, Saskatchewan S6V 7Y5
306-764-4777
http://www.siga.sk.ca/northern_lights/
index.html

**Painted Hand Casino**
510 Broadway Street West
Yorkton, Saskatchewan S3N 1B9
306-786-6777
http://www.siga.sk.ca/painted_hand/
index.html

# Appendix

# Additional Flop Games

There are other poker variations that make use of community cards. The most popular are Omaha and Omaha High-Low Eight-or-Better. These games are found in many cardrooms, both brick-and-mortar and online, and look similar to Texas Hold'em. In both games, the players receive pocket cards that are used with a three-card flop, followed by two additional community cards to form the best hand. The betting structure is also the same, with big and small blind bets to seed the pot and four rounds of betting — prior to the flop, after the flop, after the fourth card, and after the fifth card. However, these games differ from Hold'em much more than they look. If you are a regular Hold'em player and try one of these games, you might be surprised by how much the hand values change.

## Omaha

In Omaha, each player receives *four* pocket cards; at showdown, each player *must* use two and *only* two of their pocket cards, with three cards from the board to form a hand. It is the requirement that a player use two pockets cards that confuses people familiar with Hold'em. (In Hold'em, your hand can use two, one, or none of your pocket cards.) The option that Hold'em players have of "playing the board" does not exist in Omaha. If four-of-a-kind appears on the board in Omaha, the best hand you can make is a full house because only three of those four cards are playable. A pocket pair will give you a full house, otherwise your best hand is three-of-a-kind.

To see the consequences of the two pocket-card rule, imagine that your initial hand consisted of all four Aces. Should you bet and see the flop? No, four Aces is a terrible starting hand and should be folded. Only two of those Aces are playable — the other two are dead and will never appear on the board to improve your hand. Reading the board in Omaha is especially challenging because you need to figure out which two of your four pocket cards to play. Imagine holding K♦ K♥ 5♦ 7♥, and the board has K♣ 4♠ A♥ 8♥ 6♠. What is your hand? At first glance, you might think trip-Kings, but if you consider all the possibilities, you should see that your 5 and 7 completes an 8-high straight.

*Pocket Cards:*

*The Board:*

*The high hand is an 8-high straight*

Now consider holding 8♥ 9♦ 10♦ J♠ and the board has 6♠ 7♥ Q♥ J♥ 4♥. You will be staring a long time before figuring out that all you have is a pair of Jacks. You cannot complete the straight because you can *only use* two of your cards: You cannot complete the flush because you *must use* two of your cards.

In fact, any time the board shows four or five to a flush or straight, you cannot make the hand with just one pocket card. For example, you hold A♠ 9♠ 5♦ 6♠, and the board has 8♥ J♣ Q♥ K♣ 10♠. All you have is a hand with an Ace for a high card. You cannot make any of the straights because you must use two of your cards. By contrast, in Texas Hold'em, anyone having a

*Pocket Cards:*

*The Board:*

*The high hand is a pair of Jacks.*

single Ace or 9 would have a straight for this board, because you can use just one of your cards. The other card wouldn't matter.

Like Hold'em, playing high cards is important, but unlike Hold'em, starting hands are more radically altered by the flop. The greatest danger Hold'em players face in Omaha is over-valuing high pocket pairs. Your starting hand could be A♣ A♦ K♣ K♦, but if the flop came up 5♥ 4♥ 6♠, you are not the favorite. With four cards in everyone's pocket, someone could easily have two little cards, such as 3, 7 or 7, 8 or a 9, 10, and wait for an 8 to fall, and someone has two Hearts and is drawing to the flush. Your hand cannot make a flush, or a straight, and needs two perfect cards to make a boat. In Hold'em, a flop of little cards such as this probably improved no one and a pair of Aces or a pair of Kings would loom large.

To win over the long-run at Omaha, you must play starting cards that are *coordinated*; that is, have the potential for a large number of favorable flops. A hand like A♣ K♣ K♦ Q♦ could flop an Ace-high Club flush, a King-high Diamond flush, an Ace-high straight, a King-high straight, a set of Kings, Kings over a smaller pair, or Aces over, if an A, Q fell on the flop. In contrast, a hand such as A♣ 9♦ 8♠ 5♥ is less likely to hit a favorable flop. No flushes are possible with these starting cards and in the unlikely event the flop is 10, J, Q, your straight will probably lose to someone with A, K or K, 10.

As a general rule, the rank of winning hands in Omaha is higher than in Hold'em. Two-pair is not a strong holding in Omaha. The four pocket cards allow for the completion of many kinds of drawing hands. In a full ten-handed ring game, if a straight is possible, someone likely has it. The same is true for flushes, and any time the board is paired, a full house is likely. When I played in the now defunct Prince George's County Maryland cardrooms, there was bonus money given each day for the first person with Aces-full, Kings-full, etc., high hand for the afternoon, plus $500 for any royal, and $100 for any straight flush. Under these conditions, no one wanted to play anything but Omaha for high, because the higher-ranked hands generated by Omaha meant the bonus money was paid out faster.

## Omaha High-Low Eight-or-Better

This is a variant of Omaha played for a high-low split. It is played exactly like Omaha, only the low hand splits the pot with the high hand. To qualify for a low hand, you cannot have a card higher than an 8. If all hands contain at least one card higher than an 8, the high hand takes the entire pot. Aces can be played low, and flushes and straights don't count for low. That means the nut-low hand would be a wheel A, 2, 3, 4, 5, which as a 5-high straight could also be a winning high hand (or better yet, a "steel wheel" A, 2, 3, 4, 5, suited).

Obviously, the ideal in such a game is a *scoop,* meaning that you take the entire pot by having both the best low and best high hand. You can use two of your pocket cards to form your high hand, and a different two pocket cards to form your low. Imagine you hold K♣ K♥ 5♦ 4♥ and the board is K♦ 2♣ 3♠ 3♦ 8♥. For a high hand, you have Kings-full and for a low hand, you have 2♣ 3♠ 4♥ 5♦ 8♥.

Like high-only Omaha, your starting hands must be coordinated, but that requirement is different for Omaha High-Low. Coordinated for this game means starting cards that have

*Pocket Cards:*

*The Board:*

*The high hand is Kings-full, the low hand is 8-high.*

the potential for making the best high and low hand. The best starting hands have Aces, low cards, and are double suited. For example: A♥ A♦ 2♥ 3♦ has many winning high possibilities: a nut-flush if 3 Diamonds or 3 Hearts hit the board, trip aces if another Ace hit, or even Aces-full. It could also make the best possible low hand in different ways. If the board had A, 4, 5, or 3, 4, 5, or 2, 4, 5, or 2, 5, 6, it would make the "nut-low."

There are some unique features about Omaha High-Low Eight-or-Better to remember. It is common to have a "nut-low" counterfeited. For example you hold A, 2, J, K. The board after the turn is 4, 5, 6, 10. You have the best possible low now, but if the river brings a 2, an A, 3 wins low because that hand becomes 5, 4, 3, 2, A. Your low remains 6, 5, 4, 2, A. Remember, you must use two of your cards to form a low hand and the board has "counterfeited" your 2.

The other pitfall in Omaha High-Low Eight-or-Better is the possibility of being "quartered." For example, you hold A, 2, J, K against an opponent who has A, 3, 5, 6. The board is 2, 3, 4, 5, J. Both of you have a 5-high for low and split the low pot. However, your 5-high straight does not hold up for high because your opponent can complete a 6-high straight. You get one-quarter of the pot while your opponent receives three-quarters. If you bet, thinking that at worst you would get the money back with the nut-low you would be wrong. Your opponent will keep half the money you bet.

Omaha High-Low Eight-or-Better is a complex game and rising in popularity because of HORSE events. A HORSE format is a rotating mix of games in which each poker variation is played for a certain number of hands or minutes. The O in HORSE is Omaha High-Low Eight-or-Better. The other games are H = **H**old'em, R = **R**azz, S = **S**even-Card Stud, and E = Seven-Card Stud High-Low **E**ight-or-Better. The last game is a high-low split-pot version of Seven-Card Stud, with the same rule that to qualify for the low pot, your low-hand must be at least an 8-high or lower. To learn more about Seven-Card Stud High-Low Eight-or-Better visit *http://www.StudHighLow.com*.

# Glossary

**all-in**—when a player places all his or her remaining chips into the pot. Players going all-in do not call additional bets, and they cannot compete for additional bets made by other players, which go into a side pot.

**ante**—an initial contribution to the pot that all players must make to be dealt cards. In popular Seven-Card games such as Seven-Card Stud, Seven-Card Stud High-Low Eight or Better, and Razz, the ante is approximately one-fifth of the first betting limit ($0.20 in a game with $1-$2 limits). For flop games such as Hold'em, blind bets are used to seed the pot initially, but in the late stages of many tournament structures, antes are also required.

**back in**—a hand that plays out differently than intended. For example a player with a pair of kings at the beginning, who then receives four additional cards of a suit matching one of the kings, has "backed in" to a flush.

**bad beat**—an improbable loss, such as losing with a very strong hand or losing to someone's long-shot draw.

**bet**—to place money in the pot that other players must match to remain in the hand.

**bicycle**—a five-card hand consisting of A, 2, 3, 4, 5, of different suits. In high poker this is a 5-high straight. In low poker this is a 5-high low, which is the best low-hand possible. Also known as a *wheel*.

**big blind**—the player two seats to the left of the button, who must make a pre-flop bet before receiving pocket cards.

**bluffing**—betting on a weak hand in order to convince others the hand is strong.

**board**—the face-up cards on the table (see *community cards*).

**board games**—poker variants in which a fraction of the cards dealt to each player are exposed. Popular board games include Seven-Card Stud, Five-Card Stud, Razz, and Seven-Card Stud High-Low Eight or Better. Variants such as Omaha and Hold'em are not board games because only the community cards are exposed on the board. The cards dealt to each of the players are known only to them (see also *stud games*).

**boat**—alternate term for full house.

**brick**—a card dealt that does not improve the ranking of its hand.

**bring-in**—a forced bet after the initial deal. In board games such as Seven-Card Stud and Seven-Card Stud High-Low the player with the lowest exposed card must initiate betting action after the deal by making a minimum bet of approximately one-quarter of the first betting limit ($0.25 in a game with $1-$2 limits). In Razz it is the player with the highest exposed card that makes the bring-in bet.

**bubble**—the player who is knocked out one place away from being paid in a poker tournament is said to finish "on the bubble."

**button**—a small plastic disk used in casino games to mark the player in the "dealer's position." After each hand, the button rotates to the next player on the left. Because a non-playing casino employee deals the cards, the button is moved after each hand, allowing players to takes turns having the advantageous dealer position of acting last.

**call**—to match another player's bet.

**cards speak**—a rule that players do not have to correctly state the contents of their hand. The dealer will award the pot to the player showing the best cards, regardless of what statements the player made. Casino games are usually played with the *cards speak* rule.

**check**—to pass on betting.

**check-raise**—to raise another player's bet after initially checking (see *raise*).

**chips**—tokens purchased by players for use in placing bets.

**community cards**—the five cards placed face-up in the center of the table, and used by all the players to form their hands (see *board*).

**complete**—the option in the first round of betting in Stud games to raise the *bring-in* bet to the maximum allowed by the limits. For example, in a $1-$2 Stud game with a bring-in of $0.25, players acting after the bring-in bet can call the $0.25 or complete by raising to $1. At the beginning of betting, the bring-in also has the option of completing instead of making of the minimum forced $0.25 bet.

**connected cards**—a group of cards with sequential ranks.

**dead hand**—a hand that cannot improve, either because the cards needed are in other hands, or because all possible improvements will not be enough to win. Also refers to a hand, that for any reason, can no longer contest the pot. For example, players absent or disconnected when it is their turn to act will have their hands declared dead.

**dealer**—the person who deals the cards and manages the money going into the pot. In a casino, the dealer is an employee, not a player in the game.

**door-card** – the one exposed card of the initial three starting cards in Stud games.

**drawing dead**—drawing in a situation when even if the draw is made, the player still loses. For example, if you draw for a flush when someone already has a full house.

**drawing hand**—a hand that will not win unless it is improved. Having four cards to a straight or four cards to a flush are examples of drawing hands.

**eight-or-better**—the rule in many split-pot games that for a hand to win the low pot it cannot contain a card ranked higher than an 8. In the event that no low hand meets the "eight-or-better" condition the high hand is awarded the entire pot.

**flop**—the first three community cards in Hold'em, which are shown all at once.

**fold**—to drop out of a hand and forfeit all interest in the pot.

**free card**—seeing a fourth or fifth community card without having to call a bet.

**freerolling**— the ability to make bets and raises that cannot lose, but have the potential to win additional money.

**freeroll tournament**—a poker tournament with no cash entry fee, but cash prizes for the winners at the end.

**high-low split**—a poker game in which the pot is split by the players holding the highest and lowest hands. In many high-low games, the low hand must qualify to claim half the pot. A common qualification is that the low hand must not have a card higher than an eight. If no low hand qualifies, the high hand takes the entire pot.

**implied collusion**—a situation in which many players are on an improbable draw to beat the best hand.

**implied pot odds**—the ratio of the total amount of money a player expects to win to the amount of money that a player must contribute to the pot. For example, the pot may contain $50, but you expect five players to call your $10 bet. The implied odds are 10 to 1 since you expect to win $100. Contrast with *pot odds*.

**jackpot game**—a poker variant found in some casinos when an amount is taken from each pot to accumulate in a jackpot. To win the jackpot, an unlikely poker event must occur. The most common is the "bad beat jackpot," in which a player holding Aces-full or higher loses the hand. Jackpots in low-limit Hold'em games can accumulate to tens of thousands of dollars and their existence encourages loser play because players often stay in hands longer than they should in hopes of hitting the jackpot.

**jamming**—betting or raising with the intention of re-raising if that option returns before the round of betting closes.

**kicker**—a card that is part of a hand, but not part of a combination. For example, if you hold A, K and the board shows K, 8, 8, 3, Q, your hand is two pair (Kings and eights) with an Ace kicker.

**limit Hold'em**—a common variation in which the bets and raises are limited to fixed amounts in each round of betting. In $5–10 limit Hold'em, bets and raises are in increments $5 before and after the flop and $10 after the turn and river cards.

**limp**—another word for *call*, which is the act of matching another player's bet.

**live hand**—a hand that has the possibility of improving from additional cards to come.

**monster hand**—a very high-ranked hand. Aces-full, four of a kind, any straight-flush, are often referred to as monsters since losses with these kinds of hands are very infrequent.

**muck**—to give up your cards and forfeit interest in contesting the pot (see *fold*). Also refers to the pile of cards discarded by all the players during a hand.

**no-limit Hold'em**—a variation in which in any betting round, the players can bet any amount up to what they have on the table.

**nuts**—the highest possible hand that can be formed with the cards on the board.

**nut-flush**—the highest possible flush that can be formed with the cards on the board.

**nut-low**— the lowest possible hand that can be formed given the current cards on the board.

**nut-straight**—the highest possible straight that can be formed with the cards on the board.

**Omaha**—a variation of Hold'em in which players receive four pocket cards. A total of five community cards appear on the board, but the players are only allowed to use three of them to form their hand. Players must use two of their four pocket cards to make their hand.

**Omaha High-Low Eight-or-Better**—a variation of *Omaha* in which the high and low hands split the pot. Each player is allowed to form two different hands, one using any two of their pocket cards to make the best possible high, and one using any two of their pocket cards to make the best possible low. To claim the low hand, there can be no card higher than an eight. Straights and flushes do not count in determining low. If no low hand qualifies, the high hand wins the entire pot.

**outs**—cards that will improve a hand. For example, if you have four to a flush, there are nine outs for making a flush.

**overcard**—a community card that is higher than either of a player's pocket cards.

**pocket cards**—the face-down cards dealt to each player at the beginning of a hand.

**poker tournament**—an event in which players pay an entry fee to form a prize fund. Each participant is issued playing chips that have no cash value. The players who accumulate all the chips during play, win the cash prizes.

**position**—a player's turn to act in a hand relative to the other players. A player in an early position is one of the first to act; a player in a late position is one of the last. Since late position is an advantage, position rotates one seat after each hand to give players equal turns.

**post**—a pre-flop bet required when joining a game in progress or when re-entering a game if a turn in the blind position is missed.

**pot**—the total amount of money wagered on a hand.

**pot-limit Hold'em**—a variation in which in any betting round, the players can bet any amount up to what is currently in the pot.

**pot odds**—the ratio of the amount of money in the pot to the amount of money that a player must contribute to compete for the pot. For example, if you must call a $10 bet to compete for a $50 pot, the pot odds are 5 to 1.

**proposition player**—also referred to as a *prop* player, is a person paid by the house to play. The purpose is to have players available to start games or keep a game going. Proposition players play with their own money, so they must be good enough to at least break even at the table, or their pay will not cover their losses.

**quartered**— a situation in a split-pot game in which two players split half of the pot either because they tied for the best high hand or tied for the best low hand.

**qualified low**—a hand that meets the conditions for claiming the low half of the pot. Most high-low poker games have an "eight-or-better" rule as a condition for awarding half of the pot to the lowest hand. To qualify for the low pot, the five-card hand must have no cards ranked higher than an eight and no pairs. Aces are both the lowest and highest ranked cards. Straights or flushes do not disqualify a hand from being low.

**raise**—both matching and increasing a bet made by another player.

**rake**—a fraction of each pot taken by the casino as a charge for running a poker game.

**Razz**—a variation of Seven-Card Stud in which the pot is awarded to the lowest ranked hand. There is no qualifying rule to win and, unless the best low hands are identical, no split-pots. Straights and flushes do not disqualify a hand from being low in Razz. Therefore, the best possible hand in Razz is a 5-high low, which would be A, 2, 3, 4, 5. The suits would not matter in the ranking of the hand.

**river card**—the fifth and final community card in Hold'em.

**royal flush**—the highest ranked hand in poker—Ace, King, Queen, Jack, 10, all in the same suit.

**scoop**—to win the entire pot in a high-low split-pot game.

**semi-bluffing**—betting on a weak hand that has a good chance of improving.

**set**—three cards of the same rank (also referred to as *trips*).

**Seven-Card Stud**—a popular poker game in which each player receives seven cards and uses five to form their hand. Each player receives three cards initially—two face down and one face-up. The next three cards are dealt face-up and the final card face down. In contrast to Hold'em, there are no shared cards in a Stud game. Players may only use the cards they receive.

**Seven-Card Stud High-Low Eight-or-Better**— a variation of Seven-Card Stud in which the high and low hands split the pot. Each player is allowed to form two different hands, one using the five cards that form the best possible high, and one using the five cards that make the best possible low. To claim the low pot, there can be no card higher than an eight in the low hand. Straights and flushes do not count in determining low. If no low hand qualifies, the high hand wins the entire pot.

**showdown**—the act of showing cards to determine the winner of a hand.

**side pot**—a separate pot created after one player goes "all-in." Additional money wagered by the players who are not all-in goes into the *side pot*. The person going all-in cannot compete for the side pot (see *all-in*).

**slow-play**—representing a strong hand as weak by not betting in order to disguise the strength. The opposite of bluffing.

**small blind**—the person to the immediate left of the person on the button. The small blind is required to place one half a pre-flop bet before receiving their pocket cards. To see the flop, the small blind must later on match the big blind's bet plus any raises (see *big blind*). The small blind has the option of raising.

**splashing the pot**—throwing chips into the pot in such a way that the dealer is unable to count them. *Splashing the pot* is forbidden in cardroom play.

**spread-limit Hold'em**—a variation in which bets and raises are not in fixed increments, but can be any amount up to the specified limit.

**string bet**—placing a bet, then reaching for more chips in order to raise. *String bets* are forbidden in cardroom play.

**Stud games**—see *board games*.

**table stakes**—a rule requiring that all money put in play during a hand must be on the table before the hand begins.

**tapped out**—losing all the money placed on the table.

**tell**—a characteristic mannerism or behavior that indicates a player's thinking.

**trips**—three cards of the same rank (also referred to as a *set*).

**turn card**—the fourth community card in Hold'em.

**wheel**—a five-high straight: A, 2, 3, 4, 5, of mixed suits.

**wheel cards**—the cards ranked A, 2, 3, 4, 5.

**wired-pair**—two cards of the same rank with neither card exposed.

# Bibliography

Over the past decade the literature on poker has exploded. The following is a selected bibliography arranged by topic of some of the influential books. It is by no means an exhaustive list. The intent is to provide direction for those seeking more information on different aspects of Hold'em, its variants, and poker in general.

**Poker Guides**

Doyle Brunson, *Doyle Brunson's Super System: A Course in Power Poker, 3rd Edition* (New York, NY: Cardoza, 2002)

Doyle Brunson, *Doyle Brunson's Super System 2: A Course in Power Poker* (New York, NY: Cardoza, 2005)

Mike Caro, *Caro's Book of Poker Tells* (New York, NY: Cardoza, 2003)

Barry Greenstein, *Ace on the River: An Advanced Poker Guide* (Fort Collins, CO: Last Knight Publishing Company, 2005)

Matthew Hilger & Ian Taylor, *The Poker Mindset: Essential Attitudes for Poker Success* (Atlanta, GA: Dimat Enterprises, 2007)

Daniel Kimberg, *Serious Poker, 2nd Edition* (Pittsburgh, PA: Conjelco, 2002)

Matt Lessinger, *The Book of Bluffs: How to Bluff and Win at Poker* (New York, NY: Grand Central Publishing, 2005)

Alan N. Schoonmaker, *The Psychology of Poker*  (Las Vegas, NV: Two Plus Two, 2000)

David Sklansky, *The Theory of Poker* (Las Vegas, NV: Two Plus Two, 1994)

Shane Smith, *How to Beat Low-Limit Poker: How to win big money at little games* (New York, NY: Cardoza, 2008)

## Hold'em, Limit

Bob Ciaffone and Jim Brier, *Middle Limit Holdem Poker* (Saginaw MI: Bob Ciaffone, 2002)

Ed Miller, *Small Stakes Hold 'em: Winning Big With Expert Play* (Las Vegas, NV: Two Plus Two, 2004)

David Sklansky and Mason Malmuth, *Hold'em Poker for Advanced Players* (Las Vegas, NV: Two Plus Two, 1999)

Lee Smith, *Winning Low-Limit Hold'em, 3rd edition* (Pittsburgh, PA: Conjelco, 2005)

Barry Tanenbaum, *Advanced Limit Hold'em Strategy* (UK: D&B Publishing, 2007)

## Hold'em, no-limit

Matt Flynn, Sunny Mehta, and Ed Miller, *Professional No-Limit Hold 'em: Vol. I* (Las Vegas, NV: Two Plus Two, 2007)

Dan Harrington, *Cash Games: How to Win at No-Limit Hold'em Money Games Vol. 1* (Las Vegas, NV: Two Plus Two, 2008)

Dan Harrington, *Cash Games: How to Play No-Limit Hold 'em Cash Games Vol. II* (Las Vegas, NV: Two Plus Two, 2008)

Daniel Negreanu, *Power Hold'em Strategy* (New York, NY: Cardoza, 2008)

David Sklansky and Ed Miller, *No Limit Hold 'em: Theory and Practice* (Las Vegas, NV: Two Plus Two, 2006)

## Hold'em, Tournaments

Mitchell Cogert, *Tournament Poker: 101 Winning Moves: Expert Plays for No-Limit Tournaments* (Seattle, WA: CreateSpace, 2008)

Dan Harrington, *Harrington on Hold 'em Expert Strategy for No Limit Tournaments, Vol. 1: Strategic Play* (Las Vegas, NV: Two Plus Two, 2004)

Dan Harrington, *Harrington on Hold 'em Expert Strategy for No Limit Tournaments, Vol. 2: Endgame* (Las Vegas, NV: Two Plus Two, 2005)

Dan Harrington, *Harrington on Hold 'em: Expert Strategies for No Limit Tournaments, Vol. 3: The Workbook* (Las Vegas, NV: Two Plus Two, 2006)

Gus Hansen, *Every Hand Revealed* (New York, NY, Citadel, 2008)

Eric 'Rizen' Lynch, Jon 'Pearljammer' Turner, and Jon 'Apestyles' Van Fleet, *Winning Poker Tournaments One Hand at a Time Vol. I* (Atlanta, GA: Dimat Enterprises, 2008)

David Sklansky, *Tournament Poker for Advanced Players* (Las Vegas, NV: Two Plus Two, 2002)

Shane Smith, *Tournament Tips from the Poker Pros* (New York, NY: Cardoza, 2008)

Arnold Snyder, *The Poker Tournament Formula* (New York, NY: Cardoza, 2006)

Arnold Snyder, *The Poker Tournament Formula II: Advanced Strategies* (New York, NY: Cardoza, 2008)

## Hold'em, Sit&Go

Mike Matusow, *The Full Tilt Poker Strategy Guide: Tournament Edition* (New York, NY: Grand Central Publishing, 2007) Collin Moshman, *Sit 'n Go Strategy* (Las Vegas, NV: Two Plus Two, 2007)

Andy Bloch, Richard Brodie, Chris Ferguson, Ted Forrest,
    Rafe Furst, Phil Gordon, David Grey, Howard Lederer, and
Timothy Neil, *How to Beat Sit 'n' Go Poker Tournaments* (New
    York, NY: Cardoza, 2008)
Lee Nelson, Tysen Streib, and Kim Lee, *Kill Everyone:
    Advanced Strategies for No-limit Hold 'em Poker
    Tournaments and Sit-n-go's* (Las Vegas, NV: Huntington
    Press, 2007)
Phil Shaw, *Secrets of Sit 'n' Gos: Winning Strategies for
    Single-table Poker Tournaments* (UK: D&B Publishing,
    2008)

**Internet Poker**

Rory Cummins, *The Guide To Winning Hold 'em Online*
    (Otsego, MI: PageFree Publishing, 2007)
Scott Fischman, *Online Ace: A World Series of Poker
    Champion's Guide to Mastering Internet Poker* (Bristol,
    CT: ESPN, 2006)
Mark "The Red" Harlan, and Chris Derossi, *Winning at
    Internet Poker For Dummies* (New York, NY: Wiley
    Publishing, 2005)
Matthew Hilger, and Ian Taylor, *Internet Texas Hold'em:
    Winning Strategies from an Internet Pro* (Atlanta, GA:
    Dimat Enterprises, 2003)
John Vorhaus, *Killer Poker Online, Vol. 2: Advanced Strategies
    for Crushing the Internet Game* (New York, NY: Lyle
    Stuart, 2006)

**Omaha**

Bob Ciaffone, and Jim Brier, *Omaha Poker* (Saginaw, MI: Bob
    Ciaffone, 2006)
Sam Farha, *Farha on Omaha: Expert Strategy for Beating
    Cash Games and Tournaments* (Chicago, IL: Triumph
    Books, 2007)

Jeff Hwang, *Pot-Limit Omaha Poker*, (New York, NY: Citadel, 2008)

Rolf Slotboom, *Secrets of Professional Pot-Limit Omaha* (UK: D&B Publishing, 2006)

Rolf Slotboom, and Rob Hollink, *Secrets of Short-handed Pot-Limit Omaha* (UK: D&B Publishing, 2009)

**Omaha High-low**

Bill Boston, *Omaha High-Low: Play to Win With The Odds* (New York, NY: Cardoza, 2006)

Bill Boston, *Low Limit Omaha High-Low Strategies* (New York, NY: Cardoza, 2009)

Mike Cappelletti, *How to Win at Omaha High-Low Poker*, (New York, NY: Cardoza, 2003)

Shane Smith, and Don Vines, *Omaha High-Low Poker: How to Win at the Lower Limits* (New York, NY: Cardoza, 2008)

Mark Tenner, and Lou Krieger, *Winning Omaha/8 Poker* (Pittsburgh, PA: Conjelco, 2003)

**Memoirs**

Andy Bellin, *Poker Nation: A High-Stakes, Low-Life Adventure into the Heart of a Gambling Country* (New York, NY: Harper Paperbacks, 2003)

Michael Craig, *The Professor, the Banker, and the Suicide King: Inside the Richest Poker Game of All Time* (New York, NY: Grand Central Publishing, 2006)

Annie Duke, and David Diamond, *Annie Duke: How I Raised, Folded, Bluffed, Flirted, Cursed, and Won Millions at the World Series of Poker* (New York, NY: Hudson Street Press, 2005)

Katy Lederer, *Poker Face: A Girlhood Among Gamblers* (New York, NY: Three Rivers Press, 2004)

James McManus, *Positively Fifth Street: Murderers, Cheetahs, and Binion's World Series of Poker*, (New York, NY: Picador, 2004)

# Index

## A

all-in  14, 47, 60, 245

## B

bad beats  137, 140, 180, 245
bankroll  213
behavioral finance
  applied to poker  188
bet  26, 245
Billings, Darse  195
bad beats  108
baseball  201
betting  11
betting structure  13
blind
  big  11, 22, 246
  small  11, 22, 254
bluffing  125, 138, 246
board  5, 245
  reading the  11
boat  7, 245
bonuses  213
Bootcamp  212
brick-and-mortar cardrooms  43,
      48, 215-237
Brunson, Doyle  200
button  22, 246

## C

call  12, 26, 247
cardrooms  21
  buying-in  24
  games in progress  24
  leaving the game  25
  leaving the table  24
  signing up to play  24
cards  68, 73
cards speak  22, 246
Chan, Johnny  200
check  12, 26, 246
check-raise  12, 120, 124, 126, 247
  defense  122
chess
  computers  194
  correspondence  29
  differences from poker  194
  tournament  51
chess tournament  200, 201
chips  21, 24, 247
cold-calling  118
collusion  47
community cards  6, 22, 247
computer simulations
  poker  199
conduct
  in a cardroom  25

# W

tioningN269

# Intelligent Poker.com

*Articles Include...*

- Cash Game Freerolls
- Counterfeit Cards
- Poker Tournament Strategies
- Online Poker Advice
- Omaha Tips for Hold'em Players
- The Beauty of Online Poker Tournaments

## Stay Informed on Poker!

- Current information on the best online cardrooms

- Online bonus codes worth hundreds of dollars.

- Latest poker news and discussion boards

- Articles with tips from top poker pros

- Free online poker calculator to analyze decisions

- Access to interactive poker statistics

- Up-to-date regional listing of hundreds of cardrooms across the United States and Canada

## Visit
# www.IntelligentPoker.com

# ABOUT THE AUTHOR

Sam Braids has had a life-long fascination with games that combine strategic thinking and psychology. He has spent decades studying and playing poker and chess. He also holds a doctorate in experimental physics and has extensive experience teaching advanced physics and mathematics. A prolific writer on poker, he regularly contributes articles to IntelligentPoker. com and StudHighLow.com. Currently he is writing a book on Seven-Card Stud High-Low Eight-or-Better Poker. He lives near Baltimore, Maryland.

# ACKNOWLEDGEMENTS

I wish to thank Arlene Uslander for her careful and enthusiastic editing of the manuscript. I also thank Graham Van Dixhorn of Susan Kendrick Writing, for his thoughtful work writing the back cover and proofreading the book.

Any errors found in this book are mine. Don't hesitate to call errors to my attention or make other comments on this book. I enjoy hearing from my readers. E-mail your feedback to comments@intelligentpoker.com or write the publisher - Intelligent Games Publishing, P. O. Box 6705, Towson, MD 21285.

- Sam Braids